My
Country
School
Diary

. . . the clean, white, boxlike structure, shining in the sun.

My
Country School
Diary

An Adventure in

Creative Teaching

By JULIA WEBER

Foreword by FRANK W. CYR, *Professor*
of Education, Teachers College, Columbia University

Illustrations by JOHN R. KOLLMAR

HARPER & BROTHERS · NEW YORK AND LONDON

MY COUNTRY SCHOOL DIARY

FIRST EDITION

A-V

Rural schools – New Jersey

Teaching

Dedicated to

my teacher and friend

MARCIA A. EVERETT

CONTENTS

FOREWORD by Frank Cyr   xi

PRELUDE   xiii

THE FIRST YEAR

1. I LEARN TO KNOW THE CHILDREN   1

I prepare for the first day . . . I have two purposes for the first year . . . The first day . . . I learn to know the children through observing and discovering their needs . . . through personal conferences . . . through home visits . . . The daily program . . . Some needs are met through using the environment . . . through opportunities for democratic living . . . through individualized instruction . . . through opportunities for self-expression . . . through group play . . . through adjusting the school program . . . through enriched curriculum experiences . . . through housekeeping activities . . . through opportunities to initiate and plan activities . . . through parent-teacher co-operation . . . A summary.

2. THE CHILDREN GROW   32

The children expand their interests . . . They grow in their desire for order and attractiveness in their surroundings . . . in skill in using the tools of learning . . . in ability to plan their affairs . . . in ability to meet new situations with confidence and poise . . . A summary.

3. WE SUFFER GROWING PAINS   48

I continue to meet previously discovered needs . . . Problems arise through playing indoors . . . Some problems involve a mature sense of values . . . Problems arise in carrying out the hot lunch program . . . Home attitudes help to create school problems . . . Outside help solves some problems . . . I begin to learn new techniques of teaching the social studies . . . Adjustments are made in the daily program . . . We begin to study the history of our community . . . Personality difficulties are revealed through group living . . . New members present adjustment problems . . . Problems are sharpened when the home and school do not understand each other . . . A summary.

THE SECOND YEAR

4. WE MAKE A NEW BEGINNING 81

I prepare for the second year ... The program continues from the first year ... The health program is expanded to meet pressing needs ... Problems developing during the summer carry over into the school and must be faced ... We begin to rebuild group spirit and co-operative action ... We continue to provide varied experiences to meet individual and group needs ... Mothers share in evaluating the school program ... The needs of the neighborhood impinge upon the school ... Function of a one-teacher school in an isolated neighborhood ... We begin to meet a need of the neighborhood by providing wholesome recreation for the young people.

5. WE EXPERIENCE CREATIVE POWER 106

Choices need to be made in developing curriculum ... Needs are met through creative dramatization ... Outside help contributes to the enrichment of the curriculum ... The attitude of the young people improves ... The community recreates together.

6. WE STUDY OUR COMMUNITY 115

The curriculum is enriched through taking advantage of resources in the community ... A more effective daily program evolves ... The school program affects and makes some difference in the neighborhood ... My helping teacher and I together evaluate the program of the school ... In the light of the evaluation, we begin the study of our community ... The children study about the world to understand better their place in it ... I learn much through informal situations to increase my understanding of the children ... The children become more free and creative in their play ... Older children have rich learning experiences through helping the younger ones ... We conclude the study of dairying ... I evaluate the study of dairying ... I evaluate the program of the second year.

THE THIRD YEAR

7. I CONTINUE TO TRY TO PUT MY PHILOSOPHY INTO PRACTICE 148

I write my philosophy to clarify it ... The children have increased ability for recreation ... They work together for the improvement of the common life ... They find joy in their work ... They see new ways of doing things ... The children learn purposefully to control essential skills . . . I observe how the children learn to appreciate co-operation . . . The children plan to develop more efficient practice of habits of healthful living . . . They take the initiative in solving their own problems . . . Normally, new problems are always arising . . . My helping teacher and I together analyze the new problems . . . We face the new problems . . . Rich experiences make for wholesome personality development.

8. I LEARN NEW TECHNIQUES 166

I plan to evaluate all along . . . I continually study the needs of the children, to meet them . . . Abundant interests impel into many fields of rich experiencing . . . The children learn to think independently and to act on their thinking . . . I prepare in order to recognize what is significant in the experiences of the children . . . I learn to select experiences which contribute to the children's growth . . . The children learn to act in consideration of each member of the group . . . They begin to form conceptions of the responsibilities of society . . . They learn to be critical and to check sources of information . . . They develop self-confidence in their own ability and intelligence . . . They develop a sense of values to guide judgment and action . . . We begin to meet the needs of society by meeting the needs of the children . . . I make choices in selecting curriculum material . . . The children learn to appreciate the complexity of human life and its problems . . . They gather an expanding body of knowledge which helps them to understand better their own situation . . . A summary.

THE FOURTH YEAR

9. WE LEARN TO LIVE IN A DEMOCRACY 197

POSTLUDE 239

APPENDIX 249

INDEX 266

FOREWORD

By FRANK W. CYR

Professor of Education, Teachers College
Columbia University

This book will interest many readers. The general reader will enjoy the flavor of the country, of the little schoolhouse on the hill, of the wood smoke curling from the chimney, and of the children and teacher working and living together as they come to know and understand better their own little world and its place in the larger world of today.

It will be of even greater interest to those responsible for the schooling of the nearly four million children in our one- and two-teacher schools, who will see in it the unfolding of an educational program which helps pupils to develop their innate abilities, and to acquire the habits and attitudes they need in order to solve the problems of everyday life and to become healthy, useful, responsible citizens. The discerning reader will recognize here the basic problems which every teacher faces in helping a group of children to work and grow together, and in discovering effective ways such problems can be met.

The simple and direct manner in which the needs of the children are studied and met will be an inspiration and help to parents and teachers alike in dealing with small children. Teachers will find the kind of teaching they would like to do, parents the kind of education they want for their own children, school board members the kind of learning they want in their school, supervisors and superintendents the kind of education they are striving for, and teachers' colleges the kind of teaching for which they want to prepare their graduates.

This book is important in that it goes to the heart of education—the way in which learning can affect children's lives and the life of their community. Americans have a deep and abiding faith in their public schools. The pioneer forefathers set out to build a school within walking distance of every child, and the school has been constantly expanding ever since. But too often the school has been content with merely teaching the three R's or being a place where things are done for children rather than a place where children learn how to do things for themselves. In "My Country School Diary" the teacher and children are shown planning, working and living together. The teacher came to know her children, their hopes and fears, their successes and failures, their lives at home and school. Then as a wise counsellor and guide worked with them in deciding what should be done and how to go about it.

The author is particularly well-qualified to write this book. Her deep understanding of rural children, her fine conception of the way in which the school can help them to grow and develop, and her faith in the ability of the individual to meet his responsibilities are all evident throughout the book. The careful diary she kept over a four-year period in order to watch the development of each child is characteristic of the thoroughness with which she worked. Friends who encouraged her to make this diary available to others through this book may review the results with a sense of deep satisfaction.

Rural communities are being reshaped by modern transportation and communication, by modern machinery and equipment, and by the new world which these are creating. If these changes are to build a finer community life, they must be guided and used by the people who live in the country. The new problems must be solved and the new opportunities met. To do this, rural people must be effectively educated. This book points the way to the kind of learning on which such education should be built.

PRELUDE

O spare me your talk of fate! Human reason needs only to will more strongly than fate, and she is fate.

Thomas Mann—*The Magic Mountain*

This is the story of four years in a one-teacher school in an isolated mountain neighborhood. Leaving the last town, the road climbs up until suddenly the summit is reached and we can look down into a small, narrow valley along the crest of the mountain. The road, with about a dozen houses strung on either side of it, dips down and continues to wind along the bottom of the valley. At the end of the road, in a clearing in the woods, is Stony Grove School. As I turned the last bend in the road, the scene always came upon me suddenly even after I knew it well. It was pleasant on these mornings to be welcomed by the call of the ovenbird, "Teacher, teacher!" I knew I belonged here. Ever since I was a little girl I had wanted to teach in a school such as this one. That privilege has now been mine.

I kept a diary during those years at Stony Grove for, above all, I wanted to learn to be a good teacher, and writing what was happening seemed to be a good way to help me to think more clearly. Some of my friends thought that the diary should be published. I am a teacher and not a writer, but in spite of my literary shortcomings I decided to undertake the task of preparing the diary for publication because I felt I had something to say. In the next few years education has to make serious decisions concerning the direction it will take. I want to add this story to the many others which weight the balance in favor of the kind of education that will make a difference in the living of people. It is my firm conviction that education can significantly improve the quality of living.

But to make this significant difference, old methods will not do. We must have something more than book learning. We must know children, what they are like and what they need. We can best meet these needs by capitalizing on their interests, by using the resources near at hand in their environment, and by supplementing these resources where necessary. In this way we can help children to develop wholesome personalities and to meet creatively the challenges of our unpredictable world.

Since the present book is one-fourth the size of the original diary, it is necessarily somewhat of a summary. There is much more to knowing children and their backgrounds than I have been able to indicate here. I hope that you will feel this knowledge of the children and their environment buried deep within each sentence. I have not tried to give any technical treatment of such subjects as the teaching of reading. This has been adequately done by others. What I have tried to show in this book is a way of living and working with children.

The group living reached its highest quality in the fourth year. This could not have come about without the struggles of the three years preceding it. Perhaps in reading about the difficulties we had in arriving at this level of growth, you will find something of interest, some help, and perhaps even some inspiration.

Before I went to Stony Grove I taught for three years in larger schools in our county. During this time I learned to overcome many of the difficulties which are faced by every beginning teacher. But even more important than this, I was inspired by the work of the county and I learned what teaching can mean.

In our county we have the superintendent of schools who is appointed by the State Department of Public Instruction to direct the work of the schools. We have, also, three Helping Teachers, as rural supervisors in New Jersey are called, who work closely with the teachers. These four people have provided a sound and forward-looking leadership. They have studied and experimented and have taken the initiative in trying to find better ways to provide for the wholesome devel-

opment of boys and girls. There has been the closest co-operation among them in serving the children of the county.

One member of this group has been in the county for more
than twenty-five years working consistently on the belief that
children are important and that what happens to them matters
a great deal. This consideration of children has been the foundation of our educational program. The state leadership during
this time, also, has been such that the counties have been able
to work together in building a better program of education all
over the state.

Several agencies in the county co-operate in the program of
the school. Rural nurses make weekly visits to the schools. A
County Library with a well-trained librarian supplies the
schools with abundant reading materials. A home demonstration agent and a 4-H Club agent in the Agricultural Extension
Service guide the work of the 4-H clubs in the schools and
help the boys and girls as well as the adults of the community
to appreciate and to improve rural living.

The policy of the county and the contributions of these
agencies were in evidence when I went to Stony Grove. The
children were happy and had a nice relationship with their
teacher. The teacher had worked on committees sharing in the
development of the educational policies of the county. She
knew the children and was trying to meet their needs. There
was an established hot lunch program, with excellent equipment, planned by the home demonstration agent, the helping
teacher, and the teacher together. There was close co-operation between the Township Board of Education and the
County Department of Public Instruction.

Stony Grove was a good place to be in. I did not have to
conform to anything. I was in a state and a county whose
educational program for years has taken children into account.
It was a developing program in which I could have a share.
When I began to teach at Stony Grove I was ready to learn
and free to experiment to find out how a group of children and
their teacher may reach a high level of creative and democratic
living. If I have succeeded somewhat, it is because all the roads

were open to me. I had every opportunity and invaluable help to discover for myself what mental hygienists have been telling us, that human nature and the situation in which we find ourselves are not fixed but, to an important degree, are what we make them and that they can be changed. We *can* arrive at a social arrangement through which each individual can realize to the fullest his potentialities and through which, all together, we can experience a high level of human living— if we only will!

I want to express my gratitude to all these people I have mentioned. My indebtedness to them is immeasurable. I am also deeply indebted to my parents, who, humble folk though they are, have always recognized the power of education; and to my many wonderful friends, who, over the years of my life, have helped me to be a better person than I might have been, and therefore a better teacher.

Dr. Frank Cyr gently but persistently goaded me until I promised to prepare the diary for publication, and then he read and criticized the manuscript and presented it to the publisher. Dr. Fannie Dunn, Anne Hoppock, Blanche Moran, and Dr. Percy Hughes also read the manuscript and gave me helpful suggestions and criticisms. To them I am especially grateful. My thanks go also to Mr. and Mrs. Wallace Clark, who typed the manuscript and gave me editorial advice.

Most of all I am indebted to Marcia Everett. She gave unselfishly and abundantly of herself that I might become a creative teacher. This book is one tangible result of our long hours of inspiring conversations and discussions both at school and before the cheery fire in her home. She read the original diary page by page as it was written over those four years. She watched and guided our growth in this little school closely and sympathetically. Without her devoted help and friendship this book might never have been written.

My

Country

School

Diary

In this account, the names of the children, other people, and places in the community are fictitious. I have kept the names of the people in the various county agencies and of those outside the community who helped us.

1

I Learn to Know the Children

FRIDAY, JUNE 5, 1936. I visited today the little school in which I shall begin to teach next fall. It gave me a strange excited feeling as I drove up to the front door of the clean, white box-like structure, shining in the sun. I have a deep faith in one-
I prepare for the first day
teacher schools and in the opportunities they afford to prepare children for a continually developing creative and democratic life. Here I shall have an opportunity to live closely with a group of children and to learn to know them intimately. I shall have them long enough to watch them grow and develop their capacities under guidance in as rich an environment as it is possible to make for them. I paused for a moment at the door and looked around at the woods surrounding the little schoolhouse. The recent rain made the leaves shine and the woods smelled so nice. "All this will be our laboratory," I thought.

The children were preparing a circus for their annual Play Day when I entered the room. A few cast shy glances in my direction but all went on working. As the children worked, their teacher related to me significant items concerning their background, their abilities, and their emotional development. My notes from this conversation and a list of the children with their ages and grades were the only records I received.

Grade		Age Yrs.-Mo.
8	Anna Olseuski	13-5
8	Olga Prinlak	15-8
7	Ralph Jones	13-7
7	Catherine Sametis	15-2
7	Ruth Thompson	11-3
6	Sophia Sametis	10-8
6	Doris Andrews	11-3
6	Mary Olseuski	10-10
6	Frank Prinlak	14-8
5	May Andrews	9-3
5	Warren Hill	9-7
5	George Prinlak	12-4
5	Edward Veniski	10-10
4	Helen Olseuski	8-0
4	Andrew Dulio	12-2
3	Albert Hill	8-3
3	Pearl Prinlak	10-1
3	Martha Jones	8-9
3	Joseph Dunder	13-5
3	Verna Cartwright	11-2
3	Alex Cartwright	12-1
3	Gus Cartwright	13-2
2	Alice Prinlak	8-8
2	Walter Williams	7-1
2	William Sametis	7-8
Beginners		
	Richard Cartwright	8-6
	John Dunder	8-4
	Joyce Williams	5-4

MONDAY, JULY 6. I went to the schoolhouse and emptied the cupboard of its books. For the most part they are good although few in number. At the very top of the cupboard I crammed the old and out-of-date books that I know I shall never use and yet do not dare to destroy. The others, after laying aside one of each kind to take home, I stacked neatly where I could get them easily in September. I shall need to stay close to the basic texts until I have learned more about the children and also about managing a one-teacher school.

There are about a dozen books of the library type, and from their appearance I judge that the children must have read them over and over again. I'll stop at the County Library before school opens and get an armful of new books.

This first year, it seems to me, I have two purposes. The first is to learn as much as possible about the needs and abilities of the children. The second is to begin to meet **I have two** these needs and to develop these abilities **purposes for** through such opportunities as arise in our daily **the first year** living together and through the resources near at hand in the community.

MONDAY, SEPTEMBER 7.   The schoolhouse looked so alone today with the weeds growing up around it. Schoolhouses should be used in summer too. Mr. Hart was washing windows when I arrived. He told me that he comes once a year to clean the stove and the chimney, the windows, the walls, and to oil the floor. The rest of the time it is up to us to keep the place clean. I "rolled up my sleeves" and began to arrange the room and to get out the material we shall use the first day. The seats and desks are movable. Besides these, the only other furniture in the room consists of two small movable bookcases, an old organ, a teacher's desk and swivel chair. I have fallen heir to a home-made table and four chairs made from orange crates, which probably constituted the library corner in other years. There is a jacket-type stove in one corner out of the way. At the entrance end of the room there is a small hall, one side of which has a sink but no running water. This side is used as a cloak-room. The other side is a kitchen. Two built-in cupboards rise from the floor to the ceiling giving ample cupboard space for the cooking and eating utensils. There is also a two burner oil stove. (See Appendix p. 258.)

When Mr. Hart and I left, the schoolhouse looked and felt clean. The interior has been repainted this summer in soft cream yellow.

TUESDAY, SEPTEMBER 8. During the summer I reread *Four Years in a Country School* by Fannie W. Dunn and Marcia A. Everett and also became familiar with the textbooks I am to use. Today I settled down to the important task of planning for the first day. The children must feel that they have accomplished something and have had a happy time doing it so that school is worth going back to the next day. The program must allow some opportunity for me to observe the children while they are working in order that I may begin to know them and to think in terms of them. At the same time, the program must be definite enough to give me confidence so that I can laugh with the children and have them know me for a friend. So much of the success or failure of the whole year will depend on this first day. This is the outline of my plans:

9:00–9:30 Adjust seats and desks to fit the children. Distribute books and materials. (This will give the children something active to do from the beginning.)

9:30–10:30 Social Studies. For the first ten minutes make a little speech to the children. Get them to talk about themselves if possible.

Assign the first few pages in the history text to the upper grade group (6, 7, 8) and to the intermediate group (4, 5). Questions to be answered will be written on the board. These children will study while I talk with the primary grade children for twenty minutes.

Talk with the primary children about their summer fun. Little children usually get around to their pets when they talk. Try to have all the children contribute something. Plan with them to make booklets, perhaps of their pets. Let them draw a picture to describe what they have contributed to the discussion.

The primary children continue to draw their pictures while I work with the intermediate group for fifteen minutes. We shall go over the questions one by one and discuss them.

The primary children go outdoors, with a child from the intermediate group in charge. The intermediate group continues to study as I suggest to them during the discussion period. I work with the upper grade group for fifteen minutes and follow the same procedure as with the intermediate group.

10:30–10:50 Physical Education. Start the children from grades 4-8 playing Dodge Ball and then play with the primary children.

10:50–12:00 Give the primary children the Clark-Ingraham Reading Diagnostic Test. (This is for the purpose of finding out something of their reading ability.) In the meantime the older children will read the first story in their readers and answer some questions to check their comprehension. When they have finished, they will have access to the new library books I shall take to school with me.

12:00–1:00 Twenty-minute lunch period followed by outdoor play.
1:00–1:30 Devotions: Bible reading, Lord's Prayer, Salute to the flag, America.

   Music. Have the children sing songs of their own choosing from the *Golden Book of Songs*.

1:30–2:15 The older children will have a diagnostic arithmetic test. The little children will have access to the library books and then will go out to play. This period will allow me to watch the work habits of the children.

   At 2:15 the primary children go home.

2:15–2:30 Physical Education. Play a game with the upper grade children.

2:30–2:45 Spelling. Combine grades 7 and 8 and use the eighth grade words in the spelling test. Combine grades 5 and 6 and use the sixth-grade words. Use the fourth-grade words for grade 4. Take the whole class together and teach them how to study their words independently and efficiently.

2:45–3:30 Arithmetic. This will be largely individual. Each child will begin with the review lessons in the beginning of his book. I shall have further opportunity to observe the study habits of the children.

Although this program is rather formal, my attitude toward the children can be informal and friendly.

WEDNESDAY, SEPTEMBER 9. I started out with fear and trembling this morning. In spite of the fact that I was prepared and knew that the room was in order, the materials handy, and the day carefully planned, all my inadequacies lay heavily upon me. It is eleven miles to the schoolhouse from home, and as I drove along I rehearsed my speech. I would tell the children how happy I am that I shall be one of them; how fortunate we are to live in such a beautiful place and have it all to explore. I would tell them, too, that this year will be pretty much what we make it. We shall solve our problems together and try to understand each other.

The first day

I began to be afraid that the children would not understand. Perhaps I should tell a story, a humorous story, but for the life of me I could not think of a single appropriate one.

When I arrived at the schoolhouse, all the children were gathered around the door so that I could hardly get to it. They entered with me and took seats, shifting around until each found a seat that suited him. Finally, a calm settled over the place and the children looked at me expectantly. There was nothing left to do but start school. We raised and lowered desks and seats adjusting them to fit the children. Ralph and Frank supervised the job. By nine o'clock we were ready to start work. The children were silent today and for the most part did only what they were asked to do.

Some of the children stand out from the group. Ralph and Frank, the two big boys, and Anna and Ruth were willing to help wherever there was an opportunity. Martha's eyes sparkle aloud. The Hill boys have nice smiles. Olga is so big and shy and seems to feel out of place. The two little Williams children seem to be nervous. There are so many Cartwrights. Joseph Dunder, who is a borderline case, as the report from the psychological clinic indicates, was really a nuisance. All the children seem shy and retiring.

THURSDAY, SEPTEMBER 10. The order of the day was somewhat similar to that of yesterday and my main purpose was to

I learn to know the children through observing and discovering their needs

find out more about the children. During the reading periods, I heard each child read orally and I have decided how I shall group them temporarily. I discovered that the history texts are entirely too difficult for the two groups, with the exception of the eighth graders, to understand. Andrew, who should be a fourth grader, cannot read a primer. The primary children did well on their reading test, but from the fourth grade on up the reading is generally poor. Only a few of the children like to read. All looked at the pictures in the library books but only a few of the girls began to read the books. All this shows that one of my big jobs is to help these children to get the most from a printed page and to find joy in reading. I think that one reason for low reading ability here is lack of experience. I noticed that they substitute colloquialisms for certain words in their reading.

Two other needs became apparent today. First, these children do not know how nor do they like to play together. Yesterday the girls had trouble with the boys in their game of dodge ball. The girls said the boys were too rough. Today the girls asked to join the game the little children were playing. The game I had started for the boys soon broke up and they stood watching us. I invited them to join us and got a response of laughter. I noticed that Ralph seemed to be the leader and I made a mental note to figure out how I could get him on my side.

Second, these children feel insecure when they are asked to take part in an activity other than what they consider schoolwork. Most of the boys do not sing. They tell me they can't. I asked them if they would like to learn to play the harmonica. The response was fine. This will help these oversensitive boys to have some experience with music.

I got a little closer to individual children today. Warren had two crying spells because he was unable to do his work. The first time I ignored it, but the second time he was crying

I learn to know the children through personal conferences so hard that I took time from the physical education period, while the others were playing, to talk to him. I said, "Warren, we should not cry about our problems but try to solve them. Part of my job is to help you with the problems which you cannot solve by yourself. Instead of crying, won't you tell me what your troubles are?" Between two heavy sighs he said he would try.

John and Joseph Dunder were absent today. This gave me an opportunity to visit the home and get acquainted with

I learn to know the children through home visits their parents. Warren offered to go along to show me where the Dunders live and I welcomed this opportunity to get to know him better. Warren's brother, Albert, and Walter Williams wanted to go along too. After school I went first to the homes of Warren and Walter to get permission to take the boys with me. Mrs. Hill was baking bread when we arrived. The Hills bought this small farm three years ago and are fixing the house over. Warren delighted in taking me around the house to point out the improvements. I liked especially the large stone fireplace they had built in the living room. Mr. Hill is a teacher and comes home week-ends.

At the Williams' I met the mother and two other children who are not yet old enough to come to school. Mr. Williams works for the township on the roads. The Williams have a beautiful vegetable and flower garden. Mrs. Williams showed me all the fruit she had canned this week.

The Dunders live in a small shack. Mr. Dunder is the caretaker of a piece of property owned by people who live in New York. Mrs. Dunder explained to me that the boys did not feel like going to school today. I tried to tell her how important regular attendance is but she said she couldn't make the boys go if they didn't want to. I did not get very far.

Tonight, I planned carefully my daily program. This is subject to change as soon as it proves inadequate. I am ignor-

The daily program
ing grade lines to group children where they seem to fit best. This will mean fewer groups and I can spend more time with each group. Then, too, working in a larger group, the children will have opportunities for discussion, for interchange of ideas, and for

THE DAILY PROGRAM*

Time	Monday	Tuesday	Wednesday	Thursday	Friday
9:00	Social Studies with Primary Group (B-3)				Science
9:20	Social Studies—Intermediate Group (4-5)				
9:40	Social Studies—Upper Grades (6,7,8)			}	Science
10:00	Physical Education with Primary Group—Upper Grades have pupil leadership				
10:20	Reading, Group I				
10:35	Reading, Group II				
10:50	Reading, Group III				
11:05	Reading, Group IV				
11:20	Reading Group V	Reading Group VI	Reading Group V	Reading Group VI	Library
11:40	English (4-8)				Health (4-8)
12:00	Twenty minute Lunch Period and Supervised Play				
1:00	Devotions and Music				
1:30	Drill in Spelling and Arithmetic—Primary Group (mainly individual instruction)				
2:15	Physical Education for Upper Grades				
	(Primary group goes home)				
2:30	Spelling and Arithmetic Drill for Upper Grades—(mainly individual instruction)				
3:20	Clean up				

*This shows only the time spent with the teacher.

social development which they would not have if they worked alone or in small groups.

FRIDAY, SEPTEMBER 11.   Our bare school grounds is a decided contrast to the beautiful surroundings. I thought that beautifying our schoolgrounds would be a good place to start our nature study and science since it would give a practical purpose for such study. I suggested that we make some drawings of the schoolgrounds on which we can record any changes we will want to make in the future. We listed on the blackboard all the areas and stationary objects that needed to be measured. Then we divided the class (grades 4-8) into groups of two and the children went outdoors with tape measures and yardsticks while I turned my attention to the little folks.

The primary group talked about signs of fall. The children will bring in colored leaves to press, various kinds of seeds, cocoons, and fall wild flowers. Alex and Gus want to bring in an anthill in a jar, as our science book suggests, to see if the ants will hibernate. All these will go into a nature museum. We had time to make some paper windmills.

As the little folks played outside with their newly made windmills, I helped the older children with their drawings of the schoolgrounds. We made a rough drawing on the board recording the dimensions, and then together computed the scale we would have to use to make the drawing fit the paper. In the course of the conversation, the children suggested that we have a small bulb bed in front of the schoolhouse.

I set aside a special time for library reading so that I can begin to guide the children's reading. Also, this will give the children an opportunity to share what they are reading. The only way I know to help children to like to read is to have them read, and read under satisfying conditions. Upon invitation, four of the primary group volunteered to tell the rest of the children about the books they are reading. Martha did a fine job and amused the group. William and Walter were somewhat embarrassed and spoke so softly that we had difficulty hearing them.

The need for good health habits is obviously great. I thought we had better have as practical an approach as possible to begin to improve these habits. After a few introductory remarks about the importance of health in our daily living, I asked the children to list all the things involving health which they did from the time they arose in the morning until they went to bed. We had a long list on the blackboard. I pointed out that, since almost everything we do involves the practice of good health habits, health knowledge is important if we are to live well. We plan to consider each item in detail to answer the "why" of all newly initiated habits.

Play periods were better today. Everyone played except the two Andrews girls. Doris said she has a weak heart.

After school I organized our 4-H Forestry Club. This neighborhood is rich in natural resources. Children should know

Some needs are met through using the environment

a great deal about the place in which they live. It gives them roots, a feeling of security and of belonging.

The club will include the high school children who live in the neighborhood. They have been stopping at the schoolhouse each night after school. Since the town is four miles away and there are no community agencies other than the school, there is no place for them to go for recreation.

At this first meeting there were eleven of us and five high school girls. We went on a treasure hunt, for I wanted to know just how much these children did know about their natural environment. Each person who found a specimen in nature which he could identify had to stand by his specimen, as destroying it disqualified him from the team. There were two teams captained by two high school girls. We identified ninety-eight specimens. These youngsters know their nature!

As Doris usually goes home on the bus, I promised to take her home tonight so that she could stay for the club meeting. I met her mother, a quiet woman who seldom leaves her house. I found that Doris does not have a weak heart. Her mother says she is not a very healthy child. She tap dances at home all the time and it tires her out! I must encourage Doris to play with the other children. She needs this socializing experience. Mr. Andrews is not living and Mrs. Andrews gets a state pension for her children.

MONDAY, SEPTEMBER 14. There are so many details to teaching in a one-teacher school that I am afraid I shall never learn to do any of the work well unless I concentrate on a few of them at a time. For a while my major emphasis will be on reading and management. I shall try to give these children many guided reading experiences all through the day.

Management in a school of this kind should not be such a big problem. If we can get certain routine matters, such as cleaning up the room and grounds, on an efficient basis we can turn our attention to other things. Then, too, there is the problem of management on the playground which will need close supervision for a while. The children had been running aimlessly over the countryside during the noon hour and they feel that I am taking away their "recess" when I ask them to play together during the physical education periods. The school is divided into small cliques and each group has little interest in any of the others. They do not have a consciousness of their group as a whole.

Gus brought one of his pet white mice to school and we wrote a story about it which the primary group is now learning to read. It was a hard job to get the story and I had to ask many questions and to make many suggestions.

I gave the two older groups other history books that are not so difficult for them. The children have been writing answers to the questions I write on the board, but we do not use the papers in our discussions. Whenever the children cannot answer a question, we find the answer in the book and read it aloud. Then we put it into our own words and write it. This is a dull procedure, but it is a first step for these children. They are learning to read historical material, and are working for accuracy as well as for clarity in their writing. All this takes time now but will save time later.

TUESDAY, SEPTEMBER 15. Children learn to be responsible by assuming responsibilities. If they are to become intelligent

Some needs are met through providing opportunities for democratic living

citizens they must have practice in the responsibilities of citizenship. At the end of the day, I talked to the children about organizing a service club. They had no idea what the activities of such a club were so I did most of the talking. I explained that they would share in the solution of problems which affected the whole group and that we would keep trying

to make our school a better place to live in. We organized ourselves into a club and elected officers. When I asked the children what they thought a president should be like, they said that he should be kind, good, and big. They thought the vice-president should have the same qualifications and that the secretary should be a good writer. Anna is our first president, Ralph our vice-president, and Mary our secretary. Following the election, we made a list on the board of all the duties that need to be done daily and decided who was to do each one.

General Manager—Olga
Sweep room—Ralph and Edward
Sweep girls' toilet—Ruth
Sweep boys' toilet—George
Dust—Catherine and Alice
Hall Manager—Anna
Librarian—Sophia
Curator of Museum—May
Handwashing—Andrew
Stove and room temperature—Frank
Inspect desks—Warren
Raise and lower flag—Doris
Windows—Mary
Water flowers—Helen
Inspect cupboards—Verna
Overshoes and lunchboxes—Richard and Walter
Play materials—Gus
Burn papers—Alex
Host—Albert
Hostess—Martha

Names were suggested for our club and we finally decided on the "Helpers' Club."

I visited at the Olseuskis' today. Anna's mother was so happy that her daughter had been elected "head" of the class, as she called it. The kitchen is bare and there is no linoleum on the thoroughly scrubbed floor. The children wear uninteresting and ill-fitted homemade clothes, but they are spotless. Mr. Olseuski is dead and Mrs. Olseuski gets a state pension for her children. She told me that her children liked the new teacher and hoped I would visit the home often. At first the girls had refused to speak in Polish to their mother, and I learned that they had asked her not to use her native language while I was there, for they were afraid I might not like it. When I told them that I not only speak but read and write the language of my parents it cleared the atmosphere immediately.

At the Prinlaks' I was given an armful of flowers. There are eleven children in the Prinlak family. Two are working, five are in school, and four are under school age. The income is meager as it depends on the milk production of only four cows. Mrs. Prinlak looks undernourished and overworked.

WEDNESDAY, SEPTEMBER 16. The discussion of Gus's mouse was more fluent today and in no time we had a story. The children had something to write about.

> We are watching Jumbo.
> He eats apples and bread.
> He climbs up the screen.
> He makes a nest.
> He is afraid of us.
> We are going to be more quiet.

A calm settled over the children during the second half of the afternoon. Arithmetic is a great calmer of bodies, at least. I like having it at the end of the day. I helped Warren with his addition combinations today. He knew it was second-grade work but he accepted the help and did not cry.

On my way home I stopped in to see Mrs. Sametis. Mr. Sametis has a store in the city and comes home once a month. The house was upset and not very clean. There is an older girl in high school who seems to be very intelligent. The other children are well poised and interesting. I'd like to know more about their background.

Before I went home I stopped at the Hills'. We talked at great length about Warren. Warren began to show signs of sensitivity when he went to nursery school. After the Hills bought this farm and Warren started out to a new school, the changes in method were confusing to him. When he thought he could not keep up he became so emotionally concerned that this stood in the way of further learning. The boys found that he "hurt" easily and made life quite miserable for him. Albert did not mind the teasing and adjusted more easily. Perhaps, together, Mrs. Hill and I can do something for Warren.

THURSDAY, SEPTEMBER 17. Before school started this morning some of the boys had started a game of cops and robbers when Ralph suggested, "Let's play dodge ball." Before nine o'clock everyone was in the game and playing hard! They are beginning to enjoy playing together.

Walter brought his dog to school and we wrote a story about him for the pet books. The social studies for the older children still go slowly. I am using the children's social studies papers for lessons in English. We use part of the social studies period to make the necessary corrections and to learn why they need to be made. On some days, as each child in the group studies his own paper for errors, I help those who ask for help. On other days, when many children are making the same kinds of errors, I discuss these with the whole group. At times it is necessary to use suitable drill material from their English books to give the children practice in some needed skill. We use the regular period set aside for English for this purpose.

Some needs are met through individualized instruction

I like to go over the papers with the children as often as possible. It seems such a waste of time to correct papers after school, for children seldom look at them after they are corrected except to see what grade they received. Consequently, in order to focus attention on the correction of errors, I have stopped grading papers. Working closely with the children is efficient, and the valuable time after school can be spent in learning more about the children and the community, in meeting needs through clubwork, and in planning and evaluating the program of the school.

During the library period, Albert Hill told the story of Little Black Sambo in a most interesting and entertaining fashion. Two of the older children volunteered to tell about the books they are reading. This is the first time any of the older children have volunteered. All these children need to talk a great deal more.

Some needs are met through providing opportunities for self-expression

During the health period, we talked about the health practices involved in getting ready for school. Some of the children come to school without any breakfast. Most of them forget to brush their teeth. Only a few remember to bring handkerchiefs, as they say they never need to use them. I suggested that it would be a good idea to have some kind of checkup to help us form good habits. Each child began to make a chart for his notebook on squared paper with space to check each item for each day. The older children will make charts for the younger ones. Each morning the older children will check their own charts and one of them will help the little children check theirs. I shall inspect the children unobserved throughout the activities of the day. Also I shall try to encourage the children to eat good breakfasts.

We had our first club meeting today. Anna was not at all self-conscious and did well in presiding over the meeting. I had to do a great deal of prompting as to parliamentary procedure and suitable topics for discussion. The children said they were getting tired of playing dodge ball. I suggested that they draw up their own schedule of games. They elected Ralph, Ruth, and Mary to serve on a committee to plan the games for next week. The children also brought up and discussed the matter of playing fairly and being less rough.

After school I had supper at the Williams home. The children are somewhat shy and nervous. They love their mother. Mrs. Williams approves of modern methods of education.

SATURDAY, SEPTEMBER 19.　I finished going over the diagnostic tests which I gave to the older children. According to the test results, six of the children (Anna, Olga, Sophia, May, Helen, and Mary) are doing good work, and the other eight (Ralph, Ruth, Catherine, Frank, Doris, Warren, Edward, and George) are somewhat retarded. Olga and Anna did exceptionally well. The children seemed to have the most difficulty with language and with reading. Warren was the exception; he did well in both. Arithmetic seems to be the weakest subject of the brighter children. All this bears out fairly well what I have been feeling about these children.

MONDAY, SEPTEMBER 21.　I am still having difficulties with getting the children to play well together. The game committee met before school to plan the games for **Some needs are met through group play** the week. Everything was fine until the physical education period in the afternoon when Frank and George refused to play the game and, for a while, the atmosphere was unhappy. Ralph and Anna saved the day by deciding to play without these two boys. The other children followed their suggestion and they had a good game after all. Ralph is fast becoming a leader on the playground. I spoke to Frank and George and explained that it is difficult to please everyone at the same time in a group of this size and that sometimes we had to play games we did not like. If everyone played only the games he liked, there would never be enough members to play any one game well. These children need to learn to respect the rights of minorities. The preaching probably didn't do much good. They have to experience what I said before they comprehend the full meaning. They will with time, I hope.

At noon Anna and Ruth took the little children on a hike. They gathered seeds, leaves, and flowers. The boys began to prepare the ground for our bulb bed. What a peaceful noon hour!

The little children do not work so well as the older ones. The hour in the morning seems so long for them to be alone. Martha and Pearl usually manage to find something interesting to do when their regular work is finished. Albert and William never get finished because they spend too much time making faces at each other.

I was hoping to get the pet booklets finished today. When I suggested it they protested, "No, we haven't written about our bull frog and chipmunk yet." Pearl and Martha have become independent and write original stories. The others copy the group story into their notebooks after they have learned to read the story. The beginners just have a picture book.

TUESDAY, SEPTEMBER 22. Warren had another unhappy morning. Someone called him a "sissy" and he cried as if his heart would break. I talked quietly with him for a while and told him that the boys would continue to tease him as long as he reacted the way he did. He said he would try not to cry, but he knew no one liked him. I pointed out that it wasn't that the boys did not like him, they were just having a little fun at his expense. He showed me his stamp collection and asked if he could keep it at school. Warren managed to get all his work done today for the first time and in the afternoon he played like a real boy.

I visited the Veniski home today. Mr. Veniski told me in his broken English about all the troubles he has had in the past fifteen years building up his farm, but now he has four big sons to take over the work. Edward is the youngest in the family. There are strong ties in this family and they are industrious people.

WEDNESDAY, SEPTEMBER 23. I tried dividing up that long period in the morning for the little children with two fifteen-

Some needs are met through adjusting the the school program

minute story periods. Olga took half the group first and then Anna took the other half. They read to the little children. At 11:40 they went out to play. This worked much better. They settled down to business quickly, finished the job they had to do, and did their work more neatly than yesterday.

THURSDAY, SEPTEMBER 24. The children did not like the idea of keeping our animals in the hall as they could not watch them there. They suggested that we have a corner of our room for the museum. Since this necessitated some changes, we planned to rearrange the room at noon. The lightest part of the room will be used for our reading groups and the library. We found a place for our science museum in the front of the room where it will not be in the way. We set aside a place for the little children to play when they cannot go outdoors. My desk was put in the rear of the room as I seldom use it anyway. When it was all over, the room looked so nice that some of the older girls remained after school to clean the book and supply cupboard. They said it did not go well with our nice, orderly room.

After school Mrs. Dulio told me that Andrew had a serious head injury when he was seven years old. They did not expect him to live. She feels that this has definitely affected his mind. The Dulios have been here only a few months. They came from the city because it was getting too expensive to live there. They are hard workers. Besides taking care of his own farm, Mr. Dulio is caretaker of a small estate.

FRIDAY, SEPTEMBER 25. The children are mounting the leaves and flowers they have collected and identified. The older children worked quietly during the first half hour while I helped the little ones with the covers of their pet booklets. Then Anna helped the little folks cut out the letters and paste them in place, while I took the older children outside to make plans for our school grounds. Anna works so quietly and easily with the little children. She wants to be a teacher. We talked generally about how we would like our school grounds to look. When we came back into the room we divided into committees to do some reading for the various parts of our plans. There are four committees to study about perennials, shrubs, soil, and a wild-flower rock garden. The committees are to decide on appropriate plants to use and where they would like to put them.

The Helpers' Club meeting was poor. These children are so self-conscious and giggle nervously when they address "Madam President." I try to keep the meeting short and encourage the children to act quickly. Today we made two rules: we must not leave the school grounds without permission, and we must remember to come into the schoolhouse quietly.

The day's work goes much more smoothly now and there is not so much waste of time. The older children have been **Some needs are met through enriched curriculum experiences** studying about the Indians of the continent and are making a frieze to show how the Indians lived in various sections of North America. The intermediate group has been dramatizing spontaneously during the social studies periods "scenes from history" and now the children want to write a play on the life of Columbus. This work, the identifying of their nature specimens, and their library reading are activities which are beginning to take up the spare time of the children. I have not managed so well with the little children, however. They still have too much time to waste.

More trouble on the playground! Almost at the end of the physical education period, Ralph slid into home plate and Frank tagged him with the ball just before his foot touched the plate. I, as umpire, pronounced it "out." Ralph stalked off and said he wasn't going to play any more and kept his word the rest of the day. After school I talked with him. He complained that the sides were unfair and that all the big ones were on Frank's side. I reminded him that the game committee, of which he himself was a member, had approved my selection of teams. I asked him if he thought he solved the problem by refusing to play. I suggested that he bring up the matter with the game committee and rearrange the sides more fairly.

At our Forestry Club meeting we made a simple constitution, elected officers, and planned our nature hobby committees. All the members are interested in geology and want to study that together. They are also interested in animal habits.

There are two Jones girls in high school. I went home with them to meet their oldest sister, who keeps house for them. Since their mother died two years ago they are living in their grandmother's house. Mr. Jones is a mechanic in town. Martha played some hymns on the piano for me. She has learned to play them "by ear." Ralph got into old clothes and went out to play. He wasn't going to stay in with all the girls! I suddenly saw the background of some of Ralph's dislike for girls. He is the only boy in a family of five girls, four of them older than himself.

MONDAY, SEPTEMBER 28. The game committee was to meet this morning to even up the teams. The committee met, but where was Ralph? When he came in to the meeting he was very unco-operative and kept saying to each suggestion of the group, "I don't care what you do." The committee came to me for help. I suggested that they postpone the meeting until Ralph was in a better mood. When school began, the cloud lifted and at noon, when the committee met again, Ralph took an active part. Then Frank was dissatisfied and said he had the weaker team. Ralph nobly said he would change teams with him. Everything was fine.

In order to help the children to be more independent, I began to put the plans for the day's work on the blackboard. It helped some to reduce the waste of time, but the children need practice in the use of these plans. I think it will be well to go through the plans with the children each morning. Later, perhaps, we can plan the work of each day together.

Before we went outdoors to eat our lunch today I talked to the children about the paper and food that is thrown

Some needs are met through housekeeping activities

around. By the end of the day the schoolroom and grounds look very untidy. I gave Olga the job of general manager of cleanup hoping this would give her some confidence in herself and make her feel her worth to the group. She doesn't do a good job, allowing the children to do their work in a slipshod manner or to shirk their duties altogether. Part of the trouble is that the children do not know how to do their work. Catherine knows her job is to dust, but what to dust and how to dust is the problem. While the children worked individually at their arithmetic, I took each child in turn and helped him to see just what his responsibility is and how it is to be done. I helped Olga make a check sheet for herself so that she can check off the jobs as they get done. I purposely put the emphasis on the work rather than on the individual doing the work. In this way children do not criticize each other and may in time help each other to see that a job is well done.

TUESDAY, SEPTEMBER 29. It was cold enough to have a fire today. Frank took care of it all day. He is a responsible fireman and knows more about the stove than I do. He also regulated the temperature by raising and lowering the windows and adjusting the draft.

Since it was a rainy day, we had to play indoors. We played fruit basket upset and Jacob and Ruth. Helen and Martha are so noisy. They scream about everything. Joseph, of course, tops them all. Whenever the group gets active, he practically goes wild. The children have learned not to notice him, however, so he is not so much of a problem as he might be. They seem to sense that he is not responsible. There is little I can do for Joseph in a regular classroom situation. He should be in an institution where he can get the attention he needs.

This morning for the first time I went over the day's plans with the children and it did help, as the children knew what was expected of them all day. I put on the blackboard the plans for the older children only.

Plans for Today

8:55–9:05 Plan the day's work.

9:05–9:20 Group A read from mimeograph, Homes of the Indians of our County, also about permanent and temporary homes from texts. Begin to write a story on homes for booklets.

Group B begin to plan the scene of Columbus' conversation with Queen Isabella. Write what they would say.

9:20–9:40 Group B with teacher, discuss scene.

Group A continue above.

9:40–10:00 Group A with teacher, discuss Indian homes.

Group B draw a scene for the part discussed.

10:00–10:20 Play "Jacob and Ruth."

10:20–11:20 Group V read story beginning on page 87, answer the questions on the front board.

Group VI read story beginning on page 92, answer the questions on the side board.

Groups V and VI see "Things to be done" when finished with reading.

11:20–11:40 Group VI with teacher, answer questions on reading. Group V continue above.

11:40–12:00 English with teacher, correct errors in stories on Indian Homes and in the dramatization.

1:00–1:30 Harmonica lesson with teacher.

1:30–2:15 See "Things to be done."

2:15–2:30 Play.

2:30–2:45 Spelling, group 4 with teacher. Others study words misspelled in yesterday's preliminary test.

2:45–3:20 Arithmetic, see individual assignment slips. Helen and May work with teacher.

3:20–3:30 Clean up.

On another board were listed these things to be done:

Copy into notebooks words misspelled on test.

Finish arithmetic.

Work on frieze.

Identify leaves and flowers.

Plan arrangement for bulbs.

Do some work for schoolground beautification committee.

Work on social studies stories that have not been finished.

Copy health notes on good paper for notebooks.

WEDNESDAY, SEPTEMBER 30. Another rainy day kept us indoors, but the harmonicas saved the day. We had a lesson during the music period. Although the little children are not learning to play, they wanted to listen today. The children enjoyed the harmonicas so much that they asked to have another lesson during the physical education period, since it was too wet to play outdoors.

The children in group A are making rapid strides in the social studies work, and today for the first time we had a spontaneous discussion. All the children contributed. They are interested in this Indian study. So far, we have had little activity. The children remain in their seats. They work individually on sections of their frieze and will put it together later. Each child is making an illustrated notebook with stories composed from the answers to the questions we have been listing for each lesson.

During our midweek spelling test, Walter went to pieces because he thought he could not spell the words. I told him to forget about the test and just listen while the others were taking it. While the other children were correcting their errors and studying the words they had misspelled, I dictated the words slowly and carefully to Walter and encouraged him to try them. He was overjoyed to find that he could spell them all. "Next time, you won't have any trouble taking the test with the group, will you?" I asked. He did not answer but his smile said much.

THURSDAY, OCTOBER 1. I began to teach the older children an Indian dance during the afternoon physical education period and, much to my surprise and joy, not one of the big boys objected. They are having a good time studying about the Indians of our own county. We have turned aside from our texts for a while and are using mimeographed material which I have prepared.

FRIDAY, OCTOBER 2. This morning we planted the twenty bulbs in the bed after we had decided how to arrange them. The boys put up a wire fence to keep our neighbors' sheep out. The committee on the wild-flower rock garden began to make a list of the wild flowers which grow in our township. The committee on soils did some reading on types of soils and on drainage. They are getting their material from county library books. The other two committees sent to seed companies for catalogues.

We used our health period to make covers for our health booklets. I taught the children how to make letters, using squared paper. The little children are not having formal health lessons except occasionally when we need to talk about health practices for the purpose of consciously improving their habits. All day long, however, there are many opportunities for health teaching. I make suggestions to them during the health inspection. During reading periods they learn how to hold their books, how the light should fall on their work, and how to improve their sitting posture. Outdoor play, illnesses, especially colds, the use of tools, such as pencils and scissors, and the like, also provide many opportunities for health teaching and for the practice of good health habits.

Every one of the children can play the scale on his harmonica and now I shall teach them to play "America."

During the business part of our Forestry Club meeting we made plans for a picnic on Columbus Day. For the rest of the time we went outdoors and I taught the group how to make plaster of Paris casts of animal tracks. We had time only to make the negative.

After the club meeting I visited the Cartwrights. Mrs. Cartwright met me at the door of her home, which is badly in need of repair. It hasn't been painted for years. Windowpanes are missing and dirty rags are stuffed into the squares. The roof has large holes so that the rafters show. The door no longer fits the opening. All the children hid when I arrived and peeped around corners at me. Mrs. Cartwright has six children and six stepchildren. Now I have been to the homes of all the children and it certainly sheds light on the way the children get along in school.

MONDAY, OCTOBER 5. I had a conference with Olga today. This was the first of my regular conferences. Although I have conferences with individual children whenever the need for it arises, I plan to have at least one regular conference a month with each child. At this time together we can evaluate the child's work and plan a program for improvement for the next month. I hope also to encourage the children to talk to me about themselves, their personal likes and dislikes and ambitions, their worries and pleasures, and anything else they would like to tell me. Olga was dreadfully shy and I got no more from her than "Yes" and "No." Her notebook was beautifully written and organized and all her work was up to date. I commended her on her industry and she smiled, somewhat embarrassed. I asked her what she would like to concentrate on for the next month. She didn't know. I suggested that she might plan to make one good report to the group during the library period.

TUESDAY, OCTOBER 6. Olga and Anna are able to do more than the regular work for their group. Since I need to go slowly with the others, I try to make supplementary suggestions to these two girls in the way of additional reading and reports. At present they are at work on an original dramatization. Today they read it to the group. The children thought it would be nice to give it at an entertainment for their parents and friends for the purpose of making money for their hot lunch project. However, the general opinion was that the play was rather short to be given for an evening's entertainment. Sophia suggested that we have a few speeches about the life of the Indians and explain the frieze. We could also show our Indian relic collection. Edward, who had been listening in on this discussion, said, "Why can't we give our play about Columbus, too?" The two social studies groups then became one group to plan for the entertainment.

Some needs are met through opportunities to initiate and plan activities

The boys and Warren had trouble again during the morning play period. I made Warren dry his tears and sent him on an errand to our neighbors so that I could talk with the other children. While he was gone I explained to the group that it would be sad if Warren grew up to be the kind of man who would run away to cry every time someone hurt his feelings, and we were doing not one single thing to help him. "If you would just treat him the way you treat each other, I think you'll find he's not so bad after all," I suggested. From the way the children looked at me I could tell that for them this was a new way of looking at the situation. They have not learned as yet that we do have some responsibility toward our fellow human beings. By the time Warren came back, the children were working and no one looked up when he entered.

This morning, before school began, I was talking with some boys about the books they had read. Frank said he had read *Pinocchio* and liked the book so much that he would like to read it again. Several of the others felt the same way and Ralph asked, "Won't you read it to us?" Then Frank described how he had made a small wooden Pinocchio last year.

The children knew what a puppet show was but they had never seen one. It occurs to me that this would be a fine activity for these shy children. They could prepare plays for each other and have many spontaneous dramatizations. If they could forget themselves in these little dolls, it would set them free to grow in poise and in fluent use of language. They could learn co-operation and responsibility through producing a show. First, I'd better get busy and learn how to make and handle a puppet.

I had a conference with Anna tonight. Her work was just as well done as Olga's. Anna told me much about her two sisters who are housekeepers in New York City and how they are sorry they did not go to high school. They intend to see to it that the rest of the family does go. Anna did not know what she wanted to concentrate on for the next month. I suggested that she try to curb her temper when she corrects her youngest sister. We parted good friends.

WEDNESDAY, OCTOBER 7. Such arguing goes on during the physical education period! As soon as one team is losing, the members accuse the other team of cheating. The older children interrupted my game with the little children twice and finally I said, "If we cannot play together, perhaps we had better not play at all." When we got inside, I pointed out how unhappy everyone was because of the thoughtless things we were saying and doing. They think the score is all-important but having a happy time is far more important. Besides, the exercise didn't do them any good when they were all tied up inside in angry knots.

THURSDAY, OCTOBER 8. The speech yesterday didn't do any good as play time was angrier than ever, and Ralph, Frank and George "quit." While the rest went on playing, we four went into conference. "Boys," I said, "we have to solve this problem once and for all. What have you to suggest?" Frank suggested that he and Ralph choose sides alternately and then the side would be divided more evenly. I told Frank that he knew as well as I did that the sides could never be divided evenly. "But," protested Frank, "if we choose our own sides it will be our own fault if we choose a poor team and we'll have to stick by it." He also suggested that new teams be chosen each week and this changing around will be fair to everybody. Well, time will tell.

After school, I had the first mothers' meeting. They are not used to coming to the schoolhouse for meetings. Only five of the eleven mothers were there: Mrs. Olseuski, Mrs. Williams, Mrs. Cartwright, Mrs. Thompson, and Martha's oldest sister, who keeps house for the Joneses. We discussed financing the hot lunch program. I told the mothers about the entertainment we are planning. They offered to make cake and fudge to sell. Several of the children stayed and showed the mothers the things we are doing. The meeting was friendly and brief.

Some needs are met through parent-teacher co-operation

FRIDAY, OCTOBER 9. The physical education periods were fine today. Ralph and Frank chose sides alternately and the children played baseball. I played rabbit-in-the-circle with the little ones. At the end of the period Frank came up to me and said, "We had a good time, Miss Weber." Ralph's team won and kept winning all day. This gave Frank an opportunity to prove himself and he tested well.

I taught the Forestry Club how to make a positive from a negative plaster of Paris cast. In the last half hour I told the group as simply as I could the story of the formation of the earth and the building up and breaking down of rock. This was to be an introduction to our study of rocks and minerals. Some of the high school girls voluntarily took notes. They were much interested.

It is now exactly one month since the first day of school, and time, I think, for taking stock.

I have attempted this month, first, to get to know the children in this little school and something of their backgrounds, of their needs, and of their abilities. There are **A summary** twenty-eight children in twelve families. There are three Polish, one Italian, one Greek, and seven American families. All these homes, with the exception of the Veniskis', are economically insecure. In most cases the material standards of living are low. However, at the Hills', the Thompsons' and the Olseuskis' I found high spiritual standards and wholesome home living. There is a fineness about the Sametis children that makes me feel there are values in this home not to be discovered in the crude exterior of their daily living.

Generally, the children are rather loud. They read poorly. They are little individualists. They are not very clean and care little about the appearance of their room and surroundings. They are timid. However, they like to collect things, they know nature, they like to sing, they are open to suggestions, and they are happy.

Individually, there are great variations in personality as there always are. All the Olseuski children are quick, intelligent, and able. Helen is a little tomboy, our extreme extrovert. She is always arguing with someone. Anna disapproves of Helen, for Anna is very much a lady. Mary is the happy medium and is probably the best liked child in the group.

The Prinlaks are the shyest children. They have little to do with the others except when it cannot be avoided. Alice and Frank are the least shy of the Prinlaks. Pearl often acts as though she has been treated badly and is trying to get even.

The Sametis children are ready for any activity. Their language expression is beautiful. They are thin and have the poorest postures in the group. William has the blackest eyes, that just sparkle with humor.

Ralph and Martha Jones are much in need of their mother. Their oldest sister and grandmother try hard to give them what they need, but Ralph and Martha lack the love and devotion that only a mother can give. They are constantly having clashes with their grandmother, not understanding, of course, that she is responsible for the fine home they do have. Both of these children are intelligent. Martha has much initiative.

Ruth Thompson is a giggling, shy girl but likable. She contributes little to discussions as she is somewhat slow in her work and finds it difficult. Her mother is going to help me avoid mistakes in working with the community. She tactfully suggests things I should and should not do.

The Andrews girls are hard to understand. They give me the uncomfortable feeling that they do not approve of anything I do. It is the way they look at me with that quizzical expression. I must make a special effort to make friends with them. Both of the girls want to be actresses, especially dancers.

Albert Hill is a happy-go-lucky fellow, a little bit lazy and careless but otherwise well adjusted. Warren is an intelligent and highly sensitive child who is emotionally badly adjusted. Warren has an understanding mother. Both of us want to help Warren to adjust and to develop his fine abilities.

Edward Veniski is a stout, easygoing boy. His favorite expression is "I don't want to." He is quiet and so far I have learned little about him, as is usually the case with quiet children. His work is poor generally.

Curlyheaded Andrew Dulio is liked by everyone in the group. He is small for his age and everyone thinks of him as one of the little fellows. Andrew is a special friend of Ruth's.

The Dunders are a difficult problem. I have tried so hard to teach Joseph to write his name, but it seems a hopeless task. He is so loud and noisy. I can't find enough to keep him busy as his attention span is the shortest in the group. Most of the time we try to ignore his antics. I allow him to play outdoors as much as possible when the little children are not out. John seems to be learning to read. He behaves like a normal child.

The Cartwrights are over age for their group and are very slow. They are quiet children and work hard at the assigned task. They like to share in cleaning up and seem to take pride in the appearance of the classroom, more so than the other children.

The Williams are always immaculate in appearance and tastefully dressed. Mrs. Williams's sister sees to it that the children are supplied with clothes. Both of the children are the envy of the school and are popular. The big girls make a fuss over Joyce and her clothes. They treat her as if she were a special doll. It is a little hard to make friends with Walter; not that he doesn't want to be friendly, but he is as timid as a little rabbit.

I have attempted this month also to begin to meet some of the needs of the children through adjusting and enriching the daily activities.

The appearance of our room has changed and now reflects the nature of our activities. The seating arrangement is still formal. In the rear of the room in the right-hand corner is the library with a bookcase, a linoleum rug, a card table, and four orange-crate chairs. On the table are an attractive scarf and a few colorful books. In the rear of the room to the left is my desk. In the front of the room to the right is our nature corner, which now contains a jar of hibernating ants, a turtle in an aquarium, wild flowers mounted on cotton under cellophane, a booklet of waxed fall leaves, a booklet of leaf spatter prints, a collection of rocks, fungi, birds' nests, and a winter dish garden of mosses, lichens, pipsissewa, and partridge berries. In the front of the room to the left is the reading corner where I work with the reading groups. In the front center of the room is the play corner for the little children. The children have brought a few dolls and doll clothes from home, a toy bed, some blocks, some jigsaw puzzles, and a few battered toy automobiles. On one bulletin board and on a shelf under it we have gathered an exhibit of Indian relics including about twenty-five arrowheads, an ax, a mortar and pestle, slickstones, and pieces of pottery. We also have several pictures of Indians and stories to go with them. Above this bulletin board is the frieze of Indian homes.

On the other bulletin board are our game charts. Below the bulletin boards are the booklets made by the primary group containing stories and illustrations of the pets we have had at school. There is also a primary color chart and story books made by the older primary children on one of the stories in their reader. On the opposite wall under the windows are the problem charts and question charts for the intermediate and upper groups' social studies and the Indian booklets made by the older children. In the front of the room under the blackboard are booklets made by the primary children on animal homes. There is also a map made by the intermediate children to show how much of the world was known before Columbus discovered America.

In the next months I shall continue to seek to understand these boys and girls and to try to develop their capacities in socially desirable ways.

2

The Children Grow

SATURDAY, OCTOBER 10. All children, and especially these children with their limited experiences, need to develop abundant interests in order that their lives may be enriched and their time spent worthily. So far I have tried to interest them in beautifying their surroundings, in finding joy in reading through their library period, and in learning more about their natural surroundings through their Forestry Club. Another rich resource of this community is its Indian lore. I have already opened up this storehouse to the children, but in order to make the experience with it more real, I plan to take the children on an Indian trip. Today I took Catherine, Frank, Ruth, and Sophia. We visited a rock shelter and then drove up the River road which at one time was an Indian trail. I talked to them about the old Indian trail, Chief Tammenund, the squaw settlement, and the council tree. We discussed what we have already learned about the Minsi tribe, which at one time inhabited this area.

The children expand their interests

MONDAY, OCTOBER 12. This holiday morning, I took the rest of group A (Ralph, Anna, Olga, and Doris) on the Indian trip. They were much more quiet than the first group. To Olga it was a new experience to do any traveling, even this short distance. Conversation turned around nature and Indians. Ralph has been especially interested in finding fossils ever since I told the Forestry Club the story of the formation of this part of our earth. Ralph also noticed the fold in the layers of rock along the River road, and asked about it. I prompted the children to tell me what they thought and I found that they have a fair understanding of the geological development of the Gap.

This evening the Forestry Club, twenty of us, went on a picnic. The children helped to clean up after supper and we burned the rubbish. Ralph and Frank placed a huge log on the fire and we made ourselves comfortable around it. We sat for a while in silence, smelling deeply the pine-scented woods and listening to the gurgling of the brook. One of the high school girls told us several humorous stories. Then I told the group Indian legends and Skunny Wundy stories. The background for them could not have been more perfect and I was filled with the spirit of the Indian storyteller: "Listen to me, my children, while I relate to you the bravery of our hero Skunny Wundy who destroyed the witches of the swamp and turned them into hummocks of sedge."

We sang after that, all kinds of songs, camp songs, rounds, cowboy songs, old favorites, several of the nice popular tunes. All too soon it was time to go home. Mr. Thompson came in his big truck, gathered up the children and took them to their doors.

TUESDAY, OCTOBER 13. At every turning I heard "picnic" today. Everybody went around loving everybody else. What a long way we have come from the days when each one went his own way!

The intermediate children began the next unit in their history books. We discussed the meaning of problems. There are three main ones in this unit on early settlers. They will have more detailed questions to help them solve the main problem. When these questions are answered, they will use the answers to write a story summarizing the solution to the problem. I am trying to help the children to think in terms of problems to solve rather than in terms of specific questions to be answered for an assignment. This is a second step for the children.

WEDNESDAY, OCTOBER 14. Whenever I looked up from my work I found many vacant seats. The little boys were on the front porch building a playhouse from orange crates, following the plans we had made in the morning. Little girls were making clothes for pipe-cleaner dolls. Some of the older children were working on posters to advertise the entertainment or labeling their frieze. Others were at their desks working on arithmetic, spelling, or reading needs.

Physical education has been fine. We keep a weekly score instead of a daily one so that the losers always have a new chance the next day. The team that was losing yesterday at baseball won today in longball which makes the score only one point apart.

THURSDAY, OCTOBER 15. The days are so full that we have little time to give to our play practice. The children have been giving their noontime to it willingly. Rehearsals have been poor. The Indian dance is amusing, for the children are so clumsy. They are so shy that they giggle every time they feel conspicuous. On those occasions we stop and wait patiently until we can start again. I certainly have my fears for the entertainment night.

FRIDAY, OCTOBER 16. This morning during our science period I took the children on a walk to observe the fall leaves before they are all gone. We identified many of the trees and added the quaking aspen to our collection of tree friends. We noticed the many different colors of the various kinds of oaks. On top of the hill near Andrew's home we tried to identify the trees in the distance by their shape and color. The tulip trees were prominent. In the evergreen group we identified the blue spruce, hemlock, cedar, and yellow pine.

During the health period we discussed the necessity for personal cleanliness and how to keep clean. The older children learned a little about the physiology of the skin. There was just time enough left to begin to write the results of our discussion into the notebooks. Although all the children come together for the discussion, they are expected to write only as much as is within their ability. The little children are making picture books.

Our Helpers' Club meeting was simple, but good. We elected new officers for the next four weeks. We shall elect new officers each month so that as many children as possible will have the experience of holding office. Ralph is president, Olga vice-president, and Anna secretary. Ralph led the rest of the meeting well and shows promise of becoming a good leader. We discussed how well we are keeping the rules we made for ourselves. Ralph felt we should now make new ones because we have learned to follow the others fairly well, especially the rule about playing together. A whole week has gone by without a quarrel. I suggested that we should begin to make a list of all the good habits we are forming. For a while we shall concentrate on these habits: work more quietly so that we do not disturb others and keep our schoolroom and all our work clean and neat.

MONDAY, OCTOBER 19.   The little children are making booklets on homes, which will include stories about the various kinds of homes. Today they wrote their first story and made their first picture. We "talked" our stories first and I put on the board the words they needed to know how to spell. I am trying to increase their independence in story writing.

WEDNESDAY, OCTOBER 21.   This morning Ruth gave me a poem she wrote about our walk on Friday.

A Walk

> We went for a walk and had jolly old talk.
> We looked at the leaves to study the trees.
> We bent our bones to look for stones.

I shall make a manuscript page of Ruth's poem, illustrate it and put it on the bulletin board. It may stimulate others. Later perhaps we can have a newspaper and include these creative efforts.

THURSDAY, OCTOBER 22.—Martha took all the primary children outdoors and read to them for a while today. Once when I went out to be sure everything was all right I found Martha asking questions about what she had read to them. I listened for a while and heard a more active discussion than I have been able to lead!

During the morning physical education period William asked if he could teach us a game. He explained it carefully and we asked questions. The game was "Fox, are you ready?" and we enjoyed it thoroughly. For some time now the upper grade children have started a game each morning before school.

FRIDAY, OCTOBER 23. Anna came in with a poem this morning and asked if she could take paper home to illustrate her poem the way I had illustrated Ruth's.

It rained on and off this morning but that did not keep the boys from gathering logs, stumps, branches of colored leaves, mosses, and rocks for scenery for our Indian dramatization. Several of the children said the stage setting was the loveliest they had ever seen. The intermediate group is calling their play "Pictures from our history book on the life of Columbus." They built a large picture frame from birchwood within which all the action takes place. This is placed in the foreground of the set and the curtains are drawn up to it. When this play is over, the children will remove the frame to leave the space free for the Indian play. While the girls were arranging the curtains that would enclose the frame, Warren came up to tell them that they were doing it the hard way. He gave some excellent suggestions. With one bound, Warren rose in the estimation of the group.

After a play period we sat around informally and I read to the children from Milne's *When We Were Very Young*. They asked me to repeat several of the poems, especially the one about the little boy who had a penny and wanted to buy a rabbit. I had to read this one four times and the children began to recite the refrains with me.

Before the youngsters went home I gave them a brief "sermon" on how we usually conduct ourselves at an entertainment. The way those children look at me when I talk seriously to them makes me want to hug them all.

There were about fifty people present, including the children, at the entertainment this evening. We began with community singing, and how these folks love to sing! We sang some old favorites and I taught them the round, "Sweetly Sings the Donkey." The primary children sang a group of songs and were loudly applauded, much to their delight. After it was over the people stayed on and on. The children showed their parents and friends some of the interesting articles we had in our room and told them of our work. Mrs. Hill was pleasantly surprised that the children were willing to do this. We made ten dollars from our sale of homemade cake and candy.

All this week I had been warned by the children and a few parents that formerly there has been trouble with rough young men at school entertainments. Two of the chief offenders are brothers of Edward. Before we started tonight I talked with these two boys and explained to them that this play meant a great deal to the boys and girls. They had worked hard to prepare for it and wanted to make a good impression. Since the children's voices are soft, would these boys please stand by the door to see that no one talks in the hall. Fortunately, it worked and the entertainment was a peaceful and happy affair.

MONDAY, OCTOBER 26. It was cold and windy outdoors today but cozy and happy by contrast inside. For a while we watched the rain "pull" the leaves off the trees and listened to the music the wind played on the woodwinds of the neighborhood. It was all so nice. Before school we worked to clean up Friday's debris and by nine o'clock we were ready to start school with a clean schoolroom.

The Sametis children are leaving to go to the city to their father and I am heartbroken. They are just beginning to become free and natural and now they will have to make a new adjustment.

It seemed quiet and orderly to carry on our regular routine and, in a way, just a little dull.

WEDNESDAY, OCTOBER 28. I am finding it a decided advantage to take a moment now and then to observe the children at work. It especially makes me conscious of those children who usually attract little attention to themselves because they work quietly. Edward, for instance, makes no trouble but he wastes much time just looking at his book because he reads so poorly. I must provide him with some easier reading. Ralph also wastes time by playing with "stuff" he brings from home and keeps in his desk. This, evidently, is more challenging than his schoolwork. Mary and Olga work conscientiously, always doing a little more than is expected of them. Frank is like that, too, although his work is not so well done. Helen has trouble with all her neighbors. Ruth is a rather irresponsible giggler.

When I sit back to observe I always suffer pangs of conscience where the beginners are concerned. They are missing so much because I cannot spend more time with them. Consequently, they spend too much time just sitting. They need to sing, to play, to dramatize, to paint more than they do. I must find some way of giving them more experiences.

After school today we had our first 4-H Sewing Club meeting. All the girls from the intermediate and upper groups and four high school girls were present. We had a short business meeting and elected officers. We planned our projects. The younger girls will make machine-stitched pot holders to get experience in using a sewing machine. All the others will make slips for which Miss Moran the county home demonstration agent gave us patterns.

THURSDAY, OCTOBER 29. We had the second of our mothers' meetings after school. Mrs. Hill, Mrs. Olseuski, Mrs. Cartwright, and Mrs. Thompson were the only ones present. I was discouraged until the mothers informed me that this is a busy time for them. We made plans for Education Week. The mothers will come at noon on Thursday and will stay until three, when the children will be dismissed. At that time we shall have a discussion of their observations.

FRIDAY, OCTOBER 30. Today the older children made notebooks in which to record the correct forms of their language and spelling errors. They will also keep in this booklet the new words they are learning to use and the names of the books they have read. They worked with a zeal that warmed my heart.

At the Forestry Club meeting the children copied into their notebooks the Key to Rocks which I had prepared for them. A practice period followed in which they learned to use the key. We identified several rocks in our museum collection.

MONDAY, NOVEMBER 2. The beginning of a new month always means a new beginning for all of us. We started the month right by doing a good job of house cleaning. The children scrubbed their desks thoroughly, discarded the accumulation of wastepaper and neatly put their books, notebooks, and other necessary equipment into their desks. That started us off. "Why can't we clean the cupboards?" asked half a dozen children at once. Somehow they just love to clean the cupboards. Even then they did not have enough of cleaning. Ruth thought that while we were at it we might just as well get the kitchen cupboards ready for our hot lunch program. Frank scrubbed the shelves in true Dutch fashion, Warren dried them thoroughly, while Anna and Ruth relabeled the enameled cups with the names of the children. Then they scalded all the dishes, pots and pans, utensils, and the cans for staples, and placed them neatly on the shelves. When it was all finished, Warren and Frank insisted that they are going to be cooks this winter. Warren calls what we did today "playing hard." It took all day to clean the room but now it smells and feels so clean.

The children grow in their desire for order and attractiveness in their surroundings

41364

Through the emphasis on a clean room and an attractive playground, even the children are beginning to look cleaner.

WEDNESDAY, NOVEMBER 4. The vocabulary of the children is increasing slightly. We have been having fun with new words, using them at every opportunity. Their latest acquisition is "absurd."

The children grow in skill in using the tools of learning

We are spending a great deal of time on our reading, writing, and arithmetic just now, for these are areas in which the needs of these children are great. Skill in the tool subjects is important not only because of their usefulness in living, but because of emotional problems resulting from continued failure. Warren is such a good example of that. Since he has had some satisfaction through improvement in arithmetic and spelling he feels more comfortable with the group.

In reading I follow the guides in the teacher's manual, since reading specialists know better than I do how children learn to read and also what purposes can best be served through each story. However, I do adapt them because I know each boy and girl and my classroom situation better than any reading specialist.

Arithmetic, spelling, English, and writing are individual matters in our school. Each child has a notebook in which his needs are recorded. I am trying to help each child to be increasingly aware of his needs and to have a strong desire to improve. Conferences help to do this effectively.

Until recently that last drill period in the afternoon has been like a three-ring circus. The children came to me for help before they genuinely tried the work. I took a small group at a time and helped the children to become acquainted with their arithmetic texts. I showed them how their texts explain step by step the procedure for any new work. I guided them in the use of these explanations. The emphasis has been shifting from getting the correct answer to understanding the problem. Ruth said today, "I got the right answer, but I still don't understand why it's right."

Since they are working with increasing independence, I can now find time to have conferences at the end of each day. We went through Ruth's notebooks carefully today. Much of the work was carelessly done. For the next month Ruth will try to read over everything she writes and make corrections before she considers the work finished. We also talked about the flippant attitude she has toward people, especially toward those adults in the community whom she knows. I explained to her that we knew she meant nothing disrespectful by it but that it was a bad habit to get into.

FRIDAY, NOVEMBER 6. After school we had our Forestry Club meeting. During the roll call we had to answer to our names with the name of an animal. Ruth named one of the high school girls. That set us off on a long discussion on whether people were animals. We tested more rocks, using the key. This weekend Warren, Ralph, and Edward are going to hike around to find as many evidences as possible of rock being broken down into soil. Next week we shall take a trip that these boys plan for us. I also taught the children a new 4-H Club song.

MONDAY, NOVEMBER 9. At noon we put a sign on the door: "Have gone on a picnic. Will be back at one o'clock." It was such a beautiful day, we did not want to waste it. We started off toward the mountain and ate our lunch along a winding stream. As we walked back and I listened to the children's chatter I was acutely aware of their many needs and just as acutely conscious of my many shortcomings. I wanted so much to talk to them the way our state forester, Mr. Scovel, does, to open up the wonders of our natural world to them, but I just do not know enough. During the week, by the time the notebooks are carefully gone over, by the time I prepare for six reading groups and read over the social studies material and do all the other minute details of my job, it is time to go to bed. I am too tired to think of all the other nice things that need to be carefully planned. So I go on the same way, wishing there were four of me, trying to find out what goes on in each little head and heart, trying to understand and do something about it.

THURSDAY, NOVEMBER 12. This is Education Week. We reversed the order of things so that the mothers could see the children at work on social studies. Only Mrs. Thompson, Mrs. Williams, and Mrs. Dulio came. Four other mothers sent written regrets and had good reasons for not coming. I was happy about Mrs. Dulio. This is the first time she has been to the school. The older girls served tea to the mothers at three o'clock and we had a social time. Mrs. Williams has just returned from visiting relatives in South Carolina. She told us about her trip.

FRIDAY, NOVEMBER 13. We began to discuss the possibility of a newspaper, how it is organized and what we can put into it. Warren was elected editor-in-chief and Olga associate editor.

MONDAY, NOVEMBER 16. Since it was a cold day today, it was appropriate that we start to serve a hot dish. Ruth and Mary cooked capably and were conscious of the rules of sanitation. The lunch period, however, was noisy and confusing. When the afternoon session began we took a few minutes to discuss the lunch period. From now on those who have a job to do at noon will wash their hands at 11:50. They will group the desks to form tables, set out oilcloth mats, napkins, and spoons while the rest of the group is getting washed. No serving will be done until everyone has washed his hands and is in his seat. When all have been served, we shall say grace. The cooks must be sure there is water being heated for dishwashing and must leave the kitchen in order. All will remain seated while the dishes are gathered, rinsed, and stacked. The dishwasher will get two pans ready, one with warm soapy water for washing, the other with scalding water for rinsing. When the children go out to play, some will remain to wash and dry the oilcloth mats, to sweep the room and to get it in readiness for the afternoon. The dishwasher and driers will work in the kitchen. A general caretaker will wash the stove, inspect the jobs, and see that the room and the kitchen are left in good order.

We began to write the articles for our newspaper. We listed on the board all the things we wanted to write about and each child selected one article to write. We shall use our English periods for this work for a while.

TUESDAY, NOVEMBER 17. There was a decided improvement in the way our hot lunch was prepared and served and in the cleaning up afterwards. It was a conscious improvement, for many of the children said, "We were much better today, weren't we?"

WEDNESDAY, NOVEMBER 18. I was so happy about Frank today. That boy certainly warms my heart. He took it upon himself to eat his lunch with five little boys. He showed the little fellows how to hold their spoons. He made them eat the last drop of their potato chowder. He hushed all loud speaking. The boys like Frank. He is a good influence on them, especially on Albert.

FRIDAY, NOVEMBER 20. The boys took us on the Forestry Club walk and pointed out the work of wind, frost, growing plants, and water in the making of soil. When we returned we made salt crystals to see how crystallization takes place in nature. Several of the children have found quartz crystals and wondered why they always took the shape they did.

TUESDAY, NOVEMBER 24. It snowed last night, our first really big snow! How happy the children were. They made snowmen, built a fort, and had soft snowball fights. Anna was inspired to write another poem. We took time to compare the shapes of snow crystals with the shapes of quartz and salt crystals. I like to watch the children's eyes open wide with wonder.

THURSDAY, NOVEMBER 26. Much time was spent on our newspaper this morning. We organized our articles and on the blackboard planned the appearance of the paper. I shall get the master copies typed for the hectograph.

MONDAY, NOVEMBER 30.   Ralph is our dishwasher for the next two weeks. He works efficiently and for the first time the dishes were done and the kitchen in order before the afternoon session began.

The Andrews sisters are cooks and they interrupt so often to ask about every tiny detail. I must spend more time with them before school begins in the morning so that they will be able to work more independently.

TUESDAY, DECEMBER 1.   A new boy arrived today. His mother came with him and warned me that he was a mischievous boy and that I was to settle him. Fred Lutz is in the third grade. He had a pleasant morning and made friends easily.

Joseph acted badly, showing off before our new boy, because Fred was an appreciative audience. I talked with Fred later and explained that we take no notice of Joseph because he is not responsible for what he does. We know better and so we cannot do the things Joseph does.

WEDNESDAY, DECEMBER 2.   Olga and Anna hectographed our newspaper today. When they finished we had to stop work to read it. The children are pleased with the result.

We began to make Christmas cards for our parents and friends. The children are drawing them on Manila paper and painting them. I taught the children to sing "Silent Night" in two parts. They also learned to play it on their harmonicas.

FRIDAY, DECEMBER 4.   These children need to initiate and plan their activities because interest and purpose are essential to wholesome development. Through the Helpers' Club and through the conferences the children are already beginning to work and plan with purpose. Today we took another step in this direction. Each morning I have had the plans

The children grow in ability to plan their affairs

for the day on the blackboard. We would discuss these plans the first thing. This morning, however, I thought I would have the children plan their own day. We listed orally all the things that need to be done and then we organized them on the blackboard. The children felt that, since the room is still a little too cold in the morning, this would be a good time to practice singing our Christmas carols. We are using our social studies periods to get a Christmas dramatization ready. Our dramatization is to be a pageant of the Christmas story as told in the second chapter of Luke. We shall sing appropriate carols throughout the pageant.

MONDAY, DECEMBER 7. The children planned their own day quite successfully. After we had our group plans made, the children listed their individual activities. Anna planned with Andrew when they were going to work on the backdrop for the Christmas pageant. The costume committee planned a time to meet. Ralph and Warren found a time when they could clean out the woodshed to make room for the new load of wood that is coming tomorrow. Individual children had such things on their lists as "do page 72 in arithmetic . . . correct misspelled words on Friday's spelling paper . . . make a Christmas card, read a chapter in my library book." They would check off the items as they were accomplished. Several children listed more than they could possibly do in one day, so of course did not finish. At the end of the day we talked about how well we had accomplished our plans.

TUESDAY, DECEMBER 8. We practiced our pageant this morning. The choir is beginning to feel the importance of its part and now the children in the choir do not feel at all unhappy about the fact that they do not have a speaking part in the pageant. During the time we usually have for reading we began to make our Christmas gifts. The older children are painting silhouettes on glass, which they will frame for a picture. The little children are weaving rag pot holders.

FRIDAY, DECEMBER 11. These children need to develop social habits and attitudes which will enable them to get along with

The children grow in ability to meet new situations with confidence and poise

those about them and to meet new situations with confidence and poise. We have worked hard at this in our physical education and library periods. Today we had another kind of opportunity for social development. Two teachers from Columbia University came to visit us. I watched the children closely to see how they would react. They were neither bothered nor excited and at times I had the feeling that they were not even aware of the visitors. There were a few times when they showed their shyness. Ralph lost his tongue during the club meeting. I helped him over the first shock and then things went smoothly. Olga took no part in entertaining our visitors nor in general group discussion. Mary had several suggestions to give in Helpers' Club meeting but became embarrassed and Warren had to give them for her. Mary became friendly with our visitors later, however, and told them about our work. Martha, Helen, Ruth, and the Andrews girls talked freely and comfortably with them. The visitors were interested in the hot lunch and spent much time in the kitchen watching the cooks at work. When I stepped out there once, May was seriously seasoning the spaghetti and tomatoes. She looked up with a smile. There is something charming about May. She has a little sense of humor that is worth cultivating. Doris is getting more independent, too. She was opening a can of tomatoes and had difficulty making the can opener work. Ruth offered to do it for her. Doris said, "No. You just tell me how and let me do it." The visitors, with deep understanding of the place of satisfaction in the learning process, said they had never tasted such good spaghetti and tomatoes and that it was seasoned just right. The girls were so pleased.

We elected new officers for our Helpers' Club. Warren is president, Edward vice-president, and Olga secretary. I'm happy about Edward. He does so few things well. Being vice-president is not difficult, yet it carries with it some distinction and he can learn by assisting. I am glad that the group is recognizing Olga's worth. And Warren! Three months ago he was a forlorn, extremely sensitive child with practically no friends. He has not only made astounding progress in his work, but has also become the most popular child in the group.

MONDAY, DECEMBER 14. The Sametis children are back from the city and there was general rejoicing. Mrs. Sametis said the city was no place to raise her children. She could not keep track of them.

While we were planning the work for the day, the children asked to have the Sametis children tell them about the school they attended. They also wanted to hear from Warren about the puppet show he saw in New Brunswick on Friday. Sophia told some interesting things in a fairly organized way but it was Warren who held the absolute attention of the group. After he had finished Mary said, "Boy! He certainly can tell stories."

I learned today that Mrs. Sametis has four brothers: one, a doctor in Greece; one, a professor at the University of Cairo; one, an Orthodox priest in Jerusalem; and the last a salesman in New York City. Mrs. Sametis, being a girl, was the only one who did not receive an education, yet she taught herself to read not only her native Greek, but English as well. I am beginning to understand the ability of the Sametis children.

WEDNESDAY, DECEMBER 23. The last few days have been busy ones. We finished making and wrapping the gifts and we finished our cards. We put the last touches on the Christmas tree and on the stage, hung the curtains, and checked the costumes. We practiced the pageant and sang the carols. Every child was co-operative and cheerful. At last the day arrived.

The little schoolroom was bursting with people tonight. All but two of the parents were there. Mr. Hill managed to get home in time for the entertainment. Mrs. Andrews came, too! She has never been out to the schoolhouse in all the years she has lived in the neighborhood. The Andrews girls were so happy.

Dr. and Mrs. Breed, the headmaster of Blair Academy and

his wife, were there. They were impressed with the pageant and the beautiful singing. Since Dr. and Mrs. Breed wanted to help us, they gave us money toward the piano we need so much.

My dad was Santa and distributed the oranges, candy, and toys to the children and the gifts to the parents. It was such a happy evening. As I looked out over the audience I was conscious of the friendly atmosphere that prevailed. We are good friends, these people and I.

THURSDAY, DECEMBER 24. It took all morning to clean up. At one o'clock the children went home for the holidays and left the school house an empty place indeed.

In the months that have passed, many things have happened. I have watched the personalities of these children begin to

A summary   emerge and become somewhat free. I have watched them grow in ability to plan, to carry out their plans successfully, to recognize and to solve their problems. I have watched them grow in their ability to live together and to respect each other. I have encouraged many kinds of activities so that each child would be challenged by one at least and so find his place in our group.

3

We Suffer Growing Pains

MONDAY, JANUARY 4, 1937. For the next few months I shall try to enlist each child's co-operation in setting up purposes for his work. Before the holidays I used several half days to give the children achievement tests. During this last week I scored the tests and made individual graphs of the results.

These graphs were superimposed on the graphs of the results of the first test so that each child can readily see his improvement. I do not record the scores. The graphs merely indicate whether a child is high or low in the various subjects. The children have made marked improvement. Ralph made remarkable improvement in all subjects.

This morning, as the children worked independently, I took time to have a conference with each child to explain the graph and to suggest remedial measures. The children were pleased with their colorful graphs, especially since most of them indicated improvement. Improvement is a powerful incentive for continued effort. Following the conferences, each child made a progress book in which to keep his graph and my suggestions for remedial work. He will also keep in this book a page entitled "Things I have managed by myself." This month the children shall record on this page small items such as putting away games after play without being told. As they grow in management ability they shall record only those items which involve real management, such as heading a committee.

I continue to meet previously discovered needs

Before Christmas, Mrs. Wilson, a town friend of the community, said she could get a piano for us for the small sum of ten dollars. How happy we were to find that the piano, a really good one, had arrived and had already been tuned. Of course, we had to have a brief concert.

TUESDAY, JANUARY 5. Wonderful and mysterious things were going on today. The cooks took extra precautions to keep the kitchen in a sanitary condition. Ralph closed the door at two different times when it was left open by some careless child, a thing he never before left his seat to do even if he was freezing. Edward learned some multiplication combinations without being told. Catherine polished the piano. Why? It suddenly dawned upon me when I saw Anna open her progress book and record, "Jan. 5, I helped Doris serve the cups of cocoa when her tray was too full." They are all working to see how long they can make the list. This is a next step for these children.

FRIDAY, JANUARY 8. Warren presided well over the Helpers' Club meeting. He was confident and encouraged discussion. Albert said, "Mr. President, we should do something about our physical education period. It is so noisy that it gives us a **Problems arise** headache." Because of the weather we often **through play-** have to play indoors. We dance during the **ing indoors** morning period, but each child finds a game to play during the afternoon one and this is the period that gets noisy. The suggestion was made that the game committee arrange groups to play certain games. The groups will change games each day and the membership of the groups will change each week. I do not know whether this will help. The room is so small and there are so many of us that when we get interested in the games we are playing the noise just "happens."

MONDAY, JANUARY 11. The children did not like at all the groupings made by the game committee. They said they did not like to divide up into squads because it made some people unhappy. It was suggested instead that we form our own groups each day. Everyone should see to it that he becomes a part of a group and does not just stand around. We made a list of possible games. Mary will make a chart of them and put them on the bulletin board. The children will add more as the game committee finds them.

TUESDAY, JANUARY 12. The graphs and remedial work suggestions seem to be helping the children to help themselves. Edward has been sticking to the job of improving in his schoolwork and each day he reports to me how much he has done. He sings during all the music periods and at other times besides. He brings in the coal and picks up what he drops. Ralph, also, is making a conscious effort to improve. He is attentive to discussions and takes an active part in them. The dictionaries are in constant use. We shall spend much time these winter months on efforts to improve in the tools of learning.

WEDNESDAY, JANUARY 13. Since I have finished reading *Pinocchio*, we began to consider the possibility of making a puppet show of it. We listed about fifteen scenes to dramatize. Since it was obvious that we could not have them all, we planned to choose six of these. I divided the older children into six groups to write the script.

The little children are still building their house and writing stories about it. Their vocabulary chart is now so long that we had to review the words today to be sure the children were remembering them.

FRIDAY, JANUARY 15. After Forestry Club today, when we were getting ready to go home, I noticed that the fence around the bulb bed was down and that there **Some prob-** were footprints all over the bed. Catherine and **lems involve a** Sophia said the boys had been using the fence **mature sense** for high jumping. That spoiled my whole day **of values** and all the nice things that happened completely left my mind. Why should these boys do a thing like that when they had spent so much time and care in preparing it? It was not an enforced task and they had done it joyfully.

MONDAY, JANUARY 18. This morning I asked Ralph to sit down with me for a while. I explained to him what I had found on Friday. Before I had an opportunity to ask, he said, "I know who did it. George, Andrew, Helen, Albert, and Fred." "How about yourself?" I asked. He answered that neither he nor Frank had taken part. "Ralph, why didn't you tell me about this before?" I questioned. His answer made me almost glad the whole incident had occurred. "Well, Frank and I saw them jumping in the plot and knew they shouldn't be doing it, so we told them to stop. They did stop, so I didn't think I had to tell you." They had done exactly what I have been trying to teach them to do, to solve their own problems. I asked the five children to repair the damage they had done.

When my helping teacher came today, I related the whole story to her. She pointed out that the children had not yet received any satisfaction from the work they had put on the bulb bed. It takes a mature person to forgo an immediate pleasure for a greater one in the distant future. That is something these children have not yet learned. Another year, after the children have received joy from the beauty of the flowers and have had satisfaction from the praise of visitors on the appearance of their grounds, they will probably not be so thoughtless.

TUESDAY, JANUARY 19. At noon, Warren, George, and Frank had water all over the place. Every once in a while no one wants to do his job in connection with hot lunch **Problems arise** and this was one of those days. Albert had to be **in carrying** called to put the mats away. Mary washed the **out the hot** mats half clean and had to do the job over **lunch pro-** again. Catherine kept complaining about Warren **gram** and Frank. The cupboards were left in a disorderly condition, the towels were not washed, and the stove still had evidences of the lunch on it. I let it go today. Sometimes I think it is better not to talk too much.

WEDNESDAY, JANUARY 20. I helped the children in the kitchen today, showing them easier ways of doing the work. Washing towels has presented a problem, as there never seems to be enough hot water. Today, after the dishwater had been prepared, we heated water in an old pail, so that the pots which we ordinarily use for this purpose could be washed. That helped some but even then Frank said, "I can't do this job. Besides, I don't like it."

The Cartwrights have been out for some time and I learned today that they have influenza. In fact, there were only seventeen of the twenty-nine children present. This accounts for some of the trouble we have been having with hot lunch. The children keep their assigned jobs for two-week periods.

At the beginning of each two-week period I carefully super-
vise the work until the children learn how to do each job.
With so many absences the children have to do jobs other
than their own and I just cannot get around to helping them
all. It makes the work difficult and distasteful to the children.
Then, too, we do not yet have a really efficient working plan.
I'm afraid I have as much to learn as the children.

FRIDAY, JANUARY 22. When we began to plan our day's work
several children requested that we have music the first thing
this morning, as it has been crowded out the past few days.
I began to teach the group a few fundamentals about reading
music from sight. Everyone enjoyed it, probably because it
was new. Even the boys sang.

MONDAY, JANUARY 25. We have been having difficulty with
Fred. He is always having a fight with someone. Fred is old
for his years. When I visited at his home I found that he milks
six cows in the morning. He does not change his clothes before he comes to school and smells strongly of the barn. These
folks work so hard that they do not have a chance to look
around at the world in which they live. They seem to be poor
managers. Mrs. Lutz told me that she does not like this farm
and does not expect to stay. I learned later that Mrs. Lutz is
always moving. She is quite a figure at farm sales with her un-
kempt hair, men's shoes, and coarse language. The children
knew Fred's background better than I did and that is why
he has had a hard time being accepted by the group.

TUESDAY, JANUARY 26. At the end of the day I brought forth
Wilfred, the puppet clown I made this weekend. After demon-
strating how to handle a puppet, and allowing each child to
practice, I asked for volunteers to give us two-minute extem-
poraneous performances. A few brave souls, Helen, Mary,
Warren, Ruth, and Andrew, tried it. How we all laughed. We
love the little clown! All the children are eager to start work
on the puppets. They examined carefully the book on string
puppets which I had placed on the library table.

WEDNESDAY, JANUARY 27. I have been giving much of my time to the hot lunch and it takes a great deal out of me. I feel as though I were running a three-ring circus. Miss Moran told me before we started hot lunch that it would be difficult this year, for all the girls who did the work so capably in the past two years have gone on to high school. I suppose it is my job to raise another group of capable workers.

This month we have learned how not to do a great many things. Today Anna wanted to go to our neighbor's, whose sewing machine we are using, to finish a seam she did not get finished at the meeting last night. When I reminded Anna that she was supposed to be helping Ruth cook, she said, "There isn't much to do now. Ruth can do what needs to be done." Yet, with two of them watching, they allowed the rice to burn to the bottom of the pot and it took Catherine a half hour to clean it. The children told the girls what they thought of their cooking.

THURSDAY, JANUARY 28. We are progressing rapidly with our harmonica lessons. We learned to play "Yankee Doodle" today. I am also beginning to teach the children how to conduct. Several of the children directed the band and did well.

FRIDAY, JANUARY 29. This morning the intermediate group finished their history book, *Those Who Dared*. The children loved this book so much that they asked me to read the last few chapters aloud to them. When I finished the last sentence and closed the book, Mary said reverently, "That was such a beautiful book."

I've been especially interested in the "Things I have managed by myself" page of the progress books. These are some of the things the children have listed:

Helped Mary with her arithmetic
Put the shade up so that the sun would not shine in Catherine's eyes
Kept the kitchen clean
I told Pearl not to read with her lips

Picked up the waste paper from the library

Did my best in cooking

Closed the bottom door of the stove so the room would not
get too hot

Made sure that there was water on the stove for washing dishes

Tried to keep Fred from quarreling while we were playing ten-
pins

I was a good sport to be "it" when nobody else wanted to be "it"

I remembered to write up the minutes for the club meeting

Got the game started at play time

Did my best in writing my part of the Pinocchio play

Helped the primary children weave their rug

Told the girls not to play on the piano all at the same time

Told Helen not to write in her book

Put away a page of the dictionary that fell out

Kept myself busy

Picked up the coats from the floor and hung them up

MONDAY, FEBRUARY 1. As each child finished his work he began to make a heavy paper cover for his collection of the *Weekly Reader*. We have been doing little formal geography study and I felt that through this paper we would get much geography that would be somewhat meaningful to these children. I also suggested that we have a large world map on which we can locate the places we read about. I had a rather battered world map, 4′ x 9′. Sophia, Helen, and Ruth offered to trace it on some heavy brown paper.

Ralph refused to do any work today. I heard him say to Edward, "It's her job, she gets paid for it. Miss Hanson [a

**Home atti-
tudes help to
create school
problems**

former teacher of his in another school] always did her own work." I have known for some time that certain children in the room felt this way. I don't know exactly what to do about it. I don't know that anything immediate can be done. A change in outlook will take time and come about gradually.

TUESDAY, FEBRUARY 2. After Ralph, Frank, and Edward openly refused to do their jobs, I had a talk with the bigger boys after school. I tried to explain to the boys why, in a school such as ours, everyone had to share in the work. I asked them to consider how long it takes a group of us to get our school in a clean orderly condition and how long it would take one person to do it all. I always share in cleaning up even though I am not responsible for the disorder. If I had to do all the work, we would have to curtail most of our activities as it is impossible for one human being to do everything. It wouldn't be such a difficult matter to keep the place clean if we just sat in our seats all day. "After all, boys, this is your school, it will be a part of your life long after I have left it. Take pride in the things that belong to you because they show what kind of person you are." They were all hanging their heads by that time, and I was a little ashamed. Sometimes I think I talk too much.

WEDNESDAY, FEBRUARY 3. It was so good to hear Frank's "Sure enough" again. He did more than his share of work today, as did the other boys. The spirit of the whole school was different and each time one of the boys would smile at me I felt that there was a deep understanding between us. And for the first time since we have been serving hot lunch I did not feel that I was running it all.

After school the mothers had the second meeting since the New Year. At the last meeting I showed the graphs of the results of the achievement test to the mothers and explained to them how we are using the graphs. They were interested and happy about the improvement shown. After they looked at the graphs they thumbed through the rest of the progress book. We also discussed the hot lunch program and the mothers considered what else they could do to raise money for it. Mrs. Williams said she would love to be in a play again. She had not been in one since she was in high school. "Remember the fun we used to have?" she asked.

At the County Library, with the help of the librarian, we found a light humorous play, *How the Story Grew*. We had our meeting at Mrs. Thompson's tonight and Mrs. Hill read the play to us. We laughed until the tears rolled down our cheeks. Since we could not get enough mothers for the parts in the play, we invited two high school girls to take part.

THURSDAY, FEBRUARY 4. The boys wanted to stay for the sewing club meeting tonight. While some of the girls cut out their dresses and others stitched French seams in their slips, the boys sewed on the puppets. They insisted on sewing them up on the machine which Miss Moran was able to get for us. There was quite a bit of confusion as we could not find enough needles or pins and there were so many of us that we got in each other's way. The children had a wonderful time.

I met Mrs. Breed tonight and she wanted to know what else she could do for us. All of a sudden it occurred to me—a

Outside help solves some problems

young man—carpentry—why hadn't I thought of it before! "Do you suppose there is a boy at the academy who can help us make a puppet stage?" I asked. Mrs. Breed promised to find out. On the way home I thought, "Yes, that is what a teacher in a one-teacher school should do—invite others in to teach what she cannot."

Last night I spent the evening with Miss Everett, my helping teacher, to consider next steps for these children, especially in the social studies program. So far it has been formal and we

I begin to learn new techniques of teaching the social studies

have followed our texts. I have tried to make the best use of this material. However, the children have had no real purpose. The children asked no questions and did little of the planning. We asked ourselves, "How can we get these children to question? How can we help them to grow in the desire to find out things? How can we make their learning active rather than a passive accumulation of isolated facts?"

Miss Everett felt that a trip would help to fill the need for new experiences. After considering the kinds of trips possible, we decided to take the children to the Doylestown museum. This would capitalize on their interest in pioneer life, and children question and want to know more about things in which they are interested. Since neither of us had ever been to the museum, we planned to go on Saturday to see what there is for the children.

There are several things we are hoping will come out of a trip like this. We want the children to go to books to get information rather than to read assigned pages. We want the children to know more about the place in which they live. It is close at hand and available for study. Children learn more when they can see things and think of them in relation to themselves rather than abstractly. On this trip we shall listen to the children and try to find something that is challenging them.

I am going to develop this work with all the children in the intermediate and upper groups together. Since I am getting to know the children so well, I can guide the work so that each child makes the growth of which he is capable. In addition, this will give us a much longer period in which to work together.

SATURDAY, FEBRUARY 6. Miss Everett and I went to Doylestown and found the museum to be exactly what we wanted. It contains materials from pioneer life gathered in the vicinity of Doylestown. We browsed through some of the books in the museum library and found interesting information concerning earlier days in our township. We took notes.

MONDAY, FEBRUARY 8. From time to time, as we go over the plans for the day, the children make suggestions which gradually have changed the nature of our daily program. We were talking about our school grounds, and the children felt that if we intended to work outdoors in the spring we had better do some concentrated work on our plans. Warren said, "Let's begin today." He added, "Why don't we have science on Monday anyway? Everything happens on Friday." "We have science in our Forestry Club too,"

Adjustments are made in the daily program

Mary pointed out. So we planned to have our science this morning. The following program changes have now been made.

Daily: 8:55–9:10 Plan work for the day
Monday: 9:10–9:25 Science for group C (the primary group) (Social Studies, rest of the week)
          9:25–10:00 Science for groups A and B (the older children) (Social Studies, rest of the week)
Wednesday: Dancing for girls
Thursday: Dancing for boys
          (If weather is good we go outdoors on these days and make up the lesson when we cannot go out)
Friday: 11:20–11:40 Discussion of Weekly Readers and Current Events
          11:40–12:00 Library
Wednesday: 11:40–12:00 Health
Monday and Friday: Singing for the older children
          (A and B groups) Little children sing or listen in
Wednesday: Singing for the primary children. (C group) Older children help out
Tuesday and Thursday: Harmonica practice
Time spent on conferences during drill period at the end of the day.

For the past three weeks we have been studying *Home and Garden* magazines and seed catalogues and have been recording our ideas for school-grounds beautification on our individual plans. Ralph, Warren, Sophia, Anna, Ruth, and Mary have been working on two large-scale drawings of our school grounds (6′ x 3′). One will show the grounds as they are now, the other as we would like to have them. Today we discussed our various ideas. We made decisions concerning the play space, the rock garden, and the areas around the toilets. These plans will be recorded on our large drawing.

TUESDAY, FEBRUARY 9.   Mrs. Breed came to school today with Mr. Wilson, a young man who knows about puppets. Mr. Wilson took the measurements of our cloth puppets. He said he would get some soft wood and teach the boys how to carve wooden puppets to represent Pinocchio and his two wooden friends. The children surrounded him and listened with their mouths open. After he left, they said, "What a nice boy he is."

SATURDAY, FEBRUARY 13. We were delayed in leaving for Doylestown because at the last minute Mr. Prinlak would not allow his children to go. I went to the house to try to persuade him, for the Prinlaks of all the children in the school need this experience. He was afraid they would get hurt. I tried to explain how much the children would learn that they could not learn at home. That approach did not work either, for he reminded me that he had traveled over most of the countries of Europe and it had not done him any good. "Anyway, all school is nonsense and the less children have of it the better. It's Saturday today. That's not a school day." So we had to leave without the Prinlaks and I felt miserable.

At the museum the children really kept their eyes open and saw so much that we had missed last Saturday. They asked many "What's this?" questions. How eagerly they examined everything and how good they were!

On the way back from the museum we stopped at a quarry and collected talc, mica (both biotite and muscovite), serpentine, soapstone, graphite, calcite, and asbestos for our school museum. They liked the quarry so much that we could hardly get them to leave.

MONDAY, FEBRUARY 15. Ralph told me as soon as we entered the schoolhouse this morning that he and his father had looked up Doylestown on the map and had traced the route we took. Ralph retraced the route for us on our map of New Jersey and Pennsylvania and the children in turn began to talk about their impressions.

I encouraged the children to talk freely in order to discover what interested them most and what they would like to know more about. The room with the marionettes held the attention of all of them. Ralph liked the Indian relics. Sophia liked the spinning room. Anna liked the Conestoga wagon and the stagecoach. Warren liked the guns. Most of the time they were merely reminiscing. There was no indication that the children were curious to know more about anything they saw.

Mr. Wilson came today and worked with the boys from 2:30 until 4:30 and kept them enrapt. Two hours is a long time to hold the attention of children. His demonstrations were brief and to the point and then he set the children to work. He taught them how to use the knives effectively and safely. Before he left he explained to the boys exactly what they were to do during the week.

TUESDAY, FEBRUARY 16. I spent this evening with Miss Everett wondering where we go from here. The children love books, so we finally decided that Miss Everett should bring some books about the things we saw. Perhaps they would read here and there and their curiosity would be aroused.

WEDNESDAY, FEBRUARY 17. Miss Everett brought in an armful of books which she left on the library table. After lunch, the children began to look through the books. They kept bringing me pictures of the things they had seen, not only at the museum but also on the trip down, such as the Delaware Canal. Warren, Ruth, Anna, Sophia, Catherine, Doris, and May spent almost two hours with the books. Helen and Mary did not look very long. The Prinlaks, with the exception of Olga, did not look at all, which is understandable.

FRIDAY, FEBRUARY 19. After we had planned the day's work we talked about the books Miss Everett had brought. Each

We begin to study the history of our community

child showed a picture which interested him and he told a little about it. Whenever the opportunity presented itself, I asked, "I wonder if any of the older people around here have any of these things?" May said she had a dulcimer. Several children said they had wooden bowls and butter paddles. Mary said, "Maybe we can have a museum of our own." Several of the children mentioned a few old-timers in the community. I suggested that they visit these folks. Perhaps we could find some other interesting places to visit.

This afternoon we began to work on our rock garden. We have a stone row that was well covered with soil when the road was widened. It is in a shady spot at the edge of the road. There were leaves to be cleaned out and bushes to remove. It was a beautiful day to work outdoors and the children were very happy.

TUESDAY, FEBRUARY 23. The children have begun to collect material for our museum. We have a butter print, a butter mold, and an old vase. A cradle has been promised. May will bring her dulcimer.

WEDNESDAY, FEBRUARY 24. Today we talked for a while about the past in our own community. Ralph said he had heard that the road that passes in front of the schoolhouse used to be an old stagecoach road going to Oldtown. The children felt that this road over the mountain was a hard way to go to Oldtown. Why didn't they go the way we go now? I suggested that if we could find how the pioneers decided where their roads would be, that would give us the answer. We went to the books Miss Everett had brought and I distributed them according to the children's reading ability. The children worked in twos and threes to find out about travel in pioneer times. They did not know how to look for the material, so I showed them how to use the index and the table of contents. We made a list of key words on the board so that they would know to look in the index under other words besides "travel." I began to teach the children individually how to take notes.

Ruth told us that her mother knew of some people who might be able to tell us about the township. The Andrews girls and Ralph told us of two others. Ruth added that her mother suggested we go with questions so that it will be easier for people to tell us what we want to know. Mothers certainly can be a help to teachers!

FRIDAY, FEBRUARY 26.   We began to work at our puppet show in earnest today. We reread the dramatization and listed the characters. Each child chose the part he wished to take. Where there were several who wanted a part, tryouts were held and the children made the decision. Everyone wanted the part of Pinocchio, and after the tryouts Sophia was voted for the part. Anna began to cry and said that if she could not have the part of Pinocchio she would not take any part. Sophia immediately said she could have the part, but the group rose up. Ruth said, "That is the way Anna was last year. If she could not have her way she would not co-operate. It isn't fair to us and it isn't good for Anna always to have her way." It was the end of the day and all of us were tired, so I suggested that we leave the matter until Monday when we would be able to consider it in a different light. All the children are eager to take part in the dramatization except Ralph and Frank. They would rather be managers of the scenery and lights.

Personality difficulties are revealed through group living

MONDAY, MARCH 1.   About 9:30 there was a timid knock on the door, and when I opened it there stood before me a tear-stained, bedraggled little fellow. He handed me a crumpled envelope that had been sealed, but was now open. I read the note which said that the bearer was to be a new pupil in the fifth grade. The note added that I am given permission to do what I think needs to be done to handle Thomas, that Thomas has a bad temper and lies. The note warned me to keep an eye on him. "Did you read this?" I asked Thomas. He said he had. I tore the note into bits before him and said it did not mean a thing to us, that in this school we judge a person by what he does and not by what is said about him. We gave him a desk and set him to work.

I found a little time to talk to Anna today. It came about rather easily. We found ourselves alone for a few minutes during the noon hour. I said, "Anna, we have not decided about your part in the play and I would like to talk with you before the group discusses it." I explained that it wasn't necessary for me to tell her how the group felt about her, but I knew she would appreciate knowing how I felt. I pointed out several unthinking things she has done that are small matters in themselves but add up to make the kind of person folks don't like to have around. Then I recalled all the nice things she has done. I said, "You are a capable person, Anna. The group will recognize your worth if you do everything in the best way you know how." When Anna left, she said she would try to be easier to live with. She has accepted another part in the dramatization.

The mothers have been meeting twice a week after school at their various homes to practice the play. They were in a jovial mood today. Mrs. Thompson and Mrs. Williams danced the "Irish Washerwoman" for us. Inez Jones brought a cake.

THURSDAY, MARCH 4.   For the past three days we have used the social studies period to do research on travel in the pioneer days. It is a difficult task to help these children to extract the material they need. In spite of all the time we took in the beginning of the year to learn how to get material from a book, the children want to copy whole pages. Gathering material on a given topic seems to be a different matter from extracting material to answer a question.

This was a busy, trying day. I had little opportunity to go outdoors from the time I arrived at eight until after the dress rehearsal at six. The girls helped to put up the stage curtains and to arrange the setting for the mothers' play. The mothers have taken complete responsibility for the advertising, the refreshments, and the tickets. They have even ordered extra chairs from the town undertaker.

FRIDAY, MARCH 5.   While the older children worked alone at their study of travel, I spent almost an hour with the little children. Their play house is completed now. They have made and painted small wooden furniture. They have woven rugs and have made one hooked one. The girls have sewed curtains, bedding, and other household articles. We spent most of the time today finishing up the stories about their experiences in building the little house. These children have had much writing experience, which has helped them to improve in the various skills necessary for writing. All the older primary children are now writing original stories of appropriate length.

The performance was fine this evening. Ralph's brother-in-law led the community singing. Following the entertainment he played his guitar and sang cowboy songs. The oldest Same-tis girl gave a reading about an Italian organ grinder. The mothers made fifteen dollars for our hot lunch.

After the play was over, Mrs. Williams and I sat and talked about Ralph. Mrs. Williams said she is so glad there is some-one else besides herself who likes Ralph. She told me that as long as she has been in the neighborhood she has heard ter-rible stories about him. "Underneath, Ralph has some fine qualities, I'm sure," she said, "but it takes someone with a great deal of understanding and patience to bring them out." I told her that Ralph did not seem to me to be any worse than any other lively boy. In fact, he has been unusually fine at times. "He hasn't been going down to the garage this year the way he has in the past either," Mrs. Williams observed. "Those men down there tease him and use coarse language. That isn't good for any boy. And then, his father doesn't look after him the way he should."

Monday, March 8. This morning the older children dis-cussed what they have been reading about travel. Among other things they found that the early roads followed old Indian trails. They had read that industries which had to do with travel were among the earliest industries. They talked about the way coaches had to be made to be able to stand travel over rough road. I asked the children if they knew what other industries were among the early ones. They made a few guesses and expressed a desire to find out more.

Mr. Lorenzo, our 4-H Club agent, who has been interested in our school-grounds beautification project, offered to invite Mr. Blackburn, the state landscape specialist, to help us with our plans. Mr. Blackburn arrived today. He said our school-ground plan is accurate and clear. We cannot grow flowers around the schoolhouse because of the dripping from the over-hanging roof. A border around the school grounds would take about six feet away from our play space, which is small enough as it is. The woods should not be hidden from view but cleaned out. The outhouses should be painted green to put them in the background, and shrubs and firs should be planted around them. Shrubs at the corners of the school-house would give it a settled look. All these were answers to our questions. Mr. Blackburn liked our idea of a wild-flower rock garden and the rose trellises on either side of the door-way. He advised using native shrubs and told us how to plant and fertilize them. He suggested that after we landscape our school grounds the children try the same thing at home. He, too, is aware that the local community has much to offer to enrich the lives of all!

Mr. Wilson came to help the boys with the puppets. He said to Ralph, "All right, Ralph, you know how to do this now. You help these other fellows." He taught Ralph how to assign a task to each one, how to guide the work, how to correct errors. He made Ralph foreman of the work until next Monday. Mr. Wilson thinks Ralph is a fine boy and an apt pupil.

As I watched Mr. Blackburn and Mr. Wilson work with the boys and girls, I had a feeling of deep respect and appreciation for them. In a few simple terms they get across what they mean and sow the seeds for desirable changes in behavior. They seem to see their objectives so clearly and they point their efforts in a straight line toward those objectives. I'd like to be able to do that. At times I feel just like Winnie the Pooh and his friend Piglet, who go round and round a bush searching for a vague Woozle.

THURSDAY, MARCH 11. The little children have been asking to have a puppet show, too. Since string puppets are difficult, I decided to try hand puppets with them. I asked them to pick out the story they would like to dramatize. They took it so seriously and worked so hard that one of the older children commented, "It's so quiet, it seems as if all the little ones have gone home."

FRIDAY, MARCH 12. The primary children could not decide whether they would like *Joe Buys Nails* or *Hansel and Gretel* for their puppet show. They finally decided on the latter, because the scenes changed too often in *Joe Buys Nails*.

We have been having fine Forestry Club meetings in the past few weeks. We have been collecting and identifying rock specimens. Today we began to mount our individual collections on plywood.

SATURDAY, MARCH 13. This second edition of our newspaper is so long and hectographing is such a messy job that I thought it would be a better idea to bring the printers home with me rather than to try to do the work at school. Anna and Ruth came home with me last night. Olga was supposed to come but her father would not give his consent, so Ruth came in her place. This is a nice experience for these girls, for they do not have opportunities to be away from home. Anna figured how long it takes us to put out a newspaper. It took seven hours to type the paper and four and one-half hours to hectograph the thirty-five copies. Therefore it takes about twelve hours without counting the time to write the articles. But, since we have only three issues a year, we feel it is worth every bit of that time. Its value in giving purpose to much of the writing of the children, and in acquainting the community with the school, cannot be measured.

In the afternoon we tramped over Dad's farm and found quartz crystals, sandstone, shale, limestone, and flint for our collections. I wish I could do this more often. A teacher and the children can get so close in this way.

MONDAY, MARCH 15. The first thing we did this morning was to read our newspaper. When we finished, the new boy, Thomas, cried out, "Boy, that's some paper!" Everyone laughed with pleasure at his sudden exclamation.

This afternoon I taught the children a round in preparation for two-part singing. Mrs. Williams arrived about that time and told us how nice the voices sounded outside the schoolhouse. Several of the boys still sing with deep voices because they think that is the way boys ought to sing. I'm going to try to bring up the little boys with some right attitudes about music.

MONDAY, MARCH 22. We started our first two-part song today, a lovely French folk tune. The children like to sing in two parts. Some of the girls are beginning to read music from sight fairly well. Sophia is rapidly becoming our favorite conductor.

After school, my brother worked with the boys to build birch trellises on either side of the doorway of the schoolhouse.

TUESDAY, MARCH 23. The girls have found pictures of samplers in their books and said they would like to make some. Several of the boys want to make models of Conestoga wagons and stagecoaches. George expressed a desire to carve some wooden utensils. I added to the list by suggesting that some make wall hangings depicting pioneer life to add interest and beauty to our room. Anna and Sophia immediately volunteered to do this. Some of these activities were begun today.

All noon hour Frank whispered defiant phrases to Ralph. After all had gone out to play, I sat down with Frank. "What's the use?" is an important part of his vocabulary these days. I talked to him about the "use" of everything. I recalled to him the times when he had taken full part and how much happiness it had brought him. I said, "Frank, try hard to take part in everything. When you are a part of something, you don't feel so alone." When he went out he said, "I'll try."

After school, Ralph and Ruth offered to direct me to the homes of three old-timers in the community to make arrangements for interviews. Ralph told me Frank would like to go too. We four had a happy time together talking mostly about the qualities of the Ford.

THURSDAY, MARCH 25. At our Helpers' Club meeting Catherine made the motion that, since it is spring, the game committee should meet and plan our outdoor activities as it had done in the fall. The group decided that Thursday is a much better day for the club meeting, for if any committees had to meet, they could meet on Friday and we could start in without delay on Monday. A new game committee was formed. Albert was chosen, for the group felt that the little children should also be represented.

SATURDAY, MARCH 27. This morning Sophia, Catherine, Olga, George, and I started out to see Mr. Harold Small. Frank was to go with us also but Olga told us she thought Frank was not feeling well. When we arranged for an interview with Mr. Small we had left with him a list of our questions. Today he was ready to answer them. All but George took notes. Catherine was especially alert and asked many questions. Mr. Small gave us much information about the early settlement of our community. On the way home we stopped to see a log barn Mr. Small had told us about. It was put together entirely with wooden pegs and is still in excellent condition. The owner told us that the barn must be about two hundred years old.

This afternoon Doris, May, and Ruth went to the Browns' with me. Mr. and Mrs. Brown live on the site of the first settlement in Valley View and they were filled with the lore of the place. They even had the original deed, which we copied.

At 4:30 Anna, Mary, Helen, and Edward went with me to town to interview Mr. John Rayburn. He told us a great deal about the way his grandmother used to cook.

TUESDAY, MARCH 30. Every child was back after the brief Easter holiday. We had a discussion of Saturday's trips. I told the children that this was valuable information that we should get down into writing as we would probably not find it in any book, and it would be lost when the old people are gone. We organized the material by listing the topics on the blackboard. The children chose the topics they wished to write up and planned to keep the notes in their notebooks.

Frank was sullen all day long. This afternoon he played the game badly and was a poor sport. He refused to work in the rock garden when the other children were eager to do so.

WEDNESDAY, MARCH 31. These days are so beautiful that the children request each morning to be allowed to work in the rock garden. This morning we arranged a half hour outdoors for each child. We work in shifts and each squad has a "boss." How they enjoy this! They dramatize their work and become laborers. One "boss" came in today and announced that it was time for the 11:20 shift. The boys are also digging a sand pit for high jumping. They won't need garden fences for this purpose in the future.

Group VI often go over their reading together before I join them. Warren was in charge today and they taught each other much. They never skip over words they do not know. They even discuss the slightest shades of meaning. They are becoming increasingly conscious of the power of words.

THURSDAY, APRIL 1. I worked with Miss Everett last night and we both felt that the little children were not having enough dramatic play and language activity. They have had many building activities and written work but little conversation except in making plans. We thought the little children also should have some broader experiences. None of these children have ever been on a train. We know they would be interested and decided that this was a good place to start.

This morning I talked with the little children to find out how much they knew about trains and discovered that it was very little.

We took some time today to clean our kitchen cupboards and to put everything away neatly for next year as we shall not have hot lunch for the rest of this year. The children would rather have picnic lunches on these nice days.

Yesterday we began to play organized games outdoors again as we did in the fall and it became clear today that the children need to learn all over again to play together. They are so quarrelsome. Frank has been in an especially bad mood and usually starts the trouble.

MONDAY, APRIL 5. The little children made a list of all the things they want to know about trains. We wrote a group letter to several railroads to get information. The children dictated the letter, which I wrote on the board. Fred, Martha, and Verna are copying the letters for us.

The older children have begun their activities in earnest. The girls are working on their samplers and the boys are constructing articles for the museum. Anna is making a 3' x 4' wall hanging. She made her sketch today and enlarged it on brown paper. It is a picture of two barefoot boys following a Conestoga wagon. Anna spent some time looking for a picture of the clothing worn in pioneer days to make her picture accurate. She made such a fuss about it, because she had difficulty finding a picture, that Ruth and Olga helped her by doing some reading on clothing.

TUESDAY, APRIL 6. And now it is May who is unhappy! I spent some time talking with her this morning. Lately she is not taking part in games, nor is she singing. She goes around with such a gloomy look on her face. She is so unlike her usual self. All I could learn was that she felt that some of the girls were jealous of her. She doesn't know why. I encouraged her to enjoy her school activities without worrying unduly about what others think. All morning she was glum but during harmonica practice she brightened and actually took part in conducting the group.

May is not the only one who is having difficulty. The four big girls were to work on the chart of wild flowers in our township but there was an argument. Each girl accused the others of shirking their jobs. I asked them if they did not think they were old enough to plan and apportion the work without all that quarreling. They thought they were and did come to some decision.

And finally, to cap the climax, Thomas and Ralph came to blows. Thomas did something Ralph did not like and Ralph **New members** "socked" him. Thomas's temper flared up and **present ad-** he went for Ralph. I gripped Thomas's wrists **justment** and held them firmly. His eyes were red and he **problems** was gritting his teeth but he did not resist. I talked with him just as quietly as I knew how, to calm him, although I was anything but calm inside. I told him he would be so sorry afterwards if he did anything rash in a temper. When Thomas was feeling better, I talked with Ralph, who admitted his lack of self-control. I pointed out how badly we treat our new people. We don't accept them very well and we make it hard for them to adjust. Ralph said it was not because we were not trying but because the new people do such crazy things. I explained to Ralph that the new people had not had so much freedom and are only now learning to form the habits of self-control which are so necessary in a school like ours. I reminded Ralph of our own difficulties in the beginning of the year and how patient everyone had been with him, while he was learning to become a co-operating member of the group. It ended with Ralph's decision to be more patient with Thomas.

I really felt "low" tonight after all this and sought the refuge of my helping teacher friend. We talked at length about the "ups" and "downs" of this little school, and when I left Miss Everett I was encouraged. She repeated to me things I had heard many times before, but when I get all wound up in the myriad details, I lose my perspective. She helped to restore it.

If these children lived in the sheltered environment of a formal school with a benevolent despot at its head, these problems would not be revealed in school. The school would function in a fairly smooth way. Nevertheless, the problems would still be there. They would be there, ready to break out sometime later when it might be too late to solve them. What better place is there for problems to come to a head than in school where there is a mature person who, although she may have much to learn, has, at least, had some training in guiding the children in the solution of their problems. Frank, Ralph, and Thomas would be discipline problems in a formal school. Here, although they have their adjustments to make, they are beginning to make contributions to their small society. They are learning desirable ways of behaving. Our school is a natural social situation and children are learning to adjust and accept the responsibilities of citizenship. This practice should give them a "head start" when they more actively participate in the larger community.

WEDNESDAY, APRIL 7. The little children have been going through our library books to find stories about trains. When they find one they put a marker in the book and place it on the table. They managed to gather quite a collection. Even the beginners helped with this.

THURSDAY, APRIL 8. I have learned that the former teacher had difficulty with May's older sister because of self-pity. She felt that everyone disliked her and that they went out of their way to be mean to her. She is not popular in high school for the same reason. It appears that May is beginning to imitate. I wish I knew what to do about it. I talked with May during the noon hour and tried to tell her that the group likes folks who enjoy being a part of the group and who willingly do their share to keep our school happy. May has helped so much this winter and the group appreciates her good sense of humor. She really has no grounds for feeling as she does.

I was happy to see May playing with the group in the afternoon.

The questions the little folks have asked about trains are now on a chart. Today each child began to read to find answers to the questions.

Today, after all these weeks, I learned why Frank has been acting as he has. His father does not have a horse and cannot afford to buy one, nor can he afford to hire someone to do his plowing for him. He has hitched the plow to his car and while he drives the car Frank guides the plow. To say that this is hard work would be putting it mildly. For three days in the past two weeks Frank has gone home at noon, pretending to be ill, because he did not want me to know what was happening. This, then, is what is making him so bitter.

FRIDAY, APRIL 9.   It rained hard today, so we had to make our own sunshine inside. We sang first thing in the morning. How beautifully these children sing! How careful they are to enunciate properly and to put expression into their singing. They sang the Eighth Psalm to a beautiful chorale by Bach. They sing it without accompaniment and follow every suggestion in my directing. I was moved by the beauty of it.

I watched Ralph, who did not sing, but from the intent expression on his face I knew that he too was moved, as were all the other children. For a few seconds after we had finished there was silence in the room, and then—Mary blew her nose.

The little children wrote letters to their mothers asking permission to go on a train ride on Tuesday. They worked so eagerly. We discussed what we were to put into the letter, and listed on the board the words the children would need to know how to spell. Each child wrote his own letter and I helped with the corrections.

Helpers' Club meeting was quarrelsome today. There has been so much of this going on recently. The Prinlaks and the Olseuskis do not get along, and the children bring the family quarrels to school with them. The Olseuskis have trouble with Ruth, and vice versa. The Sametis children have trouble with Ruth and the Olseuskis. May has trouble with them all. It seems to be the girls just now. I've been trying to think back how all of this might have started.

MONDAY, APRIL 12.   Ralph came to school in a bad mood today. Several of the girls began to tease him and that made it worse. He played ball before school and through carelessness broke a windowpane. He ordered Ruth to clean it up, but I told him it was his job. He swept up the glass, removed the rest of the glass from the pane and scraped off the putty. The work seemed to calm him. When he came back into the room we were singing. Much to my surprise and delight, Ralph sang too.

The little ones have finished making their puppets for *Hansel and Gretel* and began to practice with them for the first time today. They were clumsy but they had such a good time.

TUESDAY, APRIL 13. The little children talked about their proposed train trip. They reviewed the questions they wanted to ask the station agent and the conductor. We discussed how we were to behave.

Miss Everett and I took the fourteen youngsters. At the station, the children bought their own tickets. They saw the mailman put the mailbag on the arm extension for the train to pick up. Andrew was allowed to flag the train. The trip took us through the Gap and the conductor pointed out places of interest. The conductor was interested in the children. He showed them the dining car and allowed them to sit in the parlor car. At Jamesburg, we watched other trains come in and learned about whistles and signals. At the five- and ten-cent store we bought some train booklets, and at a soda store we bought ice-cream cones.

While Miss Everett and I were with the little children, Miss Hoppock, another helping teacher, took the older children to interview Mr. Livingston, a long-time resident in the community. They had a picnic lunch at the stream. When we returned, the older children were eager to tell us what a fine time they'd had and the little children were just as eager to talk about their trip. We spent the next half hour exchanging experiences.

THURSDAY, APRIL 15. In social studies today the older children discussed early schools. Everyone took part and enjoyed it more than any of our discussions so far. Mr. Livingston had told the children the history of our school, what it looked like when he attended as a boy, and what games he played.

Martha wrote a story last night about the train trip and brought it to school. That made the others all want to write stories. Martha said she was going to make a train book. The others liked the idea. Martha helped the little children with the words they did not know how to spell, while I worked with the older ones.

During the club meeting the children made another decision about their play. Before this, Ralph and Frank have been choosing their teams each week. Mary suggested that others be given this privilege. The children had an orderly discussion and finally decided that Frank and Ralph would choose teams again today. Next week, the boys' first choices will select teams, the following week the second choices will have the privilege, and so on until all have had a turn to choose sides.

FRIDAY, APRIL 16. The day is not long enough for all the things we need to do! In English period we reviewed our speech errors. We made a list of sentences, using the correct form of our common speech errors. We had a list of forty-two sentences. It was interesting to see how aware of their speech the children have become. They were able to suggest sentences in rapid succession.

The tulips are blooming in our bulb bed and make a lovely patch of color. Several people have told us what an improvement the bed makes in the appearance of our school grounds. The children are very happy about it and examine the bed every morning for new blossoms.

MONDAY, APRIL 19. The little children had some dramatic play this morning. We lined up our desks in train fashion. Andrew was the engineer, William the ticket agent, and Fred the conductor. The children enjoyed it so much that they asked to play train during the physical education period.

TUESDAY, APRIL 20. The little children talked about yesterday's train play. We decided that before we played again we would plan some conversation around the trip we had taken. Martha said that our train play was hampered because no one could answer the questions of the passengers. Fred suggested that we find the answers. The children thought that we could find the answers by reading the leaflets the train companies had sent us. We divided into three groups to find out about whistles, the kitchen, and the dining car, since these interested the children most. Andrew, Alex, and Gus got out their train book and the three dark heads almost touched. Later, Andrew said, "It's lucky we read about the whistles over again, we made a lot of mistakes yesterday."

FRIDAY, APRIL 23. At the end of a perfect day something had to happen to spoil it. While the children were waiting for the bus, Thomas swore at Ralph. Ralph lost his temper and punched Thomas in the nose. He did not stay to see what happened. Tom's nose bled and I attended to it, assuring Thomas that, although Ralph had no right to do what he did, still Tom would have to expect things like that to happen to him if he went around swearing at people. "Well, he made me mad," Thomas explained.

TUESDAY, APRIL 27. Thomas was not in school yesterday and I took time to talk with Ralph to try to make him see the seriousness of what he had done.

This morning I received a note from Mrs. Lenick stating that she had reported the matter between Thomas and Ralph to the State Police. I felt miserable. They have only been here two months and I've been so busy that I have not taken time to go out there to become acquainted with Mrs. Lenick. If I had only done that, this would not have happened. She wrote that she knew all about Ralph, that no one could handle him, and that his father would do nothing to correct him. She wasn't blaming me, she was only trying to help me out. Trying to help me out! If she only knew how I have worked with Ralph. This might be the undoing of a whole year's work.

Problems are sharpened when the home and school do not understand each other

I decided to let Ralph in on the matter. I related as much of the contents of the note as I felt Ralph needed to know. We decided that it would be a good thing for both of us to have a talk with Ralph's dad before any member of the State Police did. I had dinner with the Joneses tonight and after dinner we three went into conference. I related the facts and then Mr. Jones talked with Ralph. He handled the situation well, I thought, and gave Ralph good advice. Mr. Jones thanked me for coming and said he would know now what to expect. Ralph was grateful too. He escorted me to my car, a thing he has never done before.

WEDNESDAY, APRIL 28.   A state trooper called this morning. I talked with him first and explained the situation and then he talked with Ralph. I hope the matter is settled and that Ralph is a wiser boy because of this experience.

What a time the little children had talking about what makes a steam engine go! Albert had a picture from an upper grade science book and explained exactly what makes the wheels turn around! He had studied and studied the picture until he could tell the group simply and accurately. When we played train, Albert was the engineer and answered the questions of the curious passengers. Later they added kitchen and dining-car scenes to their train play.

The older children worked hard today to get the stories written on the early days in our township. So far the children have studied the homes, food, clothing, medicine, schools, religion, and amusements of the pioneers. The museum has grown to nineteen articles. The girls have finished their samplers. The boys have made crude models of a Conestoga wagon, a stagecoach, and a log cabin. Anna has crayoned her picture on the muslin wall hanging and has pressed the wax into the fabric. The hanging is now ready for the lining. Sophia's hanging has turned out to be a huge one, 3' x 9'. It tells much of the story of pioneer life. Various members of the group are helping Sophia color her hanging.

THURSDAY, APRIL 29. Eight mothers came to the regular meeting after school. We discussed the hot lunch program for the next year. The mothers are going to report to our neighbor across the road from the school when they have any surplus vegetables this summer. Then she will call together the older girls and some of the mothers to can the vegetables. The mothers will take turns helping with the canning.

THURSDAY, JUNE 10. The activities of the past month have kept me so busy that some things had to be crowded out, among them the luxury of writing in a diary. It did seem a luxury compared to the pressing activities which demanded immediate attention. Although what I write from memory will be of less help as far as analysis and evaluation are concerned, I think as a matter of record I should summarize the events which have occurred since I last wrote.

A summary

The children worked hard on their puppet show. Mr. Wilson helped the boys build a platform which fitted over the sawhorses. He taught the boys how to build frames for the curtains and for the scenes and how to provide lighting. The girls sewed new muslin curtains. The boys painted the scenes, made the properties and the handles for the puppet strings. The children practiced diligently and learned to handle their puppets well. They forgot themselves in the little puppets and the puppets became real people.

The little folks practiced their hand puppet show and got it into good shape. On May 21, the children gave the shows to a large group of parents and teachers at the County Achievement Day program. On May 26, they gave it at the schoolhouse. Since then fame of the show has spread abroad and already folks who have not seen it are asking if we shall have another one next year.

This month we produced a seven-page newspaper, the third paper this year.

And, as if we did not have enough to do, we planned a pageant to be given at the annual Township Play Day. Each year the pupils and the teachers of the two schools in the township come together for a play day. Part of the afternoon program consists of an entertainment in which each school has a share. This year we dramatized the history of our township and presented the parents with a mimeographed copy of "Some Interesting Facts in the History of Valley View Township."

Probably the strongest impression I have of this period is of the fine spirit of co-operation which pervaded all the work. There has been a happy, busy, workshop atmosphere about the place.

As I look back over the year's work, I have the feeling that all our struggles and growing pains have not been in vain, and that all of us—children, parents, and teacher—have grown richer through our experiences in working, playing, and living together.

4

We Make a New Beginning

FRIDAY, AUGUST 27, 1937. A busy summer is over and I must now turn my attention to the new school year. I studied the

I prepare for the second year

list of thirty-one children (see Appendix, p. 251), all of them a year older than they were when I first met them. The list includes four beginners:

> Elizabeth Prinlak, age 7-8
> Florence Hill, age 5-9
> Charles Willis, age 5-1
> Eric Thompson, age 5-1

Three children have left our group: Olga is working in the city, Anna has gone on to the town high school, and Fred Lutz moved away this summer.

I regrouped the children in reading, spelling, and arithmetic. We shall have two groups in social studies as well as in science and health. For the time being we shall use the daily program we followed at the end of last year, until we work out new plans.

MONDAY, AUGUST 30. I visited the schoolhouse today. The rosebushes on the trellises have grown. Ruth said that one of them had roses on it this summer.

I stopped to say "hello" to those along the way. Ruth has had 4-H Club camp experience. She showed me her insect collection. Mr. Thompson is still working as hard as ever on the road and betweentimes he cuts and sells wood. I have not seen that man take a rest yet.

The Sametis children were glad to see me. Catherine is thin, but Sophia and William have gained weight. They have had summer boarders who rented rooms and did their own cooking. All the boarders stood around and listened while I talked with the children. Sophia has some orange crates to be used at school for making furniture. None of the children have had time to pursue their summer hobbies.

Mrs. Williams has been ill. The four children have spent little time at home. They have taken turns living with their various relatives, and this summer has been wholesome and good for them.

Martha, Inez, and their grandmother were the only ones home at the Joneses'. Ralph has spent most of the summer at the garage with his dad. I'm a little afraid of what this will mean when he starts back to school again. Martha showed me her insect collection and pressed leaves.

The Hill children rushed across the lawn to meet me. Mr. Hill was building a springhouse. Albert showed me where we can get some good modeling clay from the brook that runs past his house. Warren showed me how his stamp collection has grown. The boys have also collected caterpillars and are feeding them until they spin cocoons.

Edward helped at school this afternoon, building shelves in our tool cupboard and putting in hooks on which to hang the new set of tools I bought this summer for seven dollars from our school fund. We went to the lumber company to order lumber for a three-paneled screen, and for easels.

TUESDAY, AUGUST 31. Such things as I have seen and heard today! It is going to take every bit of courage and understanding I have to meet the problems which will come up in our living together.

The old feud between the Prinlaks and the Olseuskis has opened up again. There have been court trials, much name calling, throwing of rocks, and even some shooting. Frank, apparently, was the worst offender. The Olseuskis are asking help from me. What can I say?

At the Prinlaks' I learned that they are having a hard time making their small income do. Mr. Prinlak said to me, "If you're poor, you're poor as long as you live." Mrs. Prinlak was baking bread. Before I left she gave me four quarts of huckleberries to take home. When I hesitated, she said she had twenty-six other gallon jars filled. Frank and George went upstairs and hid when I drove up. They peeped and listened through a chimney hole all the while I was there. What can the school do for children who are so handicapped? I never felt more inadequate.

When I arrived at the Cartwrights' all the children hid and peeped out at me from behind the house. They smiled when I caught their eyes and jerked their heads out of sight again. The Cartwrights had a beautiful garden kept by the boys, but not one can of vegetables was put away.

Today, for the first time, I made the acquaintance of Thomas's father and stepmother. Mrs. Lenick seemed glad to see me and told me much of Thomas's life. After his parents were divorced, Thomas went to live with his grandmother. He went to school only when he chose. When Thomas's stepmother came to live with his father, Thomas resented her and was rude and rebellious. Mrs. Lenick is trying to make Thomas a "good" boy. She keeps him clean and has made a clean home for him. She still thinks he is a bad lot and won't amount to much.

Mrs. Dulio took me down to the cellar and showed me rows and rows of canned vegetables, wild fruits, and mushrooms which she and Andrew had gathered. She showed me where they will bury carrots and beets and the bins where apples will be stored. They have gone nowhere all summer. They have neither a radio nor newspapers. They have worked and worked on this little rented farm, hoping to save enough to be able to buy a small place of their own. Yet with all the hardships there is happiness in this home. When Andrew looks at his mother there is a loving light in his eyes. Mrs. Dulio calls him "my curlyhead." Their philosophy is simple: work hard and do not worry about what you cannot help.

Going to the Andrews' was like finding an oasis in the desert. The girls are eager for school to start, they have ideas about things to do. Mrs. Andrews talked about the nice summer they have had. They went to the movies quite frequently. Doris had her tonsils out. The atmosphere was happy and pleasant.

On the way home, I met Mrs. Ramsey. She has been sending her little daughter to the town school, but this year she wants Irene to attend Stony Grove because she has heard so much about it. Irene is six years old. She will bring our enrollment up to thirty-two.

And now, as I look back over the past two days, I'm just a little frightened at the task before me. Perhaps the best way to start would be to assume that we shall continue to live in school as we did in June. After that —?

SATURDAY, SEPTEMBER 4. Anna, Helen, Ruth, Sophia, and Catherine saw me drive up to the schoolhouse to clean this morning and came to help. We washed all the furniture and cupboards, took the books out of the closet and arranged the room. At the end of the day we rode to town and purchased material for curtains and cupboard hangings.

WEDNESDAY, SEPTEMBER 8. When I arrived, the little children were gathered around the door. The older boys were near the

The program continues from the first year

back of the schoolhouse, just a little shy to meet me on the first day of school. I set them to work at once raising and lowering seats and desks to fit the children, and they began to feel at home.

Irene was bright and cheerful today and told us she likes our school. Charles Willis cried all day long and had an "accident." He is as immature as a three-year-old. Eric hung on to Ruth practically all day, much to Ruth's disgust. Elizabeth and Florence made friends and adjusted quickly.

Last year we had talked much of certain inconveniences in our room. Before school closed we made a list of these and what we intended to do about them. One of our biggest problems was to find a place for the little children to play, where they could really talk and move. This year, with five additional desks, to find room for the little children is an even greater problem. Another of my big problems was to find ways of meeting the needs of the large boys who are over age for their grade and learn slowly. They need manual activities which will stimulate them to learn in order to be able to carry out the activities. To attempt to solve both these problems, I suggested to the children that we build a playhouse outdoors, large enough for several children to play in at one time.

Another problem was to make use of our puppet-show table so that it would "pay rent" for all the room it took. We needed a screen to separate the kitchen from the cloakroom. We wanted curtains to make our room more homelike. We needed more easels. At nine o'clock we were ready to make some plans.

> Make easels from wallpaper sample book racks and plywood—Edward and Ralph
>
> Cover puppet-show table with inlaid linoleum—Frank
>
> Make three-paneled screen frame—Warren and George
>
> Make a skirt for the puppet-show table, two cupboard curtains and window curtains—Catherine, Sophia, May, Doris, Ruth, Helen, and Mary
>
> Make orange-crate furniture for the playhouse—Alex, Gus, Andrew, Joseph, and Walter
>
> Make cushions and cushion covers for chairs, dye rags for a rug—Verna, Alice, Martha, Pearl, and Joyce
>
> Make two looms for the rag rugs—Albert and William
>
> Tear rags for rugs—John and Richard
>
> Make bedding for crib—Florence, Elizabeth, and Irene

Before school, I helped Mary understand how to make the bedding for the crib and she helped the little girls with this. The older boys needed little help from me. I merely approved their measurements before they began to saw the lumber. Ruth helped the little girls with the cushions. I spent most of the time with the boys who were making the orange-crate furniture. We had a workshop until ten o'clock.

After the physical education period we began to talk about our summer activities. Mary made some drawings. Martha and Ralph have some insects. Catherine and Sophia have butterflies. William has some fossils. Frank made two airplanes and repaired two clocks. Ralph learned some new swimming strokes. Other children began hobbies but did not complete them.

I talked to the children about my summer experiences as a demonstration teacher in a one-teacher school in Michigan. I showed them the diary which the children in Michigan had kept, and the fossils which I brought back with me. We compared them with William's fossils.

The health needs of these children are so great that I feel it is necessary to concentrate on them for a while. I plan to use the last half hour of each morning for this.

The health program is expanded to meet pressing needs Last year, many of our difficulties occurred in the afternoon after the noon play period. This year perhaps a quiet rest period for the first fifteen minutes will calm them for the afternoon's work. During the health period we discussed this matter of resting.

The rest period was successful today. Several children who did not want to rest their heads on their desks, read easy books. We all became so relaxed that we kept yawning during the music period. We sang our old favorites today.

I started the little children on the review of the addition and subtraction combinations while the older ones continued the work they had begun in the morning. Each child has a pack of cards of combinations and as he completes one it is checked off on his record sheet.

Late in the afternoon the older children began the review in their arithmetic books. And so ended a busy and interesting day.

THURSDAY, SEPTEMBER 9. Yesterday the children were glad to be back in school again and were too interested to get into

Problems developing during the summer carry over into the school and must be faced

trouble. It seemed as if we had never been away. Today, the effects of their summer experiences entered the schoolhouse.

We have no balls. Our good one was lost at the Township Play Day last spring. The other two need patching. We have a soft baseball, but no bat. Since there was no equipment to play with at noon, the boys stood around doing

nothing. I suggested that we all get together and begin to clear the space at the edge of the woods for the playhouse. The boys pretended they did not hear. Only George remarked, "It's too much like work." They walked around to the back of the schoolhouse and began to tease the little boys. Albert, who thinks he is one of the big boys now that he is in the upper group, enjoyed the rough treatment and encouraged the attention he was getting until the boys hurt him. I called the boys in and talked to them. I pointed out that it would have been a happier noon hour if they had helped with the playhouse instead of fooling the way they had. Ralph said, "Why should we help with the playhouse? We aren't going to use it." I tried to explain that there are some things we do for the general welfare of all even though we get no direct benefit from it except the satisfaction that comes from helping. The boys did not react and tried to outdo each other with smart comments. We had to call an end to our conference with nothing accomplished and, I'm afraid, much harm done. As I look back now I realize what a mistake I made. I might have spoken individually to Ralph and Frank, who were the leaders, when they did not have a supporting audience. But I think it would have been better not to have made a speech at all. The only thing to do now is to get the balls fixed as quickly as possible, to get a bat, and to teach many new games. I'll have the younger boys start on the playhouse and when the older boys become interested, as they eventually will, we'll invite them to join. This, of course, is what I should have done in the first place. Fortunately for teachers, boys forget easily.

All the boys refused to play during the physical education period. Frank said, "It's too much like work. I do plenty of that at home." He was angry that he was not on Ralph's team. He said it was that way all last year and if he couldn't be on Ralph's side this year he wouldn't play. I talked for a while with Ralph, who was in a little better mood, and managed to get him to start a game while I went into conference with Frank. I said, "Frank, what has happened to your fair judgment? Last year you helped us work out our playground problems. I don't have to tell you what is wrong with having the two biggest boys on one team." I invited him to join in the game, but he wouldn't so I left him sitting on the steps watching us.

During the health lesson I brought up this matter of continual bickering on the playground. We discussed the relation of the attitude of the mind to general health. We talked about the unhealthy effects of idleness. Although the children listened attentively and contributed to the discussion, this lesson caused most of the trouble during the noon play period. They kept referring to our discussion of the trouble we can get into when we are idle. They tested it—to see how much trouble they could get into.

FRIDAY, SEPTEMBER 10. Today was much better than yesterday. The work period in the morning always seems to go well. The children like what they are doing.

At noon all the younger boys began to clear the space for the playhouse. The older boys watched most of the time. I'm sure they would have helped today if I had not made an issue of this matter yesterday.

After school, as usual I inspected the toilets and to my dismay found obscene marking in the fresh paint in the boys' toilet. I could not tell whose writing it was.

MONDAY, SEPTEMBER 13. This morning I talked to the boys as they arrived at school. As I expected, no one knew anything about the markings. By a process of elimination I knew that one or all of the four big boys were responsible for it. While the others played outdoors I talked to the boys. I told them that it was too bad that we had to spoil the appearance of our newly painted toilets. I took this opportunity for some sex education. The boys listened attentively. I sent them out to repaint the defaced area.

It rained today, so we could not go outdoors to play. I made several suggestions about things to do and then joined a small group at the table who were examining fossils with a lens and tripod microscope. We were absorbed and before we knew it Ralph, Frank, Edward, and George were interested too. Ralph cracked a few large rocks open and we found many tiny shells embedded in the rock. It was a pleasant twenty minutes.

The noon hour was not so happy, however. The little children found quiet games to play and the older boys proceeded to break up the games. Albert was interested in studying the fossils with the hand lens. Ralph went up to him and grabbed the lens. Since Albert was not willing to give it up, there was a tussle in which the frame around the lens was broken. I told Ralph simply that he would have to buy a new one (10¢). Since the situation was getting no better, I asked the children to take their seats and to rest quietly. George and Edward did not like that and refused to work the rest of the afternoon. They just sat in their seats and sulked. I know I must do something positive about this situation, but what?

And Joseph! He hangs around the older boys and imitates them. He shouts at the top of his lungs and stamps around. He is getting too old to be easily taken care of in a public school.

Charles's father agrees with me that it would be better to keep Charles out of school another year especially since he cannot dress himself. I gave Mr. Willis a list of things to teach Charles before next year.

There was one other bright spot besides the morning play period. After we sang two songs, we shortened the music period to leave time for some original stories. Catherine told the nicest, most refreshing story about a little rabbit who would not obey his mother. Every child in the group thoroughly enjoyed it. They asked me to read to them. I read a fable from Aesop, similar to Catherine's story.

TUESDAY, SEPTEMBER 14. Last night I thought my problem through carefully. The children are having their difficulties, it's true, but so am I. I want so much to meet genuinely the needs of these boys and girls, but I'm having such a struggle. I've done more things wrong than I have done right since school began, it seems. This work taxes my ingenuity and patience heavily. How easy it would be to settle the problem by going back to an autocratically managed school. But I am not willing to give up the purposes of a democratic one, and these purposes cannot be accomplished by force.

I must give the children more challenging work to do. If I can keep them busy and interested perhaps I can guide their energies into more worth-while channels. I have had the two balls patched and bought a bat with money from the school fund. Ruth took the baseball home to restring it.

Using the social studies period to make improvements in the appearance and efficiency of our room has been good. In addition to this, I decided to capitalize on the interest of the children in my trip to Michigan to give them something more definite to do. This morning I listed on the board the interesting things I saw in Michigan: many fossils, windmills, barns with round roofs and lightning rods, fields of wheat and corn, square farms and straight roads, sheep and hogs, oil fields, much flat country, few trees, and many lakes. We talked about the meaning of these. We found a map in our geographies and traced the route I took. Ruth read that I went through part of the corn belt. She explained that more corn was raised here than in any other part of the United States. The children studied the map and found that more wheat is raised in part of this region than in any other part of the United States. More cherries are raised here, more automobiles are manufactured, more flour is milled than in any other region of the world. I had the children encircle this region with their fingers and told them that for convenience in discussing it we call it the "North Central States." I asked the children to read to try to find out why it is that this region is important in so many ways.

While I was with the other children, the little girls, under the direction of Verna, sewed cushion covers and did some weaving on the rugs, while the little boys, under the direction of Gus, painted the orange-crate furniture they had made. They put this work aside to plan for the playhouse. The children planned to make it seven feet square and six feet high. They want a peaked roof. At first they wanted windows all around the house until Andrew suggested that it would be too drafty. He suggested that we enclose entirely the north and east sides as his father had done with the chicken coop. We made a working diagram and then went outdoors to mark out the site of the house with wooden pegs and strings.

WEDNESDAY, SEPTEMBER 15. The older children set up some problems based on yesterday's discussion:

    I   How did the fossils get to Michigan?
   II   Why is this region such good farming land?
  III   How can they raise so much corn and wheat?
   IV   How did these cities become so large?

The children began to read in their geographies to solve the first problem. I gave them some help with the index.

THURSDAY, SEPTEMBER 16. Albert, Pearl, and Martha are working with the older children this year. They were having trouble with using maps. While the older group continued to work on Problem I, I helped them with map study. I gave them maps of the United States on which they are outlining the North Central States and labeling them. The primary children continued the work they were doing yesterday.

This was the day the school doctor was to come to examine the children. We used the health period to prepare for him. I read to the children the story of the way Admiral Byrd picked his men for his trip to Antarctica. We discussed the value in frequent physical examinations and why it is a good thing to discover early any physical defects we might have which need correcting. Appropriately enough, the nurse and doctor arrived just as we had finished. I watched as the doctor examined the children and the nurse made notations on the health cards. Now and then I pointed out to the doctor observations I had made and he checked carefully to verify them. I shall work with the parents to have these defects corrected as soon as possible.

The children began to make their new progress books today. They wanted them to be extra nice, so we had an art lesson on border designs.

After school the girls went to our neighbor's to sew the rest of the curtains, as our machine is not working properly. Andrew, Gus, Alex, and I went to the lumber company to order lumber and to get some advice. Mr. Oaks figured up the bill on the adding machine, which interested the boys very much. On the way home, Andrew said, "Twenty-seven dollars is a lot of money. We will probably have to give two plays to raise it." Before we left, while I was helping the girls to get started, the boys washed their hands and faces, combed their hair, and brushed their shoes.

This morning, Frank carried to school, for a distance of two miles, a heavy rock filled with fossils. The children spent a great deal of time examining it with the hand lens and microscope and pointed out unusually good forms. We have some turtle eggs in our museum. Four hatched today while the children watched. It fascinated them. George brought two chipmunks that we are watching.

MONDAY, SEPTEMBER 20. This morning we took a walk to observe how seeds are disseminated. We identified as many of the seeds as possible and brought back for our museum examples of the various means of dissemination.

During our health period we discussed what makes a walk enjoyable. We talked about pace, rhythm, position of the feet, weight, carriage and posture, proper shoes, and finally the ability to appreciate and enjoy what we see. Because Ruth's feet ached when our walk was over, we drew an outline of her foot and found that her shoes are too small for her. All the children will make this test tonight.

This afternoon the boys decided they would like to build a log cabin in the woods. I heartily welcomed the plan as the first really absorbing interest they have had this year. The little children organized a game of center catch ball. A pleasant noon hour went all too quickly.

THURSDAY, SEPTEMBER 23. After school we had a Forestry Club meeting to mount the specimens we gathered this summer. Surprisingly enough, the older boys gave up their plan to remain after school and work on their cabin in order to attend the Forestry Club meeting. Ralph had no collection of his own to mount, so he helped mount the seeds we gathered during our walk on Monday. Martha, Catherine, Sophia, and Verna were identifying insects. Albert began to build a cocoon cage. Ruth made a chart to mount her bird feathers. Warren cut small square boards on which he is going to mount his birds' nests.

FRIDAY, SEPTEMBER 24. In the science lesson this morning we discussed what happens when a seed falls to the ground, how a plant makes seed, and the purpose of the flower. We discussed pollination and photosynthesis. Mary and Helen are going to make a chart of the plant cycle.

The boys want to work on their log cabin during physical education periods and they asked me for permission. I told

We begin to rebuild group spirit and co-operative action

them that it was up to the girls because it would be spoiling their game. The girls said they wanted to be fair but they felt the boys needed the group play. It finally worked out this way. The boys would use the morning physical education period to work on the cabin until they get a good start. In the meantime the girls can play with the little ones. In the afternoon, however, we would play together as usual. It gave me a little thrill to watch these boys and girls peacefully considering their problem and coming to such a wise decision satisfactory to all. We had to start again this year—but not from the very beginning!

SATURDAY, SEPTEMBER 25. The boys and some of the girls came to the schoolhouse to begin working on the playhouse. It is a big job and we had quite a time with the foundation. It took all morning and part of the afternoon to get the foundation of stones level and to make it fit the sill. We put up double posts in the four corners, the top plates, and the center nailing pieces. We braced the posts. The children learned about the first steps in constructing a house and how to use a level. Andrew said he never realized a carpenter had such hard work to do.

WEDNESDAY, SEPTEMBER 29. During the social studies periods these days the larger primary boys are nailing the boards on the side of their house, while the smaller boys are working on the orange-crate furniture. The little girls are weaving their rag rugs and sewing bedding for the crib, curtains for the cupboards, and cushions and cushion covers for the chairs for the playhouse. I work with the little children for the first half hour to be sure they will know what to do while I work with the older children. Verna usually takes charge of the little ones when I am not with them. The older primary boys help the younger ones.

The older children in the meantime, gather information which we discuss later. At present we are discussing Problem III, How can they raise so much corn and wheat in the North Central States? The children are especially interested in the machines used to harvest the wheat.

For our health lesson today we discussed posture. We reviewed correct sitting, standing, and walking postures and how to take restful postures while working. We practiced the postures to get the feel of them and gave helpful suggestions to each other. The Sametis children have poor postures.

Catherine asked the children to remind her every time they saw her slouch.

After school the girls met to reorganize their sewing club. Only five girls were present. Most of the girls do not like to sew. They elected their officers, decided on Thursday for their meeting day and planned the next few meetings.

FRIDAY, OCTOBER 1. After school we had a Forestry Club meeting. Only Ralph, Warren, Sophia, Catherine, and Ruth stayed. We have so few members in our clubs this year. They seem to think the clubs are too much bother. Yet, they need this so much. Those who did stay to the meeting had a good time because they really wanted to be there. Ralph is making a collection of twig specimens.

SATURDAY, OCTOBER 2. My dad had to help us today. He put up the corner rafters and taught the four big boys how to put up the center ones. Since there wasn't enough work for all the boys, those who could not help raked the school grounds and burned the debris. The big boys like to work with my dad and are happy about being able to work on the house. Yesterday I explained to the boys that the roof would be too hard for the younger boys to build and that we would need their help. They answered, "Sure, we'll do it."

TUESDAY, OCTOBER 5. Frank came in with a cheery smile and asked if he could help with the playhouse. The four big boys started in immediately to measure and saw the boards and to nail them in place on the roof.

The little children have said nothing so far about making a booklet in which to record the experiences of building the playhouse. I brought up the subject today and only Albert said he thought he would rather not write stories. When the children got their bright paper for covers he changed his mind. The five- and six-year-olds made pictures showing how we cleared the site for the house. Joyce wrote under her picture, "We will make a house." The rest wrote original stories about the plans they had made.

WEDNESDAY, OCTOBER 6. The boys were here bright and early to help with the house. They have completely forgotten about the log cabin and are putting all their energies into building a nice playhouse for the little children.

The children want to give *Robin Hood* for their puppet show this year. I began to read it to them yesterday. They gather around me and we have a happy time. Ralph manages to get a seat right at my elbow. He loves the story.

We continue to provide varied experiences to meet individual and group needs

During that nice half hour while the children rest, I read an Uncle Remus story. They learned an English round, "Come, Follow." There was time left for Ralph, Martha, and Alice to tell original stories. Albert told one that was almost poetry. The best of the original stories will be written up for the school newspaper.

WEDNESDAY, OCTOBER 13. We had an art lesson today in which the children made charcoal sketches of trees. Pearl and the Hill boys got the feeling very nicely.

The children finished tracing the world map on the back of oilcloth. It is nine feet wide. Today they nailed it to a wooden rod and hung it on the wall.

The children have been learning many new games and the physical education periods have been happy.

THURSDAY, OCTOBER 14. The children feel that it is taking too long to finish the articles they are making for the room. They asked to have a whole day to work on these things and to get their notebooks in order. Each person made a list of the things he had to do. Some were working on their social studies problems. Some were getting their reading up to date. A few girls were sewing curtains. Two boys were putting oilcloth on the kitchen cupboard shelves. George was enameling the oil stove. Alex, Gus, and Andrew were putting siding on the playhouse. Catherine and Sophia were transferring their drawings to unbleached muslin for the hall screen. I spent practically the whole day with the little children helping them with their reading, spelling, and arithmetic.

After school all the children remained to Forestry Club and it seemed like old times again. The children are still mounting the specimens they gathered this summer.

FRIDAY, OCTOBER 15. Yesterday was so successful and, since there were still many loose ends to catch up, we repeated yesterday's procedure. Mr. Oaks from the lumber company was passing this way and stopped in to see how the playhouse was progressing. He was in the hall ten minutes before we knew he was there. Mr. Oaks was so interested in what he saw that he did not want to disturb us. He smiled and said, "Perfect discipline!" It made me feel so happy for now, at least, we are getting back the fine spirit we had in this school last spring. This spirit is beginning to spread, too, for tonight three of the high school girls joined the Sewing Club.

At the meeting we studied the Sears, Roebuck catalogue and sent for samples of materials for dresses. The girls are beginning to assemble their sewing boxes.

SATURDAY, OCTOBER 16. This morning I took some of the girls to Weston to select patterns for their dresses. Again I was made aware of the limited experiences of the children. They had never been on an elevator nor through revolving doors. They stopped to examine everything and were full of questions. The woman who showed the girls the patterns has some understanding of children, for she was patient and helpful.

MONDAY, OCTOBER 18. As soon as Frank arrived at school he wanted to know if there was something he could do. He is general manager of cleanup for the next two weeks, so I took him around and showed him what needed to be checked.

We spent most of the afternoon getting the curtains up and putting the room in order. The girls were eager to complete the new hall screen, so they remained after school to press the crayon scenes into the muslin and to tack the muslin to the frame. We stayed until 6:30 to finish up. I thank heaven for understanding and appreciative mothers!

My dad helped the boys with the roof today. It is too difficult for them to do alone. Frank slipped him an apple, indirectly, the way he usually slips one to me now and then these days. Working with my dad put Ralph in such good spirit that he stayed to help Catherine, Sophia, and Ruth nail the muslin to the frame.

TUESDAY, OCTOBER 19. This morning when the girls arrived, they began to look at the room critically to see that everything was right. It is a cozy room. Near the stove is our puppet stage made over into a worktable. The top is covered with brown battleship linoleum. A pleated skirt of brown, orange, and cream print percale is hung around it. Under this table we store the bulky materials with which we are working, our orange crates and lumber. In the front of the room, to one side, is our piano standing away from the wall to make a museum corner. On top of the piano is a black bowl filled with colored autumn leaves. Also in the front of the room are the two easels already showing signs of use. Around the room are hung the "works" coming from the easels. On the back bulletin board are charcoal sketches of trees, neatly mounted. On the wall are hangings which Anna and Sophia made last year. Under the windows on one side of the room are the problem and vocabulary charts for social studies and a few maps of the North Central States. The shelves in the kitchen are covered with brown, tan, and cream checked oilcloth. The screen showing fall, winter, and spring scenes on its three panels separates the cloakroom from the kitchen. The striped orange, green, and cream net curtains give a rosy glow to the room even on this dull day. The girls looked around, heaved a sigh of satisfaction, and exclaimed, "Doesn't it look nice, Miss Weber?" (See Appendix, p. 259.)

WEDNESDAY, OCTOBER 20. After school, Irene had a birthday party and all the primary children were invited to attend. Mrs.

Ramsey, a friend of hers, and I transported the children over the mountain and back into the woods to the charming stone house which Mr. and Mrs. Ramsey and their caretaker have built. We ate ice cream and cake. Following the refreshments we took a long walk in the woods. When we returned we sat on the floor and had a song fest. William said he wanted to sing the three-part "Amaryllis." I said, "You can't do that, none of the older ones are here." But they did it! They also sang the three-part round "Come, Follow" and did not need the older children to help them! I was as amazed as Mrs. Ramsey. I suppose you never cease to learn new things about the ability of children.

The trip home was delightful. Albert, Florence, Joyce, Walter, William, Eric, Pearl, and Elizabeth were in my car. The moon came up and took all our attention. William wanted to know if the moon was hot. Albert knew the answer and explained about reflected light. He also told about the mountains and craters that form the face of the "man-in-the moon." They had fun with the moon. "Look, Miss Weber, the moon has a hat on," observed Florence when the moon went behind a cloud. "Now it has a mustache." "Now it's in jail." "Now it's playing peekaboo." Albert and Florence were the last ones off. When we left Eric, Albert said, "Let's sing and find out how many songs it is from Thompson's to our place." We sang and found the distance to be three songs long.

FRIDAY, OCTOBER 22. During the health lesson we talked about the necessity of taking a bath frequently. We have several children in the group who need this lesson very much. These children have to carry water from a distance and taking a bath is hard work. We talked about sponge baths and how it is possible to keep clean even though it is not possible to immerse the whole body in water.

Fourteen members were present at the Sewing Club tonight, which includes all the eligible girls in the neighborhood. The samples came from Sears, Roebuck and we examined them for quality and price. We rubbed them to see if they had a filler and then washed them to test for shrinking and fading. We talked a little about the colors suitable to our skin and hair coloring. Before the meeting was over we filled out order blanks and money order slips, and sent for the materials.

SATURDAY, OCTOBER 23. This morning I took to Weston those girls who did not go last week. They selected patterns for blouses and dresses.

MONDAY, OCTOBER 25. In social studies this morning we began to compare the North Central States with New Jersey and the Northeastern States. The children listed nine differences. The children have made nice notebooks about the North Central States and have a fair grasp of the content.

WEDNESDAY, OCTOBER 27. The first of our mothers' meetings was held today. Three committees remained after school to help. One committee prepared tea and cookies for refreshments, and cocoa for the little children who must accompany their mothers. Another committee prepared games for these small children to play. The third committee was responsible for making the mothers comfortable and for acquainting them with our work. There were eight mothers present. Inez watched Ralph explain our work to Mrs. Thompson, Mrs. Williams, and Mrs. Hill. She said, "I never expected to see Ralph do a thing like that."

Mothers share in evaluating the school program

MONDAY, NOVEMBER 1. The children are becoming more interested in what is going on in the world since they are getting the *Current Events* papers and *My Weekly Reader*. We are recording on the world map all the places we read about. Helen put China and Japan and Japanese territory on the map and explained it to us today. Since the Philippines are so near Japan, we got into a discussion of the relation between the United States and its possessions. The children thought it would be a good idea to number the places on our map and to have a key which will tell the story of these places.

The key will be in the form of a book with a page explaining each number on the map.

THURSDAY, NOVEMBER 4.   This week the big boys have put the tar paper on the roof of the little house to make it waterproof and have put the screens in the windows. Today, Frank and George helped the Cartwright boys and Andrew to put down the floor. They finished hinging the door. Walter and William shellacked all the knots and the boys began to paint the house.

This week has been calm. All are happily working and playing together. Ruth is a good general manager and she sees to it that the room is always clean and in order. Ralph is a good president, and the children accept his authority. Mary is a capable child. She reads to the little children every day and is teaching them nursery rhymes. The primary children work in clay, which we got from the Hills' stream, and paint at the easels. They create stories, dramatize stories they read, and have rhythms twice a week. They are eagerly watching the progress on their playhouse and are impatiently waiting for it to be finished. The little children are getting more attention than they did last year.

FRIDAY, NOVEMBER 5.   There was an interesting Helpers' Club meeting this afternoon. The children felt that, even though we were careful not to disturb others by unnecessary talking, there was still too much noise in the room. They made several suggestions to remedy the situation. Part of the noise was made by the beginners pounding clay at the clay table. Mary was asked to teach the little children how to mold their clay with less noise. It was also decided to move the table to a part of the room where it would not be disturbing to have the little children work. The children set aside several periods appropriate for sharpening pencils so that this would not go on all day long. Ruth demonstrated how to open and close desks with less noise. Frank was appointed by the president to oil the seats to prevent squeaking.

After school the Sewing Club met. Two of the high school

girls brought dresses to be made over and fitted. Martha and Pearl began to make pot holders, since they have never sewed.

MONDAY, NOVEMBER 8.   This morning I stopped in town to buy more paint for the playhouse. It made me a little late and I knew I could not finish all the work I had to do before school started. Ralph and Edward were standing outside and I called to them, "Boys, will you please make the fire this morning so that we can get started on time? I have so many things to do." Edward grumbled but did come in and clean out the ashes. Then, mumbling "I did my share," he left. Ralph did not come in at all. As the other boys arrived, Ralph advised them, "Don't fix the fire for Miss Weber. Let her do it herself." In spite of that, five boys made the fire. Because of all the fuss, school began ten minutes late and we made up the time at noon. The big boys did not like it. I thought it best to ignore the matter. Perhaps it is only a temporary thing.

TUESDAY, NOVEMBER 9.   The boys were cheerful this morning and we had a happy time until noon. A group of boys sat in the playhouse to eat their lunch. It wasn't long before Joseph came to me, crying. Frank had pushed him against the wire screen and the edge had torn loose. Frank said Joseph did it deliberately, but the Cartwrights and Warren protested that Frank was not telling the truth. As calmly as I could I said, "Frank, you will have to repair the screen and you will not be able to eat in the playhouse for a while." When I left, Frank and Ralph came out of the house and began to stone it. Frank deliberately pulled out another screen. I became angry and lost my temper. I can't remember what I said and I certainly hope no one else can either. When I came to, I found myself the center of an amazed and bewildered group of children. After sending the other children off to play, I sat down with Ralph and Frank. I told them I was sorry I had lost my temper and that now we had to decide what to do.

The boys offered to repair the damage. Everything was all right the rest of the afternoon but I was miserable about the mistake I had made. None of us felt like talking. It was a quiet and sad afternoon. As I look back, I know I was only feeling sorry for myself and treated this affair as a show of ingratitude on the part of the boys. Boys don't go out of their way to be ungrateful. It's something else that is making them behave as they do.

WEDNESDAY, NOVEMBER 10. This was the first day of the hunting season and Mr. Jones took Ralph with him. Without Ralph, Frank had no moral support and there was no trouble. He was silent but it was not a rebellious silence, as he willingly performed the few tasks I gave him. Several children told me this morning that Frank had shouted all the way home last night that if I ever went to his house again he would shoot all my tires off. I wish I knew how to find out what is troubling him. The attitude of the group is that of quiet sympathy. I have them with me.

THURSDAY, NOVEMBER 11. Frank went hunting today, and everything went well with Ralph. After school Ralph asked if he could ride with me to the garage. On our way I had an opportunity to talk with him. He has made up his mind that he isn't going to be a member of any of our clubs. When I asked him why, he answered, "What's the good of it?" We said little else. I knew that words would not convince Ralph of the good of anything.

FRIDAY, NOVEMBER 12. This morning I asked Ralph to get a bucket of coal. When he returned, he asked, "Miss Weber, in my spare time, may I clean out the coal house? We can't get into it to get coal."

When we were washing our hands for lunch, Frank stepped aside so that all the girls could wash their hands first. Then he said, "Go ahead, Miss Weber, I can wait." This afternoon he asked, "When are we going to work on the little house again?"

I was beginning to feel happy once more when the two oldest Jones girls came to visit. They arrived while we were playing outdoors. Martha and Ralph began to show off so that it spoiled the game for everyone. The Jones girls enjoyed the show and laughed until the tears ran down their cheeks. Ralph had already begun to clean out the coal shed. After school he went home with his sisters and left the wood and boxes out on the school grounds. Because we could not leave these outdoors until Monday, the girls who remained after school put them back into the shed.

The needs of the neighborhood impinge upon the school

Mrs. Olseuski came to visit after school. She complained about the Prinlaks and said that this past week they have been almost unbearable with their swearing and general nastiness. She threatened to move. Another neighbor is going to report the matter to the State Police if it keeps up.

SATURDAY, NOVEMBER 13. I did a great deal of thinking today. So many of our school problems this year have grown out of the larger problems of the neighborhood. It seems, then, that if the school is to make desirable changes in the living of the children, it must make changes in the community.

What is the function of a one-teacher school in an isolated neighborhood? Its first and most important function, I think, is to shape the curriculum to meet the needs of the children who come to it. In order to be able to do this the school must also extend its activities to meet the needs of the youth and the adults. These include the need for wholesome recreation and opportunities for study, for higher standards of personal and public health, for opportunities to learn better home economics and agriculture, for spiritual refreshment and beauty in their lives, and for co-operation among their members in order to find solutions to their common problems.

Function of a one-teacher school in an isolated neighborhood

It is clear that the school cannot do the whole job, but the school must do whatever it can to improve the living in the neighborhood, for outside forces can be so powerful that they thwart the work of the school. Where do I start?

The young people are unsympathetic with the program of the elementary school because they do not understand it. They, especially Ralph's sisters, cast aspersions on the little school. These young people know no other recreation except walking the roads and fooling with each other. Perhaps if we could get together for social times at the schoolhouse it would make a difference in their attitudes. At least, it is a place to begin.

THURSDAY, NOVEMBER 18. Tonight we had our first young people's meeting at the schoolhouse. There were ten present.

We begin to meet a need of the neighborhood by providing wholesome recreation for the young people

I taught them three country dances: "Shoo fly, don't bother me," "Yankee Doodle," and "A-hunting we will go." They want to learn social dancing. We selected a committee to get the victrola, records, and needles. All seemed to have a happy time, although it was a loud one.

WEDNESDAY, NOVEMBER 24. We have spent the past three days catching up. The boys finished painting the playhouse. The little children have furnished it with a linoleum rug, two rag rugs, a table, four orange-crate chairs with cushions, a doll crib, a trunk, and a cupboard. They have finished their booklets about the house and these are displayed around the room. The older children also finished their booklets about the Northeastern States. They have spent much time on their newspaper, writing articles and sketching illustrations.

MONDAY, NOVEMBER 29. It was like a spring morning. Last night we had a warm rain and the little peepers in the swamp began their noises. I felt the warm breeze blow across my face and the next thing I knew I was wide awake, refreshed, and ready for work. Vacations are good! Perhaps that is why the day went so well. Eric volunteered a shy "good morning" for the first time. Many children were willing to help with the morning tasks.

The little children spent almost two hours in their playhouse today. This group play is especially important because these children live so far apart and school time is the only time they have for getting together. Florence was the mother and Richard the father. Joyce and Elizabeth were big sisters. Eric kept a store in the woods. Irene became a visiting relative. They washed doll clothes and strung them on a line. Richard carried the water. At noon the children came to me and said they needed a stove, dishes, and things to clean with. We are going to make what we can and buy the rest from our fund.

After school Warren, Ralph, and I met to assemble the newspaper. The boys wrote a good editorial. After we had finished, Ralph wanted to read the poetry the children had written. So we three read and enjoyed the creative efforts of our little group.

5

We Experience Creative Power

TUESDAY, NOVEMBER 30. As usual during the month of December we are to use the social studies period to prepare a dramatization for Christmas.

Choices need to be made in developing curriculum

We live in an everchanging world. To be able to live effectively in such a world, it is necessary to meet it creatively. All of us have unused resources of creative power within us. Before we can release creative powers, all the inhibitions we have built up through fear of criticism and through a feeling of inadequacy must be broken down. This is a major responsibility of the school.

These boys and girls, shy and retiring, need to have a con-
Needs are met through creative dramatization
sciousness of themselves as creative individuals. They need to develop confidence and poise and become free. We shall work through creative dramatization, since that is a medium in which I feel fairly comfortable.

WEDNESDAY, DECEMBER 1. This morning I told the children the story of the French legend, "The Sabot of Little Wolff." I gave it with as much detail as possible, describing scenes and inserting conversation. The children were impressed by it.

For a while we talked in general terms about how we could work the story out and about the possible scenes.

The first scene will be at the home of little Wolff and his aunt. In a bare shabby room they are having their supper. All through the scene Wolff's aunt nags at him, for she hates the child and considers him a burden. Little Wolff begs to be allowed to go caroling with his schoolmates and finally his aunt consents. Albert and Catherine were chosen to make a beginning in developing the dialogue. Their attempt was stiff and colorless. The children felt that Catherine was overdoing the part and it did not seem real. Albert was very much himself and not at all like Wolff. We tried Mary and William next. William made the children sit up and take notice. They decided then and there that he was a natural for the part. Other children took turns at these parts and gradually we added more and more to the dialogue and began to develop the characterization.

I watched the eager, absorbed expressions on the faces of the children. There was no embarrassed giggling and many of the children were aggressive in their desire to take part.

THURSDAY, DECEMBER 2. We continued the dramatization today, paying more attention to the characterization. Warren was little Wolff and acted like a spoiled, begging child. The group did not think it was good. What kind of a boy is Wolff?

What would a boy like this say to his aunt? How would he say it? We asked similar questions about Wolff's aunt. We talked a little about the reason some movie stars can give a sincere delineation of a character. They know and understand the character so well that they forget themselves and become the character. The children have been reading in their *Current Events* about the amount of research Paul Muni does before he acts a part. The next time Catherine and William did so well that their efforts were applauded. The feeling was good but the language was crude. We spent some time talking about appropriate words to express what we want the audience to understand. We talked about the length of sentences. The children have been using such short sentences that the dialogue is choppy.

FRIDAY, DECEMBER 3. We got into the second scene today and concentrated on working out the plot. We planned to make this a street scene in which Wolff meets his classmates. While they are waiting for the schoolmaster they taunt Wolff. When the schoolmaster arrives they start off to the church leaving Wolff to tag along behind. Ralph asked to be the schoolmaster and added much to the part. Edward and George were the only boys who did not care to contribute. I think it is from shyness rather than from lack of interest.

After we had a general idea about the plot, several boys stood in the front of the room and began to work out the conversation. It moved slowly because the boys were thinking up speeches and reciting monologues. Ruth suggested that they should listen to each other and follow up leads. Before the boys tried again, we thought about some of the things they might say and this time the conversation was more smooth.

MONDAY, DECEMBER 6. The children are happy about their third scene, a church scene, and expect to make it beautiful. The exterior of the church will need to be shown, for we must show a small child asleep on the church steps. The children thought it would be no fun for the audience to watch a stone wall all the time they were listening to the church service. They planned to have a large stained-glass window through which the audience would be able to see the shadows of the worshipers.

We began to develop the conversation which the boys have as they leave the church. Wolff, who is the last one to leave, sees that the feet of the little child are bare. He leaves one of his own shoes so that the Christ Child may leave a gift for the sleeping boy when He passes that way on Christmas Eve. The children had a difficult time to keep in character. How would these boys who taunted Wolff react to the child on the church steps? Would they be indifferent? Would they be curious or cruel? Would all the boys react in the same way? We gave each boy a background at that point and made up a life story for him. This was much fun. Each boy chose the part he thought he understood and they went through the scene again. It made a great difference and the children were pleased with themselves. They are becoming excited about the dramatization and keep making suggestions all day long. They interrupted so many times that I had to ask them to jot down their ideas and save them until we work again on the dramatization.

The program is simple these days. We work on the dramatization for an hour in the morning. The little children contribute or listen for a half hour, after which one of the older children takes them into the hall. They are teaching the little children the Christmas story as found in Luke 2:8-20, which they will recite in the church scene of the dramatization. When the little children begin to get tired, the one in charge reads to them or the children practice the familiar carols.

After the morning physical education period the room assumes a calm as everyone settles down to the reading program. As the children finish their reading they begin to work on their Christmas gifts. The older children are making pin trays, sewing baskets, and handkerchief cases of raffia and cord. The little children are painting tins for canisters and matchboxes. Some of the little boys are making breadboards from plywood.

At 11:30 on two days we have health lessons and on the other three days the geography and history necessary for an informed discussion of current events. The little children listen and contribute to the health discussion, but they play in the little house on the other three days if the weather permits. The older children take turns being with the little ones in the playhouse. They help the little children plan what they will do but do not interfere with their play. They read or work and keep an eye on the little ones so that they do not form bad habits.

After lunch we rest for fifteen minutes, and then learn carols for a half hour. While the little children have their drill period in spelling and arithmetic, the older ones do any work that has to be done in connection with their health and current events and then continue to work on their Christmas gifts.

At the end of the day the upper groups have spelling and arithmetic as usual.

TUESDAY, DECEMBER 7. We outlined the last two scenes today. In scene four, Wolff is reprimanded by his aunt for giving away his shoe. He is sent to bed with the threat that the Christ Child will leave in his remaining shoe something with which to whip him in the morning. In the last scene, Wolff and his aunt find their fireplace filled with gifts and both of Wolff's shoes. There is a clamor outside and they find the whole village laughing at the boys who expected fine gifts but received nothing but rods. A priest enters then and tells that he found on the church steps, where last night a child lay asleep, a circle of gold encrusted with precious stones. The people bow before the miracle. The children like this last scene and have not questioned its validity. Frank asked to be the priest and took the part with understanding. We now have the outline of the whole play. It needs to be worked over and the details carefully planned.

WEDNESDAY, DECEMBER 8. We spent most of our time working out the conversation for the last scene. All but George are taking part. George said he would like to take care of the scenery. We made him property manager.

The Christmas spirit is in the air. It makes all of us considerate and cheerful. The boys went out this noon for material to make wreaths for the windows. They talked in low, quiet tones as they worked. This hour was such a contrast to some of the noisy noon hours we have had.

THURSDAY, DECEMBER 9. The dramatization has become an important thing in the lives of the children. Catherine came today with an old black dress which she thought suitable for Wolff's aunt. We talked about the costuming of the other characters. This will not be difficult. The properties present a greater problem. The children drew sketches of the various scenes to get an idea of what we would need and how we could best arrange the properties.

FRIDAY, DECEMBER 10. We moved the furniture from the front of the room in order to have space to practice and a place to put the properties. The boys brought some laths and began to construct the framework for the large fireplace.

Most of our time was spent on the first scene. We decided today to have William and Catherine take the parts of little Wolff and his aunt. The children are not memorizing their parts. I note down the lines as they are worked out and read to them what they have developed so far. They begin here and try to improve it.

The boys followed the action closely and were concerned with the position of the fireplace. They decided finally to have it at the side of the scene slightly slanted so that the audience could see the iron kettle and the fire. This would leave room for a crude wooden table and a bench.

MONDAY, DECEMBER 13. The boys covered the framework of the fireplace with brown wrapping paper and began to paint it to look like a stone fireplace. Some of them began to build the table.

The children now know five French carols in two parts which they will sing during the dramatization: "Shepherds,

Shake Off Your Drowsy Sleep," "Gascon Carol," "Angels
Sweet We Heard on High," "Bring a Torch, Jeannette Isabella," "Noel Let Us Sing Now." We spent much time prac-
ticing the familiar carols which the audience will sing with us.
A musician friend of mine will be at the school tomorrow to
practice with us and we want to be ready for him.

TUESDAY, DECEMBER 14. We sang a good part of the day,
stopping only for breath now and then. The children were
fascinated by the cello. Mr. Raeppel told the
children simply and with humor about the
place of the cello in the family of stringed instruments and how it is played. The children
showered him with questions. It was the boys
who showed the greatest interest.

**Outside help
contributes to
the enrich-
ment of the
curriculum**

We sang the nine Christmas carols with piano and cello
accompaniment and then we had to sing them all over again.
The children could not seem to get enough of music. Mary
conducted the group for a while and then Sophia took the
baton. When Mr. Atwood, the county superintendent, arrived
late in the afternoon we wanted to sing the carols for him.
We played some of them on the harmonica, for Mr. Atwood
says that is one of his favorite instruments. We have been
having harmonica practice after school.

The little children would not go home at two o'clock. They
begged to stay as long as the older ones did. The children
know nothing about concert etiquette, so it was not conven-
tion but genuine interest that made them sit motionless for
such long periods and listen without a sound or the squeak of
a chair. Ralph did not once take his eyes off Mr. Raeppel.
Frank smiled his nice smile after each number and said, "Play
us another one." I felt as if the millennium had come!

WEDNESDAY, DECEMBER 15. It was difficult to get settled
today. The children kept wanting to sing. I taught them an
old Latin carol with the Latin words, "Quem Pastores." We
thought this would fit nicely into the church scene. We
worked out a simple program for the church service.

The girls began to make the properties for this scene. They covered the large puppet-show frame with brown paper and began to draw the framework for two windows. The boys are working on a street lamp for the second scene. They plan to have the room darkened. The only light will be from a kerosene carriage lamp set in the street lamp the boys are making.

THURSDAY, DECEMBER 16. It was icy today and this kept the little ones home. It gave us a splendid opportunity to turn the school into a workshop and to get our properties made. The boys succeeded in making the street lamp look like the ones we usually see on Christmas cards. It is on a post taller than the boys. They took precautions to make it sturdy so that there would be no danger of accident. Frank gave us instructions about blowing out the lamp before we remove it from the post at the end of the scene.

FRIDAY, DECEMBER 17. The girls cut the design in the church windows and pasted varicolored cellophane pieces over the openings. The little children watched the procedure with wonder and admiration. Sophia stood back and exclaimed, "Just think, Miss Weber, all that work and the people will only look at it for about five or ten minutes." Doris, who stood beside her, retorted, "Yes, but they won't forget it in a hurry." Deep down inside of me I knew that our work this month had not been in vain.

MONDAY, DECEMBER 20. The boys went for the tree today and brought back a twelve-foot cedar. The little children made some decorations for it and we trimmed it this afternoon. We wrapped the Christmas gifts the children have made for their parents and put these under the tree.

We put the finishing touches on the properties and smoothed the rough places in the dramatization.

TUESDAY, DECEMBER 21. We went through the program just as we are going to have it on Thursday night. There were many hitches in moving the properties, for the room is so tiny. Everyone got into everyone else's way but I did not hear one cross word spoken. It was "Will you please move to one side, Helen?" and "Be careful not to poke your elbow through the church window." We put our heads together and almost mathematically we planned how the properties should be moved. Each child knew exactly what his responsibility would be. This afternoon we repeated the performance and I sat at the back of the room, a relaxed, appreciative audience.

WEDNESDAY, DECEMBER 22. We thought about our voices especially today. We practiced saying certain lines in the dramatization by changing the emphasis on the words and giving various meanings. We chose the emphasis that gave the correct impression. We practiced vowel sounds in words such as "down" and consonant sounds in words such as "nothing." We practiced lines which expressed anger, surprise, ridicule, and the like to make them real.

THURSDAY, DECEMBER 23. We went through the program once this morning and then we cleaned the room and organized it for tonight.

The little room was crowded with proud parents and friends tonight. The young people were strung along the back

The attitude of the young people improves of the room. They have been meeting every Thursday night at the schoolhouse. At the last meeting I talked to them about the amount of preparation the children have put into this dramatization and how much it means to them. I called on them to help keep the hall clear and to quell any disturbance. Since the children knew exactly what to do, I was able to sit in the audience and I had an opportunity to watch the faces of the young people. They were surprised and pleased with the performance and at times expressed incredulity that their little brothers and sisters could possibly be doing what they were.

While we were having the community singing at the end

of the dramatization, Edward's brother, who at one time was

The community re-creates together a leader in creating disturbances at school entertainments, slipped out to put on a Santa Claus suit. He came in jingling his bells and the children recognized him at once. They enjoyed watching him distribute the gifts to the parents. Dr. and Mrs. Breed gave the children candy and oranges.

This was a happy evening. Every man, woman, and child in that little place had an active part in the program.

After the program Edward's brother (Santa Claus) and I piled the older children into the station wagon and my car and started out to make the round of the homes, singing carols at each one. We were invited in and given cakes and candy. All the parents were prepared for us; the secret had leaked out.

6

We Study Our Community

SATURDAY, FEBRUARY 12. During the Christmas holidays the children and I had a rare opportunity to feel something of the romance of our country. This year marks the 150th anniversary of the Ordinance of 1787, the opening of the Northwest Territory. To celebrate the occasion, a group of young people are traveling from Massachusetts to the Ohio country

The curriculum is enriched through taking advantage of resources in the community in pioneer fashion. They are stopping at various points along the way to give a pageant. Mr. Hill and I provided the transportation for the older children to see it. In the pageant the young men made the laws that would govern them when they arrived in the new country. The children were much impressed with the enthusiasm and the debating with which these laws were made. Catherine said, "That is just the way we make laws for ourselves in our Helpers' Club."

The intermediate children were especially interested in the clothes the young men wore, the way they traveled, and the hardships they met. They looked up the Northwest Territory on a map and traced the route the young folks are taking. Albert wanted to know why the pioneers chose this territory. Did they know about it before they left Massachusetts? The older children, on the other hand, were more interested in the way the laws were made.

The children divided into two groups to do some research along the lines of their interests. The groups came together for reports and discussions.

The intermediate children produced a movie on the settlement of the Northwest. They kept notes on their research, from which they drew necessary information for their movie.

The older children studied the Ordinance of 1787. We spent some time considering how fine it was that a group of ordinary men could get together to decide how they wanted to live and to govern themselves. The laws they made seemed sensible to us. I asked the children, "Where do you suppose they got their ideas?" The children said they thought the men must have known from past experience that this was what they wanted. We then examined the governments set up by the Mayflower Compact, Virginia, Massachusetts Bay Colony, Maryland, Carolina, Georgia, and Connecticut. We began to compare the governments of these colonies with the Ordinance of 1787. We found that the Ordinance was a fine document picking the best from all the colonies and adding even more democratic measures.

We also compared our present government with that of the one set up by the Ordinance. We listed the things we have that early governments did not have. Catherine said that Constitution gave us a better form of government than the pioneers had. I asked the children if they knew how we got our Constitution. Ralph said it was because the colonists needed a plan to run the affairs of the country. I told them that the colonists already had a plan. What about the Articles of Confederation? They did not know about the Articles so we looked them up. Our history book gave a list of the defects of the Articles of Confederation. Ruth said, "That is why the soldiers had to go out to the Northwest. The government was not strong enough to collect taxes and so had no money to pay its debts." I asked if the Constitution remedied these defects. The children said that it made a head who had power to carry out laws. It made a representative lawmaking body and courts for trials. We examined the duties of these three branches of our national government and the system of checks and balances.

In their reading the children found that the Constitution was not accepted at first because it made no mention of the rights for which the colonists had fought. The Bill of Rights was added. The children studied this carefully and made a list of all the rights it provided. This led them to compare the state and national governments and their functions. We made a list of all the ways the state and national governments touch us in our township. To understand our township government, we interviewed the chairman of the Township Committee and the president of the Board of Education. We visited also the County Court House and interviewed the county superintendent of schools. The warden took the children through the county jail. We also saw the surrogate's and the county clerk's offices and learned something of county government. Through all this the children have begun to build a fairly clear picture of what government means.

The primary children during this period have been studying the community. We followed the outline in the *New Jersey Handbook of Social Studies*. This included a study of the school and the physical aspects of the environment. The children made a map of their neighborhood and learned to use it. They studied about the workers in the community and the services that are provided. They spent some time learning about homes and extended this study to include homes of animals and birds. They built birdhouses and feeding stations

TENTATIVE DAILY PROGRAM

	Monday	Tuesday	Wednesday	Thursday	Friday
8:55– 9:05	Plan together the day's work..				
9:05– 9:20	*Social Studies and Science*				
	Teacher works with little children on social studies, science, and health. (Upper group study for social studies or do activities in connection with it.)				
9:20–10:00	Teacher works with older children on social studies and science. (Little children continue work planned with teacher the previous period. For the last 20 minutes, or when their work is done, they paint, play with clay, play in their play corner, or read.)				
10:00–10:20	*Physical Education*				
	Teacher plays with the little children. (Older children play alone with the president in charge.)				
10:20–10:35	*Reading*				
	Teacher works with five- and six-year-olds. (All others read.)				
10:35–10:50	Teacher works with group II. (All others read.)				
10:50–11:10	Group III with teacher	Group IV	Group III	Group IV	Discussion of *Current*
11:10–11:30	Group V with teacher	Group VI	Group V	Group VI	*Events*
	(As the little children finish the seatwork after the time spent with the teacher, they continue the kinds of activities they had in the morning. As the older children finish their reading, they read for the health, science, and current events discussions and write up discussions and problems in their notebooks. This is planned carefully each morning.)				
11:30–12:00	*Health*	*English*	*Art*	*Story Hour*	*Library*
	Teacher with upper group. (Little children read and tell stories to each other with an older child in charge. Also dramatize.)			Teacher with little ones. (O l d e r g r o u p, s t u d y English.)	All read and share experiences
1:00– 1:15	Rest..				
1:15– 1:30	*Music*				
	Teacher with little ones	Teacher with older ones. (L i t t l e ones sing with an o l d e r child.)	Teacher with little ones Rhythms	Teacher with older ones. (L i t t l e ones sing with an o l d e r child.)	Teacher with little ones
1:30– 2:05	*Drill*				
	Teacher with little children. (Older children work on individual needs and work started during the reading period.)				
2:05– 2:20	*Physical Education*				
	Teacher with older children. Little children go home at 2:05.				
2:20– 3:20	*Drill*				
	Teacher works with older children on spelling, arithmetic, and writing. Mainly individual work. Children come together in small groups for supervised study of spelling and for new work in arithmetic.				
3:20– 3:30	*Clean up*...				
	The Helpers' Club Meeting is usually held on Thursday at 2:20 although it is frequently necessary to change this to fit in with our other plans.				

and began to feed the birds that stay with us during the winter.

I am gradually learning what to do with little children in a one-teacher school. The older children work with purpose

**A more effec-
tive daily
program
evolves**

when they are not with the teacher but younger children, whose attention span is much shorter, cannot profitably spend long periods of time alone. I am beginning to use the older children to help in such a way that they, as well as the little children, will benefit. Gradually a more effective daily program has evolved.

In our health lessons we made a fairly intensive study of food values. These lessons are beginning to influence the

**The school
program
affects and
makes some
difference in
the neighbor-
hood**

eating habits of the children. Most of them do have good breakfasts and we no longer have anyone in the group who comes to school without having eaten something. When I visited Mrs. Sametis, I heard that the girls are eating greens they refused in the past. They are helping their mother prepare the greens in nutritious and palatable ways.

The hot lunch program has not had a hitch in it for a long time. Everyone likes to work in the kitchen. The kitchen crew this week named the large pot "Mr." and the small pot "Mrs." The cups are all the children with single ears. They gleefully wash each child inside and out. They are proud of the way the kitchen looks and the way they are able to finish their work before the afternoon session begins. Ralph was supposed to be dishwasher this week, but since he was not in school Frank volunteered to wash dishes, evidence enough that working in the kitchen is fun.

The easels have been in use constantly. The children painted so many snow scenes that we do not have space for them in the room. We mounted them and made a book called *Winter Scenes*.

This month I found time at the end of each day to give Ralph and Catherine some help with English grammar. There are certain things which the high school will require and I am trying to help them to get those things. They worked so willingly with me and even did extra work at home.

Yet, with all of this, somehow the work of this past month has not been so satisfying as it was during the month of December. Miss Everett and I have been working together all week and she has been helping me to analyze the situation.

My helping teacher and I together evaluate the program of the school
Because the children have learned a satisfying way of acting and because there have been no pressing problems, the work of the school has gone along smoothly enough, but the trouble is that we have remained on one level. I suppose psychologists would say we have reached a plateau in the curve of learning. I know that I am not using in my teaching all that I know about good education. It's terribly hard. To know the words is one thing, but to be able to translate the words into action is a much more difficult thing.

Together Miss Everett and I considered how we could more significantly affect the living of the children. We think that the children should be helped to understand the experiences they are having in their immediate environment. Because they will be dealing with actual situations, the children can learn to make the necessary adjustments to their environment and even to make desirable changes in it. They can use what they learn in this way to begin to understand the wider communities of the county, state, and world.

I have already used the resources of the community to provide educative experiences for the children. We have gone out together to explore and to get an increased understanding and appreciation of the flora and fauna and geology of our neighborhood. We have explored the neighborhood for its Indian lore and early history. We have investigated it for an increased understanding of the government from the local to the national as it affects us in our daily living. Miss Everett suggested that perhaps now the children ought to find out more about their present-day community. Perhaps in analyzing the community we can find a way of meeting the needs of its members.

Miss Everett made the following outline to help me get started. She also got some census figures for us.

How Is Valley View Township Today
Different From The Valley View of Colonial Days

I. What were the most important occupations in colonial days and now?
Why have there been changes in occupations and in ways of working?

Experiences	Related Activities	Problems	Content— Other Problems
1. Secure and study records showing numbers of people and occupations. 2. Make a chart with two columns. On one side work carried on in past. On other side work done now. 3. Make maps showing Valley View, showing loss of territory, from time to time. (See beginning of children's history of last year. This partly explains loss of territory.) 4. Make bar and line graphs showing relative size of population in Valley View at various times. 5. List questions arising.	1. Make a map of township, locating homes of as many people as possible and indicate their work. Large map Small map	1. How many people live now in Valley View? How occupied? 2. Are there fewer or more people? Why? 3. Have some occupations disappeared? Why? 4. Have some increased and some decreased in importance? Why? 5. Are there new occupations? Why? 6. Will population continue to decrease? Should there be new occupations or new emphasis on some we have? 7. Why are there fewer schools and no church as there used to be?	There are markedly fewer people. 1. Area has decreased (new twps. made). 2. Villages have disappeared. Ind. Rev.—coming of rr. increased competition. 3. Fewer children stay at home. Why? 4. Farmers are fewer. Why? a. Nature of surface (conservation). b. Coming of competition (rr.). c. Change from home sufficiency to interdependence. d. National farm problems. *Some occupations have disappeared:* tannery post office grist mill blacksmith shop brick kiln sawmill cooper shop molasses factory clover mill wool and flax factory (See reasons for disappearance of villages.)

TUESDAY, FEBRUARY 15. To get the children started on the study of our present-day community, I had written on the board the question, "How is Valley View today different from Valley View of colonial days?" Several of the children had copies of the booklet we made last year about the early history of our township. I listed on the board the differences the children noted.

In the light of the evaluation we begin the study of our community

> "There are fewer people." (Ruth)
>
> "There are more modern homes." (Mary)
>
> There are cars and better means of transportation, and especially better roads." (Warren)
>
> "We have better equipment to work with." (Warren)

I asked Warren what he meant by this and he explained:

> "It is easier to get things because they are made by machine and because certain people do things for everybody."
>
> "The government has to help us today." (Thomas)
>
> "People help others, they do not make things only for themselves." (Helen)
>
> "We take milk to the creamery and do not produce only enough for ourselves." (Catherine, illustrating Helen's point)

I explained that when this is done it is called specialized farming. In early days farming was general. We illustrated with general and specialized farms in our neighborhood.

> "There were towns before where there are only fields and woods now. People have gone away." (Sophia)
>
> "There were tanneries and grist mills in those days and we don't have these now." (Warren)

I listed on the board the following census figures:

Years	Population
1810–1820	3360
1820–1830	1962
1830–1840	1957
1840–1850	727
1850–1860	792
1860–1870	638
1870–1880	538

Years	Population
1880–1890	503
1890–1900	400
1900–1910	405
1930	331

The population from 1810 to 1930 in Valley View decreased markedly, whereas the population in the county for the same period increased from 13,170 to 43,187. Sophia asked why this happened. I turned the question back to the group. These were some of the remarks they made:

"We read that in early days people were not very careful of land because there was so much of it and they moved on when it was used up. Perhaps the land in Valley View became less usable and the people went in search of better land." (Mary)

"Perhaps they went West to spread out, as many people in the East did." (Albert, thinking of his recent study of the movement westward)

"There was a great decrease in the population between 1840-1850. Perhaps the gold rush took some." (Warren)

"Farming did not pay because it was cheaper to get things from the West where soil and transportation were better." (Sophia, reading from our Valley View booklet)

Since the time was almost up, I suggested to the group that we list the questions growing out of our discussion to be answered later.

1. Why are there fewer people in Valley View?
2. Will there be even fewer people in years to come?
3. What happens to the young people who grow up here?
4. What jobs do we have today that we did not have before?
5. What jobs did the early people have that we don't have?
6. Do we have any jobs that the early settlers had?

I asked Warren to be our secretary and to jot down notes of our discussion. He needs the practice.

WEDNESDAY, FEBRUARY 16. The children reviewed briefly what we did yesterday. We read over our problems and began to think how we could find answers to them. Frank suggested that to answer the fourth question we would need to make two lists, one showing what work is done today and the other showing what work was done in the past. He said this would help us answer the other questions. I suggested to the group that pictures and graphs help us to see things clearly. The size of Valley View has decreased as well as the population. May, Helen, George, and Edward are making maps to show the area of Valley View at various times. Sophia, Ruth, Thomas, and Warren are making a list of the occupations in the community at present. Mary, Albert, and Doris are going through the Valley View booklet to list the occupations the early settlers carried on.

THURSDAY, FEBRUARY 24. The primary children have been continuing their study of the community services provided. Today William asked if we were going to build a post office. While I worked with the older ones, the primary children looked through the books in our library to find information on the post office.

The committees in the upper group reported on their findings and on the charts they had made. Ruth reported for her group and pointed out that dairying is the most important present-day industry in our township. I chose to follow this up because a more intensive study of the dairy industry seems to have great learning possibilities. Through it they may be able to see social trends, and why their community is what it is. I asked the children if this was so in the early days. Ralph said, "No. In the early days each family supplied its own needs." "Didn't they have anything to sell?" I asked. "Oh yes," answered Ralph, "they had some surplus milk which they made into butter and took to market along with other crops." Warren added, in answer to my question, that the reason they took butter instead of milk was because the milk would have been sour by the time they got it to the city. In the course of the discussion they gave these reasons for the growth of the dairy industry in Valley View:

Rocky ground makes it less suitable for other farming but it is good pasture land.

There are larger markets; people in New York and Newark need milk and can't keep cows.

There are better roads and better means of transportation that make it possible to get milk to the city in good shape.

There are better means of handling milk which make it profitable to produce for others.

These problems came up in the course of the discussion and May will add them to the problem chart:

Why was dairying not important as a specialized industry in the early days of Valley View?

Why has dairying developed as a specialized industry since?

How is dairying carried on now?

What modern methods are used on dairy farms?

What does surface and climate have to do with the development of dairying in certain regions?

Where are the markets for the milk produced in Valley View and in other parts of New Jersey?

How do good roads help?

TUESDAY, MARCH 1. The primary group made plans to visit the town post office. Alice said it will be important for them to keep their eyes and ears open and to learn all they can. They made a list of questions they want to ask the postmaster. The children are beginning to read what they found in the library about the post office. I helped each child select a story he could read.

To answer their question about the relation between dairy regions and the physical features and markets, the older children knew they had to find out where the dairy regions are and what characteristics of the regions make them suitable for dairying. The children formed working groups to map out the dairy regions in our county, state, and in the world.

The children study about the world to understand better their place in it

WEDNESDAY, MARCH 2. This morning we left the older children making their maps of the dairy regions while the rest of us went to the post office in town. The postmaster took the children through the building and answered their questions. He gave them money order blanks and samples of the cancel stamp. The children saw how mail is sorted and put into bags to be taken to the train. They examined the letter slots and windows and asked about the purpose of each.

When we returned, the older children were happy to be able to tell us that they behaved well and accomplished much work. "We were very busy all the time, Miss Weber," commented their president.

THURSDAY, MARCH 3. This morning the little folks made plans for their own post office. They want it in the corner of the room where the easels are now and they will build it of orange crates. Alice acted as secretary and made a list of all the things to be done.

FRIDAY, MARCH 4. The children conducted a fine club meeting today. I take little part in the discussion these days, and the children have stopped turning around to address me when they make their motions and comments. In fact, they seem to forget I am there.

Sewing meetings are happy times. Each week as we sew we talk, and I am learning some innermost secrets. I know how

I learn much through informal situations to increase my understanding of the children

the girls feel toward each member of their families, what their pet likes and dislikes are, what they think the future holds for them, what they think about marriage, divorce, friendship, love, and raising children; what books they like to read, how they feel about money, and many other things. I have had many opportunities for providing wholesome sex education.

MONDAY, MARCH 7. George and Edward are helping the younger boys with the building of the post office. The rest of the little children selected from the list what they wanted to do.

The older children have finished their maps of the dairy regions of the world and are now studying these for facts about surface, climate, the number of and nearness to markets, and the kind of roads and transportation.

TUESDAY, MARCH 8. We had a review of what we have learned about Valley View by answering as far as we could each question on our list. During a discussion of modern dairy methods two questions were raised:

> How does a milking machine work?
> How do they pasteurize milk?

THURSDAY, MARCH 10. In order to find out what modern methods are used on a dairy farm, the children plan to visit the best dairy farm in the township. We listed the things we want to find out when we visit.

> How is milk tested?
> How does a milking machine work?
> How do they cool the milk?
> How much milk does Mr. Raymond get?
> How many cows does he have?
> What does he do with the milk to prepare it for the creamery?
> How long does it take to milk?
> What does he have to do before he can sell his milk?
> Must there be a certain number of cows?
> What does he feed the cows to get the best milk?
> What standards does milk have to reach before the creamery will accept it?
> How is a cow tested for tuberculosis? What happens if the cow doesn't pass?
> How must a farmer care for a cow in order to have it give the most milk?
> How does Mr. Raymond's milk test?
> Does Mr. Raymond belong to the Dairymen's League?
> If so, what does it do for him?

After school, Ralph and I went to Mr. Raymond's to make arrangements for an interview. We left our questions with him so that he would have an opportunity to prepare for us.

THURSDAY, MARCH 17.   The ice on the roads has kept many children at home during the past three days. I was able to spend much time with each child on his individual needs, and many difficulties have been cleared up. The children enjoyed the first two days and commented often, "I wish it were always like this." But yesterday they began to miss their classmates and the stimulation of group discussion. Catherine exclaimed, "It's just like being a hermit, always working by yourself. I wouldn't like to be a hermit, would you, Miss Weber?"

Too much rain and stormy weather have a bad effect on me and it carries over to the children. Children react to and reflect every mood of the teacher. We were all on edge and tense today, and in spite of the fact that I made a desperate effort to appear calm, I found myself speaking in curt, abrupt sentences. The storm within us seemed to pass away as we sang.

Tonight we went to see the movie *Snow White and the Seven Dwarfs*. The children would not leave until they had seen it twice. The witch did not seem to bother them. The children were fairly bursting with joy at the little animals. Helen could hardly contain herself. She kept saying over and over, "Oh, I love them, I love them."

MONDAY, MARCH 21.   The first day of spring was beautiful and warm. Before school began we sat around informally and talked about the signs of spring we have seen.

While we were eating at noon, I announced to the children, "It's spring and I'm working in the rock garden today. Who wants to work with me?" Sophia and Ruth volunteered. We were surprised when we got out to the garden to see how many tiny plants were already coming up. Verna got excited and began to jump up and down shouting, "Come and see, come and see what we have in our garden!" May, William, and Mary came to see. Later Catherine, Alice and the rest of the little people joined us. Before long even Ralph came to see if he could help. We were all sorry when the noon hour was over.

The little children are playing in their house again. Today they prepared a hand puppet show with Martha's help. They

The children become more free and creative in their play

wrote invitations to the older children to visit at their "home" to see the show. Martha helped them with the spelling. Even Andrew, Alex, Gus, Verna, Pearl, and May play house. Andrew loves to play but he says sometimes the girls are too "bossy."

TUESDAY, MARCH 22. We all have spring fever badly. Six teachers from another county were visiting today and none of us felt at all like working. We lengthened the play periods and shortened the work periods but even that did not help. Every once in a while one of the children would quietly leave the room, wander around outside in an attempt to wake up, and then come in to work again. But it was of no use. After our visitors left we just gave up entirely and went out to the garden to work. The older boys carefully removed the mulch from the bulb bed while the rest of the group cleaned the rock garden of weeds and leaves and swept the paths of stone slabs clean.

WEDNESDAY, MARCH 23. The children made up for yesterday by working like little Trojans.

We had an interview with Mr. Raymond. He was fine with the children. We sat in the living room while he answered the children's questions. Each child was responsible for taking notes on certain ones. Mr. Raymond took us to the barn to show us how he milks a cow by machine, how he takes care of his equipment, how he feeds and cares for his cows. Martha, Helen, and Warren asked questions continually.

THURSDAY, MARCH 24. This morning we reviewed what we had learned at Mr. Raymond's. Ralph wanted to know what happens to Mr. Raymond's milk when it goes to the creamery. We planned to visit the creamery to find the answers to these questions:

Do they make anything from the milk?
How do they pasteurize milk?
How is the butterfat test made?
How do they bottle milk?
How do they weigh milk?

MONDAY, MARCH 28. The older children have been spending much time searching for information about the dairy regions of the world. Today we sat in a comfortable group with our notes and maps before us and made the following statements of our findings. This is the list Warren gave to me:

1. The dairy regions are mostly in the North Temperate Zone.
2. There are some dairy regions, but not as many, in the South Temperate Zone.
3. There are no dairy regions in the dry parts of the world, with one exception. In South America where there is little rainfall and it is warm, there is just enough dairying to supply the white population with milk.
4. Dairying regions are in rolling upland and forested areas. They are often where it is difficult to do farming, but the soil is good enough for forage crops and pasture.
5. Dairying is also carried on in low flat places where the land is good for agriculture. In these places they prefer dairying to raising crops because
    The countries are small, and large areas are needed to raise bread crops profitably. It is easier to raise only what they need for cattle.
    They can get bread crops from other countries where it is cheaper to raise them.

The children compared the wheat belt and the corn belt in this country to illustrate these last statements. Another question came out of the discussion:

If milk is so important in our diet, what do they do for milk in countries where dairying is not carried on?

TUESDAY, MARCH 29. The older children began to search for information to answer the question they asked yesterday.

During the noon hours the children are occupied with a marble tournament which they have organized. Helen and Ralph paired off the group. The winners of these pairs were paired off again. This will go on until only one pair is left and the champion determined. As the children have been eliminated from the contest they have organized games of their own. Sometimes I think these children do not need a teacher, they go ahead and do so many things themselves!

WEDNESDAY, MARCH 30. The little folks have finally finished their post office. Today they learned letter form and wrote their first letters to each other. They chose a postmaster who sold them stamps, canceled the stamps, and distributed the letters from the mailboxes.

The older children brought their notes to the group discussion to answer the question, "What is done to get milk in regions where dairying is not carried on?" We discussed the camels of Arabia, the yak of India, the reindeer of Lapland, the goat of Italy, and something of the way the people of those countries live. They found that the surface features of the countries, the climate, the amount of food they can raise, the wealth of the country (necessity of using the same animal for labor as well as to obtain milk), all determine which animals are used.

We found today that it will not be possible for us to visit the creamery; it is closed for repairs. We decided to add the questions we had intended to ask at the creamery to the list of questions we will ask at the Walker Gordon farm tomorrow.

THURSDAY, MARCH 31. At Plainsboro, our guide took us to the bottling plant, the barns, the dehydrator, and the rotolactor. We had our lunch here and each child was given a half pint of milk. Our guide told us that when some of their American customers travel in Europe they miss the milk so much that they have the Walker Gordon Company send milk to them. Of course the children wanted to know how they do that. They received literature to take with them. Martha said she was going to read all of it to her grandmother. If this trip does nothing more than to establish a better relationship between Martha and her grandmother, it will have been worth while.

MONDAY, APRIL 4. This morning the children discussed what they saw at the Walker Gordon dairy. We stated our purpose for visiting and made the following list of reasons why this dairy is considered the finest in the world:

> There is absolute cleanliness in everything.
> They maintain a good herd giving good milk through proper feeding and care.
> There is a system of complete cooperation among the workers which makes the whole run smoothly.

Frank was impressed by the fact that the feed is weighed and mixed to give the cows the proper amount of vitamins and other necessary food elements. He said they take better care of the animals than we do of ourselves.

I was happy to hear Warren say that Mr. Raymond does all the things that the Walker Gordon dairy does except on a much smaller scale.

TUESDAY, APRIL 5. We reviewed all we have learned about the dairy industry so far. The children are beginning to see that our township is favorable for dairying. I asked them if they thought we should have more dairying to add to our income. We could not answer this question to our satisfaction. I suggested that we might ask Mr. Raab, the county agricultural agent, to help us. Ruth, our secretary, will write him a letter asking him to visit our school.

MONDAY, APRIL 11. We began to plan for our visit with Mr. Raab and listed the following questions which we want to discuss with him:

> What dairies are there in our region? Do they belong to cooperatives?
> From the standpoint of conservation would it be advisable to have more dairy farms in Valley View?
> If Valley View had more dairy farms could all the milk be used or would there be a surplus?
> Is it good to belong to the Dairymen's League?
> What is the difference between private creameries and Dairymen's League creameries?

How is the price of milk determined?
What is the State Milk Control Board and what does it do?

I suggested to the children that we would understand better what Mr. Raab tells us if we do some reading and have some understanding of the marketing of milk.

A new German family by the name of Mann moved into the neighborhood this week. Henry came to school today. He seems to be a fine youngster and the group accepted him wholeheartedly. Warren and Henry became fast friends. I worked with Henry and found that he will fit well into the older primary group.

TUESDAY, APRIL 12.   In our discussion today we began with surplus milk. We found that the New York milk shed, which includes our region, is the largest market in the world. It has the smallest surplus. But, in spite of that, we cannot afford to have a surplus because the cost of labor is higher in the East to compete with industrial labor, feed has to be bought because land is scarce, maintenance costs are high because of rightful rigid Board of Health requirements. Three children in the group gave illustrations of these, showing that their parents cannot afford to hire help, they must buy part of their feed, and they have to meet a long list of requirements, such as putting in electric coolers. All this makes their net income low.

One paper stated that farmers have surplus milk because they do not regulate their seasonal production to meet market needs. If dairy farmers would co-operate they could regulate their production and everyone would benefit. Edward said that was so: that his father gets half price for surplus milk. His father has more surplus milk in June because the cows have calves about that time. Also, the cows are getting out to pasture in June and are producing more milk because of better feed. I asked what the Walker Gordon dairy does about this. The children answered that they feed the cows the same way all year round and they have new cows ready to replace old ones so that the quantity and quality of the milk remains uniform. Mr. Raymond does this also.

The Sametis children said they could not see why there should be a surplus. Why couldn't they sell more milk and not charge so much? Last winter when they were in the city they could not drink all the milk they wanted because they could not afford to buy it. This was one of the reasons they returned, for they can keep a cow here.

WEDNESDAY, APRIL 13. We continued the discussion of surplus today. Edward told us that the creamery counts as surplus anything that is not sold as fluid milk. We talked for a while about what is done with surplus milk, how butter and cheese and other milk products are made. We got into an interesting discussion when Martha read that lactic acid-producing bacilli were added to butter to make it "come." The children knew what lactic acid meant and that bacilli had to be raised, but no one knew how. Sophia said perhaps they just use some old butter. Her mother uses a piece of cheese to start the curds when she is making new cheese. Mary and Edward said their mother used a piece of dough saved from the last batch of bread to use as yeast for new bread.

Yesterday the children found some interesting stories in their readers about the history of cheese, the kinds of cheeses, and how they are made. Warren will bring some Edam cheese for us to sample.

THURSDAY, APRIL 14. We had a party this morning. The refreshments were little red balls of Edam cheese, which the group enjoyed.

The question came up yesterday, "What did people do with their surplus milk in colonial days?" To answer this question we learned about the first milk train, early refrigeration, modern transportation, and modern refrigeration. The coming of the railroad was important to the growth of the dairy industry.

WEDNESDAY, APRIL 20. Before school this morning Sophia and Catherine came to me overjoyed that the flowers in our bulb bed are blossoming. They and Ruth had been up to visit the wild-flower rock garden during the holidays and had a list of fourteen wild plants that are growing. The boys got a long rope and jumped to their heart's content—"All in together, boys." I talked with Frank and Doris about work they are to help the little children with today.

At nine o'clock, Doris and I went out to the little house with the five- and six-year-olds. We planned where to lay out a yard and how large it would be. While we were doing this, Eric said, "Miss Weber, my father is plowing the garden today." Immediately Irene said, "Oh, could we have a garden? It would be fun to watch things grow." Florence told us that her mother was making a rock garden. Richard advised that it would not be hard for us to have one because there is a rock pile behind the little house. I asked them what they would like to do first. They planned to clean up the sticks and papers, to outline their yard with field stones, and to make a walk of flat stones up to the door. Then I left Doris in charge after cautioning her that she should not allow the little children to lift large rocks and that the children should do their own planning.

During these first ten minutes, the rest of the primary group wrote letters to Walter and Joyce who have moved away and who have written to us to tell us about their new school. When I came in from outdoors I helped the children with their letters. By ten, all the letters were finished but not all had been recopied. Some of them were interesting and of considerable length.

At ten o'clock we were ready to play. The older children played sticks and stones. The little children and I played "I'm on Tommy Tiddler's Ground." They would not play though until I had inspected their morning's work. There was a square of stones at the front of the house and the yard was neatly swept. They stopped ten minutes early to wash their hands, to rest, and to view their work. "They think it's nice," said Doris.

After the play period the whole school settled down to read.

The five- and six-year-olds and I looked at books and talked about them.

Group II prepared carefully while I was with Group I and were able to read their story nicely. Following their reading period they had some follow-up work in their workbooks and then Frank took them outdoors to build window boxes. Andrew and Gus had experience in sawing and nailing. Verna measured the boards. During these thirty minutes the five- and six-year-olds played in the little house.

At 11:10 Verna and Gus joined us in the practice of *Robin Hood*. Andrew joined Albert, Martha, Alice, and Mary in the practice of *Winnie the Pooh*, which will be the primary children's share in the show. Until we have the puppet show on May 12, we want to have a half hour of practice each day. We are taking this time from our reading period so that I will meet with groups III, IV, V, and VI only once a week instead of twice. They will meet once a week by themselves and will also do silent reading which will be checked for comprehension. We will use the following program:

Monday
III meet with me
IV meet by themselves
V and VI have silent reading, checked for comprehension

Tuesday
V meet with me
VI meet by themselves
III and IV have silent reading, checked for comprehension

Wednesday
IV meet with me
III meet by themselves
V and VI have silent reading, checked for comprehension

Thursday
VI meet with me
V meet by themselves
III and IV have silent reading, checked for comprehension

At 11:30 the primary children chose easy books from the library and went outdoors with Warren. They read silently until they were ready to read to each other.

After the rest period, the little children had rhythms. They sat on the rugs and I played the ball-bouncing rhythm. They recognized it and took turns bouncing the ball to music. Also in response to music they interpreted the movements of animals. The older children, in the meantime, worked at various tasks. Warren and Ralph worked on the scenes for the puppet stage. Ruth wrote an article to add to the current events notebook which goes with our world map. Helen, Martha, and Albert strung puppets. Catherine embroidered the features on the owl puppet. A committee met to apportion the duties of cleanup for the rest of the year. The children turned to these tasks whenever their regular work was finished.

From 1:30 to 2:00 the five- and six-year-olds played in the little house. Irene joined them after she had practiced writing some spelling words. She wants very much to write. I dictated new spelling words to the rest of the primary group. They went over their words carefully to find which ones they will need to study. In the little time that was left I helped them individually with their arithmetic.

At two, the primary children went home and I played baseball with the older ones. After play I helped the older groups with arithmetic.

In the 4-H Forestry Club manual there is a description of the study of a plot of ground about one-fourth of an acre in size. Children study the plot to learn about everything in it: plants, animals, water life, and the like. We found a plot in the woods that seems to have "everything" in it. It began to rain, so we could not explore it. We were rewarded, however, for we saw a double rainbow, the first any of us had ever seen. The children asked how a rainbow is formed. Warren knew and told the group. None of us knew why there should be two bows and I suggested that we look it up when we have an opportunity.

While we were waiting for the rain to stop we discussed how we would go about studying the plot. Catherine said we should go through it first to find everything we know. Warren thought we should make a diagram of the plot and put on it the things we find. I asked Warren what he meant by "things we find." He suggested holes where there might be animals, holes in trees, swamps, fields, woods. I asked if we could put on it the wildlife we found. "No," was the answer. "The map would not be big enough." Ralph said, "We could make a big map." Albert said that we could not carry this around with us. Ralph added that we could have our own maps to take with us and a big map to work on at school.

THURSDAY, APRIL 21. Ralph brought a beautiful bouquet of Juneberry blossoms to school. He asked Sophia to arrange them for him and even got the vase for her. We all went out to the garden to see what is new. Wild geranium, marsh marigold, and lady-slipper are up. I spent a little time making some plans with May, who will work with the little children today.

The primary children worked with Frank on the window boxes. Verna and Alice painted one. William, Andrew, and Henry sawed, hammered, and measured and made another box. Frank works well with the little children. He never does anything for them that they can learn to do themselves.

The older children talked about their newspaper. The children decided that the first paper was much better than the second one because we began to write the articles sooner, we had many interesting things we wanted to write about, and everyone co-operated and contributed. They suggested that we begin immediately to prepare for our third paper. Mary said we should be reminded about it every day. Warren thought it would be a good idea to have a chart on the bulletin board with everyone's name. As we make a contribution we can record next to our names the nature of the contribution. Mary added that if we have enough articles we can select the best and have a really good paper. May will make the chart for us.

We made a list of interesting school events to write about for our newspaper. When we had completed the list, Ruth said, "We ought to learn how to write a good book review." "Yes, and an article too," added Warren with a laugh. "Let's do that tomorrow," Mary said.

After school, sixteen enthusiastic youngsters remained for the plot study. The number had swelled since yesterday. Albert summarized for the newcomers what we had planned before. We gathered up tablets and pencils and Ralph led us to the woods. We lost no time in bounding the plot. As the children sketched the plot on their tablets, they talked. "Miss Weber, can we have plots of our own?"—this from Ralph. "Perhaps my dad will take us on nature hikes this summer. He knows a lot about nature," mused Warren. Ralph almost made me stop breathing when he said, "Maybe my dad will too. I'll ask him."

FRIDAY, APRIL 22. The older children made a list of standards for a good article. Ruth, who is our secretary, is making a neat copy for the bulletin board so that the children can copy the list into their progress books when they have the time. The children spent the rest of the period evaluating the articles they wrote yesterday in the light of the standards they set up today.

After the reading period the little folks voluntarily had a club meeting of their own in the playhouse. Alice helped them and gave me this list of rules the little children made for themselves.

1. Finish the steps.
2. Not to break any toys.
3. We are not to pull the stones out of the steps.
4. We are not to break the bed.
5. Not to say bad words.
6. Clean your shoes when you come in.

TUESDAY, APRIL 26. I went outdoors with the little ones and Florence told the story of the Gingerbread Man. It was fun to dramatize it today because we had the whole school grounds to run in. To my surprise, Irene said that she wanted to be the cow. She has always wanted to be the most important character. The older children, in the meantime, worked on their newspaper articles. When I came in, Doris gave me her paper and said, "Miss Weber, I went over it according to our rules, and I think it's all right." There wasn't a single mistake in it! It was also well written.

WEDNESDAY, APRIL 27. Frank worked with the primary group making window boxes. He takes his responsibility seri-

Older children have rich learning experiences through helping the younger ones

ously and reports to me how the work progresses. Today he said, "Miss Weber, sometimes they shout at each other when they get in each other's way. I told them that wasn't nice. William wouldn't work for a while because Verna pushed him. I made her say she was sorry and then they had to shake hands. Everything is all right now."

THURSDAY, APRIL 28. The little folks did not want to come in to help plan the day's work. They wanted to get started on their garden. We excused them and Edward helped them dig and rake and plant nasturtium seeds.

Mr. Raab came to answer our questions. He gave the children a general idea of dairying in Valley View as compared with other regions in the county. He helped them to understand co-operatives and their value, how the price for milk is determined, and the work of the Milk Control Board in

We conclude the study of dairying

New Jersey. The children learned that if more soil were kept in grass instead of being plowed, more dairying would be desirable in Valley View. That would improve the ground instead

of destroying it. But if keeping more cows would mean plowing more ground for corn, then it would run the farms down.

As far as surplus is concerned, New Jersey does not produce enough milk. The county agent told us that it produces only 40 per cent of the milk it consumes. But it has to meet competition from the rest of the milk shed, which includes part of Pennsylvania and New York. Mr. Raab told us, too, that the cost of starting a dairy farm is so great that it is improbable that more will develop in the township. Those dairies now in existence were started many years ago. Throughout the study the children have made the following generalizations:

1. Co-operative dairying insures markets.
2. Co-operative dairying keeps the quality of milk high.

3. Dairying is desirable in Valley View both from the standpoint of returns and conservation.

4. Some land is being plowed which should be used for pasture or woodland.

5. Specialized farming has resulted from better transportation, better machinery, more scientific methods.

6. There is something wrong with the method of distribution when many people in the city cannot have milk to drink because they can't buy it, and farmers have a surplus and can't sell it.

7. Milk is an important part of our diet.

8. Cows produce better quality and greater quantity when properly fed and cared for.

9. Milk is clean and safe when it reaches our homes and should be kept that way.

Mr. Raab came ten minutes before the play period, so the children did not get out to play until late in the afternoon. Not a child spoke about it. No sooner had Mr. Raab said, "I guess that's all," than Ralph asked him if he wanted to play long ball with us. Mr. Raab said he had fifteen minutes. They lost no time getting out. With common consent they put Mr. Raab on the side with the fewer players. Thomas stationed Mr. Raab on long base saying, "You can catch the ball because you are so tall and we won't have to run down the road every time." We had a happy play time.

I tried to analyze the value of our study of dairying. The children became aware of one of the ways in which the people

I evaluate the study of dairying in our community make a living and the problems connected with it. They discussed these problems with their parents so that they too have become increasingly aware of them— enough so, that Edward's father called in the county agricultural agent for advice.

They have begun to understand that there are economic problems, some of which arise through lack of co-operative action, while others are a result of gradual developments throughout the history of our nation. The children are becoming aware of the inconsistencies of surpluses and conditions of dire want, of the struggles of labor, of price controls.

They are beginning to feel the impact of the great community of the world on our own little neighborhood.

They are seeing how climate, surface, and transportation in other parts of our country and in the world affect an industry in our community. They are seeing how the growth of our country has affected us. They are beginning to appreciate the scientific advances in public health, farming, industry, and transportation.

To be sure, the children can do little about these situations as yet, but these learnings are important in the formation of attitudes which will condition their actions as they grow older. This "intellectualizing" must not be allowed to go beyond the genuine understanding of the children or it becomes merely propaganda or verbalizing that is dangerous.

The children could actually see in the community the things they were studying about. The time spent in school was used in reading and discussion to prepare them for intelligent observation, and afterwards to try to understand what was seen. Books have been used to interpret and extend their experiences.

The social contacts of the children are very limited. The trips taken during this study have given them practice in conventional behavior in public. Using maps and planning and taking their trips have made the children more observant and alert. Not only have they been helped to find meaning in their immediate environment, but their environment has been extended, their horizon broadened.

FRIDAY, APRIL 29. We used the science period to go over what the children learned about their plot yesterday. They had discovered nineteen holes which might be homes of mice, snakes, chipmunks, or other small animals and insects. Helen suggested that we draw what we see because if we draw them accurately we would have to know exactly what the things looked like, whether they had four legs or scales. Warren suggested that if we read we will know what to look for. They decided to keep notebooks of the information they gather.

"How are you going to study the plot?" I asked. "Do all of you want to study one thing or do you want to divide into committees?" Catherine thought it would be better to study one thing at a time, then everyone would know everything about everything. Helen said, "Let everyone do what he wants." Albert stood up and made a long speech, for him: "I think we should divide up into committees. There are not enough weeks left to study everything. If we have committees we can cover more ground." He sat down and then got up immediately. "And besides, we can learn about the other things by listening to each other and by reading each other's books." Mary added, "Then everyone will be doing what he wants and we won't waste time. It will help us to know all the things we can look for in our plots this summer." The children chose what they wished to study.

THURSDAY, MAY 5. At our plot, the committee groups carried out the plans they had made last week. The water life group examined, sketched, read about, and took notes on the appearance and habits of a spotted newt. The flower group listed all the flowers they already knew. May studied the salient features of five trees. She can now tell the difference between two white oaks and between the wild cherry and the cherry birch.

FRIDAY, MAY 13. The end of the school year always seems to be the busiest time. What every teacher in a one-teacher school needs is a good secretary who can spend her time recording, and then the teacher can be free to evaluate and plan.

The children gave the puppet shows of *Winnie the Pooh* and *Robin Hood* last night and tonight—to a packed house both evenings. News of last year's show had spread and the townspeople came up on the hill in goodly numbers. It gave all of us satisfaction to produce something that would cause the town to go out of its way to see. Many of the visitors spoke about the fine way the children managed themselves. There were stage, lights, and property managers to see that the dramatization moved along efficiently. Each child knew exactly what his job was to be.

There was no need for a prompter, for what the children did not remember they improvised. This added several amusing touches. In the second scene, when Robin Hood and Little John met on the narrow bridge and had their famous argument about which one should make way for the other, Robin Hood left the bridge for a while to cut himself a cudgel. Behind the scenes the children had some difficulty adjusting the cudgel so that it would stay in Robin Hood's hand. This meant that Little John was left standing on the bridge for a much longer period than we had planned. Ralph was equal to the situation. First Little John began to tap his foot impatiently. Then he scratched his head. Finally he walked back and forth on the bridge in so lifelike a manner that the audience lost all control. Ralph did not need to speak a word. The pantomime his puppet played expressed the whole story. From then on, the audience took a wholehearted part and the children responded in a way that was a surprise even to me. The town hardware store proprietor slapped his thighs, doubled up with laughter, made comments to his neighbors, and said that this was the best performance he had ever seen in his whole life.

The children sang five English ballads about Robin Hood's time. These songs have become great favorites.

When the show was over, the audience moved behind the scenes in a body and the children put on demonstrations. There was no showing off and they accepted their many compliments gracefully. My, but they were happy! They have a new confidence in themselves that was never there before.

Incidentally, we made $60!

MONDAY, MAY 16. After the puppet show was out of the way, we began to plan for the annual Township Play Day. We chose to dramatize *Rip Van Winkle*. This is suitable for outdoors because most of it can be in pantomime. There can be much action, music, singing, dancing, games, and stunts. These can be drawn largely from what the children have been learning all year, and every child will have opportunity to take part.

The little children have been making up games this spring. They told me about their newest one today and I think it is good. They call it "Around the Tree Trunk."

THURSDAY, MAY 19. We had an unusual stroke of luck today. As we were studying our plot, Warren came running up to us, shaking with excitement. "Come quickly," he was saying. "See what Albert found." We followed at his heels and found Albert in a clearing holding what seemed like a huge mass of feathers which was emitting the most raucous sounds. We gathered around and made observations. The bird was obviously only a baby although it was a huge one, overflowing both of Albert's hands. It was black and white, with a red crest. We could tell from its tongue, tail feathers, and claws that it was a woodpecker, but we had never seen one like this before. We were startled by the familiar raucous sound overhead. There was the mother flying back and forth, scolding us but not daring to come close. Albert set the bird gently on the ground and we moved off to a distance to see what would happen. The young woodpecker hopped slowly up a long inclined tree stump and entered the end of it. The mother followed. We left the birds to the peace of their sanctuary.

When we arrived at the schoolhouse and looked in our bird book we found that we had made the acquaintance of a pileated woodpecker, a comparatively rare bird.

MONDAY, JUNE 6. The last two weeks have flown by. Most of our time has been spent on the *Rip Van Winkle* dramatization for play day. It is in good shape now.

Last week we began to refinish our desks. The children used glass, reinforced with tape so as not to cut their hands, to scrape off the old varnish and enough of the wood to give the desks a smooth surface. They sanded the desks with coarse and then fine sandpaper. We used dark-oak varnish stain for refinishing. Most of the desks are finished and look new. The children are proud of them.

While we were working on the desks the children talked about other improvements we need in our room. Above all, they feel the need for more bookcases. The librarians have a hard time keeping the books in order because there is no place to put them. We also need museum shelves and a cupboard for the little children's toys. We decided to make these stationary and to build them right into the room. The boys felt that we could not very well use school time for this as it would interfere with the other things going on, the room would be upset for too long a period of time, and besides this kind of work can best be done in long periods with no interruption. We made plans to do this work in August before school starts and after I get back from summer school.

FRIDAY, JUNE 10. We had our Township Play Day and the dramatization of *Rip Van Winkle* was well received. It was very picturesque outdoors. The dwarfs with their colorful peaked hats came out of the woods and over the fences and scurried around like busy little mice. Dame Van Winkle was popular with the audience as Catherine once again displayed her dramatic powers. The little children playing with Rip were natural, and Thomas made Rip a lovable character. It was a pleasant way to end the school year.

The diary notes of this past year clearly show what a struggle it has been for me to try to meet the needs of these boys and girls. Yet, with Miss Everett helping me all along to analyze and evaluate the situation, I feel that I have learned a little more and I know that some gains have been made.

I evaluate the program of the second year

I believe so firmly that a democracy is the best social arrangement that I have tried in spite of all obstacles to develop democratic thinking and acting in our everyday living together. We are accomplishing this, for as I look back over this year it seems to me that the outstanding characteristic of our work is the strong sense of group membership which has developed. There has been continually increasing democratic participation. The children have begun to share all the responsibilities and duties of their school life which they are capable of undertaking. I believe we are making a genuine beginning of what Harap has called "ability and inclination to co-operate in doing the work of the world and finding enjoyment in it."

7

I Continue to Try to Put My Philosophy into Practice

THURSDAY, AUGUST 18, 1938.   I am home from summer school and all settled. At last I have had some spare time and a quiet room so that I have been able to put into words what I believe about the direction in which I think our society should go, about the place of the school in this society, and about the children we teach, what they are like, how they learn, and the school's responsibility toward them.

I write my philosophy to clarify it

It seems to me that in teaching we must keep in mind some social goals determined by our idea of the kind of society we want. We teachers have to have a picture, broadening as our own lives broaden, as to what we think is a good way of life for people. Then in the light of these values we must study our children to see how their lives may improve and develop in these desired directions. As it becomes apparent what our children need, we must try to provide the kind of program that will meet their needs.

FRIDAY, AUGUST 19.   I made the rounds of the homes today to get reacquainted and to thank the children for the many fine letters they sent me. Thomas scraped the floor of a large room, removed the varnish, and then refinished it this summer. The Andrews girls were refinishing furniture when I arrived.

Mr. Jones took Martha and Ralph to the circus, the zoo, and
The children have increased ability for recreation
for Sunday rides. The Hills took trips to the seashore and to New York. The Mann and the Hill boys spent much time playing circus and store. The Sametis children saw two movies, *Hoosier Schoolboy* and *Kidnapped*. They also visited the Planetarium and the Natural History Museum. Practically all the children found time to pursue their hobbies. The influence of the school is clearly seen in these recreation programs! The outlook for the new year is for the most part encouraging.

THURSDAY, FRIDAY, AND SATURDAY, AUGUST 25, 26, 27. All the older boys met these three days to build the cupboards we
The children work together for the improvement of the common life
had planned before school closed last spring. Ralph joined us in spite of the fact that he will be in high school and not with us to enjoy them. His present attitude is so different from that which he had at the beginning of last year when he refused to help with the playhouse because he would not be playing in it.

While we were waiting for the lumber to arrive, we made diagrams of the cupboards to scale. The eight boys were divided into three groups, one group to work on the library shelves, one to work on museum shelves, and the last to work on the toy cupboard. Each group measured and sawed the lumber according to their plans, put up the shelves, sandpapered the boards and painted them.

While we were working, several men stopped to watch us.
The children find joy in their work
They thought the boys were doing a surprisingly fine job. The boys are proud of the shelves and feel that they add considerably to the attractiveness and efficiency of our room.

FRIDAY AND TUESDAY, SEPTEMBER 2, 6. The older girls came to the schoolhouse to help clean and to get the room ready for the first day of school.

WEDNESDAY, SEPTEMBER 7. School officially opened today although most of the children have already attended. There are thirty-one children this year. (See Appendix, p. 252.) Clarence Cartwright and Charles Willis are the beginners. Bertha Schmidt is a new girl from the city and she will be in the primary group. Sally Lenick, who will also be in the primary group, is from the city, too. Her parents are caretakers of some property in the township. Sally is a cousin to Thomas.

While the children rested this afternoon, I read to them the story of Ferdinand, the Bull. The children enjoyed it and thought it would make a good puppet show.

The children see new ways of doing things

Albert said it wasn't long enough. Warren wanted to know why we couldn't have four or five short dramatizations instead of one long one this year.

We spent much time outdoors cleaning up the school grounds of papers, broken branches, and cans left by picnickers.

THURSDAY, SEPTEMBER 8. During the planning period this morning I drew the attention of the children to the weed patch behind the schoolhouse and suggested that it would improve the appearance of the school grounds if we cleaned it up and put a lawn there. While Alex and Gus worked with the little children, and Andrew and Edward patched the torn places in the muslin shades in the little house, the rest of us went to work on the weed patch. The girls began to pull weeds around the girls' toilet and the boys around the boys' toilet. As we worked, the suggestion was made that we have a contest to see whether the boys or the girls would do the better job.

Ten o'clock came all too soon and the children prepared to play in their respective groups. The children take it for granted now that they are going to play together.

Henry informed me today that he did not yet know the

alphabet and felt that he should. Some of the other children said they had to think hard when they looked up a word in the dictionary as it was difficult to remember whether "p" came in the first half of the alphabet or the second, or how near the end "t" came, etc. During the spelling period, Henry settled down to the task of learning the alphabet while the others had dictionary study. The middle group of children found in their dictionaries certain words I had written on the board. They recorded the page on which they found the word. They also put words into alphabetical order. The older children did not need this practice, so they learned to use the key or guide words to find a word in the dictionary. They also noted all the things a dictionary tells about a word besides its meaning.

The children learn purposefully to control essential skills

Last spring the children took the window boxes home to care for them over the summer. I brought them back to the schoolhouse after school today and put them in their places. The children had taken good care of them and the petunias are lovely.

FRIDAY, SEPTEMBER 9. When we went out to work on the weed patch, the girls compared their progress with that of the boys and it did not compare favorably. Doris said, "We can't do a good job because the brambles scratch our bare legs. The boys have long trousers and they don't mind." Thomas suggested that the boys would clear out the brambles if the girls wanted them to. Doris offered that, in turn, the girls would pull the weeds on the boys' side where there weren't any brambles. "Well," said May, "we can't have a contest if we are going to help each other." "What's the difference," retorted Thomas. "The work will be done better." The children learned a valuable lesson today.

I observe how the children learn to appreciate co-operation

After play time, the little children and I made plans about playing in the playhouse. In five minutes we had chosen a mother, father, children, schoolteacher and relatives, and had planned a play program. May went outdoors with the little children to be available if needed. She was quiet and gentle with them.

For two years now we have been trying to get someone to help us fill in the hollow spots on the school grounds and especially to terrace the section in front of the schoolhouse for a lawn. We have not been successful as no one seems to have any jurisdiction over this. The parents are all too busy to help us. This morning we hit upon the idea of writing a letter to the head of the WPA in our township to ask him for advice about getting help from that source.

Our nice, new, hard-covered notebooks arrived today. Last year we had so many different notebooks before we finished that the children expressed a desire to have only one and to tab the sections the way I do mine.

WEDNESDAY, SEPTEMBER 14. While half of the primary children played in the playhouse, the other half made large paintings at the easels. Then they changed about. It was Sally who had the most wonderful time with her picture, which was a portrait of her Negro doll. Sally told us, "She has pigtails and I call her 'Sunshine.' I have a duck, too. He sticks out his chest and thinks he's boss." The children want to see her doll, so she will bring it tomorrow.

Eric does not play well with the little ones. He pinches them and twists their arms. He is especially unkind to Charles. At first, I thought the other children teased him, but I watched closely today and found that it wasn't so. Eric is dominated by his two older sisters. This may be causing him to "take it out" on those smaller than himself. I'm not sure. If it's true, he needs a harmless outlet for his resentment.

At 11:30 Doris read to the little folks outdoors while the older children had a lesson in manuscript writing. They want to make a collection of their original poetry.

I read the life of Mozart and asked the children if they

would like to dramatize this story for an entertainment in October. Albert said he would like to hear about the lives of other musicians first.

THURSDAY, SEPTEMBER 15. I read the stories of Bach and Haydn to the children. They like the Mozart story best.

The primary children talked about Sally's doll, and we made a chart story. All the children learned to read the story. While I had reading lessons with groups IV and V, the little children played in their playhouse.

At 11:30 we stopped to learn the poem, "The Wind Has Such a Rainy Sound." We talked about the poet's meaning and tried to read the poem to convey that meaning. Warren said this poem was different from the poem last week because it was stormy and sad. Henry said it was "full of worry."

The little folks this year are eager to learn. Often one of them will stop playing and will take his seat to practice writing his name. Or we will find them in the library corner thumbing the picture books. Charles asks every day, "When am I going to read?"

FRIDAY, SEPTEMBER 16. Mr. Riley answered our letter today and said that in order to get the school grounds filled in we would have to get the Board of Education to draw up a legal project for it.

MONDAY, SEPTEMBER 19. During the health lesson, we summarized all the things we did last year to keep healthy. We
The children plan to develop more efficient practice of habits of healthful living
will make a check list of those which need special attention this year, and then consider them one by one until we have formed new and better habits through an intelligent understanding of the reasons for them.

I noticed today that, although the children worked continually, some did not have their work done at the appropriate time. When I investigated further I found that they did have work done which was not due for a while. They do the things they like to do first. Tomorrow I shall have to help them plan study schedules for themselves. It seems to be necessary to go through this procedure every year.

TUESDAY, SEPTEMBER 20. We spent some time in discussing and planning study programs. Each person worked out a study program satisfactory for him. These will go into their notebooks to be referred to when necessary.

MONDAY, SEPTEMBER 26. With the older children I introduced a study of the fruit industry. Our county is becoming important in the apple-raising industry. Since we have an apple orchard in our township, I thought we could use this resource to bring out certain understandings which the children did not get in the study of dairying. Apple raising may be a solution to some of the economic problems of the community.

We talked about the orchard owned by Martha's grandmother and the growth of the apple industry as a specialized industry. We discussed the value of fruit in our diet, how it was cared for in early days, and how we care for fruit today. I asked if it is possible for us to have fresh fruit all year round? Warren said it was possible to buy it in the store but we couldn't always afford fresh fruit in winter because of the price. I asked if canned fruit would be just as good. No one knew. Sophia said that oranges were inexpensive last year but she could not give a reason. Warren thought this was inconsistent because oranges travel a great distance to get to us. He had read also that oranges were hand picked and it must take a long time. I asked, "Do you suppose the pickers get paid very much when oranges sell for fifty cents a crate?" We did not go into this more deeply. All I tried to do today was to open up many aspects of the fruit industry. We touched upon the food value in fruit, the growth of the fruit industry, prices, the fact that labor has something to do with prices, the value of fresh and canned fruit, proper canning and care of fruit.

Tuesday, September 27. For the past few mornings the children have been bringing in news about the European crisis which they get from their newspapers and radios. We spend fifteen or twenty profitable minutes each morning discussing these items.

The upper group began to make a bibliography for their fruit study. The older ones in the group worked by themselves, for they had learned to do this last spring. I helped the younger ones.

Tuesday, October 4. I had to spend more time with the older children this morning teaching them to use their study time profitably.

At the end of the day, instead of having arithmetic, a committee called a special meeting of the Helper's Club to ask for Thomas's resignation. They said he was not ready to be president as he does not try to help the group. This was the result of a series of disturbances. Thomas would not play unless the game suited him. When he did play his decisions were unfair. Also, he has been unusually loud in the room. Andrew made the motion to ask Thomas to resign and the group moved unanimously. The children have come a long way in being able to make decisions and to solve the problems which arise in their daily living.

The children take the initiative in solving their own problems

A new problem is arising which will need to be carefully handled, for it is one which the children cannot solve without help. Ruth, Doris, Mary, May, and Sophia have matured rapidly since last spring. Ruth and May spend considerable time on the subject of boys. The girls would rather sit around during the noon hour to talk about coming and past movies than to play a game. They do their work carelessly and inefficiently. May has accused me of losing her papers and then she finds them tucked away in one of her books. All the girls are growing and developing rapidly.

Normally, new problems are always arising

Ruth seems to be the leader of the group. I have never been

able to convince myself that retarding is ever right. When Ruth was approaching her last year in the elementary school her mother felt that, since she was improving so rapidly and there was hope that she would be a good student in high school, perhaps it would be a good idea to keep her in the elementary school a year longer. Since Ruth agreed with her mother, we decided to do this. This year, I am firmly convinced that we made a mistake. Although Ruth has learned much, she should be with children who are physically and emotionally as mature as she is.

FRIDAY, OCTOBER 7.   In discussing the marketing of apples, Martha told us that her grandmother sells her apples to Mr. Scott, who buys a good part of the apples in the county and resells them. I suggested to the children that we visit Mr. Scott and today we made a list of the questions we want to ask.

WEDNESDAY, OCTOBER 12.   At 12:30 today the children in the upper group started out for Scott's farm. Mr. Scott took them around the orchard. When we returned to the buildings the children saw the cider press, cider filter, the icebox, the storage room, and the room where the apples were sized, graded, and packed.

From Scott's we went to Valley Lake for a picnic supper. Thomas said this was mixing pleasure with business. We sang awhile, played baseball and then, because it was getting dark, we started for home. This was a happy, profitable day.

THURSDAY, OCTOBER 13.   I've been rereading my diary notes and find them meager and lacking in adequate evaluation. The study of the fruit industry is not really challenging the children, and I am doing nothing satisfactory for these adolescent girls. Besides trying to teach, I am taking that long trip in to New York every weekend for courses. Although it is early in the school year I feel rather tired and not too ambitious. My energies are not properly directed.

SATURDAY, OCTOBER 15. As usual when I get to a low ebb, I went to see Miss Everett. Problems have a way of clearing up when I talk them over with her. Miss Everett suggested that the course I am taking would be more effective and less burdensome if it were related to my work. We did some thinking about what problem I should choose for study. We began by asking ourselves, "What next for the children?" They have done some studying of the agricultural phase of their community. They have noted changes that have come about since the beginning of the community. The question of what brought about these changes has come up frequently but has never been adequately answered. We thought the children could profit by considering the answers to this question. In this way they could get a better understanding of the changing world and especially the changes brought about by the Industrial Revolution.

My helping teacher and I together analyze the new problems

There are pressing health needs and the problem of meeting the particular needs of the adolescent girls.

It seems to us that these needs might be met through a study of textiles. In working out such a study with the children I can begin to experiment with some new techniques. I can get help with this and with the problems that arise all along from my professor in the curriculum course. Then, the paper that I write for the course can be the story and evaluation of the children's project.

Miss Everett felt that, since the children were not really interested in the fruit industry, it would be better to bring the study to as rapid and satisfying a conclusion as possible. Many of the learnings we expected the children to get in this study, we can get in the study of textiles.

MONDAY, DECEMBER 26. For two months I have not kept a diary because it just got to be one thing too many added to all the other things I had to do. Today, though, I want to record the impressions I have of this period.

Things we did in this period:

1. Completed the study of the apple industry.
2. Issued the first number of the newspaper.
3. Gave a play on the life of Mozart.
4. Sang over the radio.
5. Gave Dickens's *Christmas Carol* for our Christmas entertainment.
6. Sang Polish, Swedish, French, Italian, Russian, Hungarian, and German carols in the native languages.
7. Made many useful Christmas gifts.

The situation:

At the end of October matters were a little strained, but the tension gradually disappeared as December approached. Most of this trouble, I am sure, was due to the fact that I was tired and was not as sensitive to what went on as I should have been. The club meetings began to reflect my attitude. The children fussed and found fault with each other. Then one day in the beginning of November, I reprimanded Ruth for talking in a sharp tone of voice and she said, "That's the way you talk to us." It was a shock, but it made me realize what was happening. At the next club meeting we brought the problem out into the open. We tried to see why we were acting as we were. None of us could say how it all started but we could see that one unkind word had led to another and that, now that we were not co-operating as we should, the situation was bound to get worse. At the end of the discussion, Mary wrote in her minutes book, "It was decided that we should all try very hard to be more kind to each other."

About the children:

Ruth, Sophia, May, and Doris make a little clique, behaving like typical adolescents. They are interested in themselves

We face the new problems

primarily, in their clothes and their hair, and then in movies and their favorite screen stars. School is not vital to them. Ruth was continually criticizing everything I did at the end of October. She refused to help in keeping the room in order. On November 2 we sat down on the grass together to talk things over. It was much the same kind of talk I had with Ralph about the same subject the first year. The elementary school girls and boys are not eligible to the Young People's Club but on this day I made an exception of Ruth and invited her to join us. It was easy to explain it to the other children on the ground that Ruth really would be in high school if she had not chosen to remain with us another year. Ruth suddenly began to want to manage things. We gave her the opportunity to take full responsibility for the refreshments for the Mozart play. She selected her committee, made a list of refreshments needed, assigned to the members of the group what each should bring, and managed the sale of refreshments the night of the entertainment with no help from me! As soon as Ruth became more co-operative, the other girls did also.

May is becoming more like her sister and reflects her dislike for school. I feel badly about this, for May was on the way to becoming a fine, well-adjusted child. I feel that I have helped her less than anyone else in the group. Her sister Doris has changed from a quiet girl to a loud one. On November 10, I visited at their home and was coldly received. I miss the warm welcome with which they greeted me when their mother was alive.

I invited Edna, an older sister who is looking after the family, to visit us. She did get to one Young People's meeting and I spent considerable time with her telling her about our school program. The oldest sister, who is a nurse, visited them for the Christmas holidays and Edna brought her to our entertainment. Blanche came up to me after the performance and said it was the finest dramatization by children she had ever seen. Blanche has helped to give Edna a new point of view.

Sophia is not so mature as the other three and imitates them because she wants to belong.

Mary is not well liked by the clique because she tells them bluntly what she thinks of them. It makes her lonesome at times, so she joins the group and pretends there is nothing between them and that she is having a good time. It works on the surface but Mary has told me in conference that she isn't always happy when she is acting that way. The boys like Mary, though, and think the other girls are "silly." She is also popular with the little folks.

Thomas has made a splendid improvement since he came to

this school. He came as a cowed, frightened little boy who was ready to fight for his rights at the slightest provocation. Last year at some time or other he wanted to beat up every boy in the group, especially Ralph. This year, although he still displays his temper, these outbursts are becoming less frequent. He is beginning to adjust to our little group and to contribute to it. The children, after having removed Thomas from office in October, elected him president in November to give him another chance. Thomas made the most of his opportunities and was re-elected to a second term in December.

A college student came to visit in December. He is to come to observe our work several times. When Thomas heard this he became conscious of the obscene markings in the boys' toilet recently put here by some older boys outside of the neighborhood. He got his "gang" together, planed off the markings, and collected twenty-one cents which he gave me to buy paint for them to use.

Henry worries continually for fear he will make a little mistake. He watches the clock for fear he will not get his work finished. He works so slowly that often he has no time left to enjoy other activities. He wants to be accepted by the group. This fall the boys teased him good-naturedly during the lunch period and he was not able to finish the substantial lunch which his mother provided for him. He did not want his mother to speak to me for fear the boys would dislike him. Mrs. Mann talked it over with me in Henry's presence. I talked with Henry and told him that the boys liked him and would respect a little show of courage. At the next club meeting Henry brought up the matter. It was discussed and cleared up. Mrs. Mann and her mother-in-law are anxious that Henry do everything well. The pressure is a little too great. We are working on this together.

Warren, Albert, Martha, Mary, Thomas, and Henry make the greatest contributions to discussions that call for any use of abstract ideas.

Pearl, Alice, Elizabeth, Warren, Albert, Martha, Mary,

Helen, Thomas, Henry, and Andrew contribute most in the way of practical suggestions and good hard work.

The little children are active. They have come a long way from shyness. They are interested in all kinds of things, love to play, and ask many questions. They do not always get along well together. Eric and Irene do not like Charles and sometimes make life miserable for him. Irene doesn't like to work in school. I suspect that she is pushed a little too much at home as her mother is eager for her to excel in everything.

Sally is good for this group. She abundantly enjoys living and is such an uninhibited child that her joy shines out all over her. She makes up poems, songs, and dances, and never ceases to find something fascinating to do.

The Cartwrights have been absent more than half the time because of lack of proper clothing. They work hard when they are in school, but are painfully shy. I paid special attention to them during the Christmas gift-making period. Alex made a tie-dyed bureau scarf which he hemmed and fringed himself. Gus made a batik wall hanging and lined it. Without a doubt these are the only lovely things in their house. Verna came for a few days and made a batik which she did not have time to line. Richard and Clarence made stenciled table mats and needle holders.

About the parents:

Mrs. Thompson is co-operative and sympathetic with Ruth, and we are trying to help Eric to be more secure by praising him for things he does well. We try not to be continually correcting him.

Mrs. Hill and Mrs. Lenick (Thomas's mother) thank me over and over again for what the school has been able to do for their children. I have been taking Thomas's graphs of improvement to Mrs. Lenick and she is beginning to think there is hope for Thomas and that he is learning something. She thinks he is getting to be a much better boy.

Mrs. Sametis is always asking for advice, for she is hurt by the critical attitude of the children toward her. She does not understand what is happening to her girls and it worries her much more than it should.

Mrs. Olseuski is always offering to help when she can.

Mrs. Dulio is generous in her contributions to the hot lunch.

The Prinlaks are always urging their children to co-operate in everything and to help their teacher because she does so much for them. And they do help!

I spent two happy afternoons with Mrs. Ramsey during this period and got better acquainted with her. She told me the fascinating story of her life: how her parents had to flee from Russia during the Revolution, how her mother nursed the Finnish peasants until she had money to bring her family to this country. She told about her happy childhood and about her college education with a major in chemistry, and about her twin sister who is now the wife of a philharmonic orchestra conductor.

I also got to know Sally's mother. She is young, and ambitious for Sally. She is sorry Sally has to go to a country school because it is making a tomboy of her. Sally went to a private school in the city where she was learning to be a little lady. I told her how much Sally loves everything she does and what a wholesome, well-adjusted child she is. Sally loves her big cousin Thomas, who is gentle with her.

On the whole, the attitude of the parents is fine. They are co-operative, friendly, and sympathetic, and I have a deep sense of obligation to them.

About the study of the apple industry:

We came to the conclusion that apple orchards would be profitable in our township. The physical aspects are so favorable that our county produces a moist, flavorful apple that is in great demand. The county does not produce enough apples to meet the demand. Roads and marketing facilities also are favorable. There is adequate information available about the production of apples. There is no great outlay of capital required to start a small orchard but there would be no returns for about seven years.

This study did not hold the children the way the study of dairying did. I still have much to learn about putting into practice the phrase "Purpose is at the heart of a wholesome learning experience."

About the play on the life of Mozart:

This was one of the most interesting dramatizations I have ever helped the children give. It was developed creatively as we have developed the Christmas dramatizations in the past. Several different children took the part of Mozart throughout the play, showing him at various ages, from three to fourteen. Sally was Mozart at the age of three. In the first scene the Mozart family celebrates the anniversary of the fortieth birthday of Leopold Mozart. It is in this scene that Wolfgang says the lines which have become famous: "Dear Papa, I love you very, very much; after God, next comes my papa." Sally stood up on a chair, put her arms around Thomas's neck, said her lines genuinely, and then kissed him on the cheek. Both youngsters were entirely unself-conscious. They were not Thomas and Sally, but Leopold Mozart and his three-year-old son Wolfgang! It was so real that no one in the audience laughed.

Irene was Wolfgang at the age of six. In the second scene Leopold and his friend came upon Mozart busily writing. The following conversation ensued:

LEOPOLD: And what ever are you doing, Wolferl?
WOLFGANG: Oh, papa, a piano sonata, but it isn't finished.
LEOPOLD: Never mind that, let us see it. It must be something very fine. Look, my dear Schachtner. See how correct and orderly it all is, all written according to rule. One could never play it for it seems to be too difficult.

I shall never forget how Irene looked when she raised her little head and earnestly said to Thomas, "But it is a sonata, papa, and one must practice it first, of course, but this is the way it should go." Playing the theme from the Sonata in A marked Irene's piano debut. You would think she really believed she was Mozart!

Throughout the dramatization there was opportunity to

include the music of Mozart, which the children studied, and before the dramatization the children sang several songs set to his music. The children gave a sincere performance and the audience liked it.

About singing on the radio:

Each month station WEST has been putting on a half hour educational program, the material for which is drawn from the county. The children were asked to sing in December. They presented this program:

Choral Speaking:
Soap Bubbles
The Wind Has Such a Rainy Sound
Little White Horses
The Main Deep

Folk Songs:
Irish—The Galway Piper
Italian—To Italy
German—Little Dustman
Russian—Cossack Horsemen

From the Works of the Masters:
Brahms—In Poland There's an Inn
Haydn—The Winds
Mozart—Sleep and Rest
Beethoven—Night and Day
Bach—The Eighth Psalm

Christmas Carols:
Silent Night
Bring a Torch, Jeanette Isabella
O Sanctissima

They were happy to receive several telegrams telling them how well they had done. Proud parents listening in at home were happy too. The children were fascinated by the station and asked many questions which were answered by the sympathetic station staff. This was a worth-while experience for the children.

About the Christmas dramatization:

Thomas climaxed his dramatic career with his creative interpretation of Scrooge in Dickens's *Christmas Carol.*

Rich experiences make for wholesome personality development
Everyone in the audience congratulated him and Dr. and Mrs. Breed shook hands with him. The next morning while we were cleaning up he said to me modestly, "I must have been pretty good last night." He was good! The whole community has a new respect for Thomas and Thomas has a new respect for himself.

In the second scene, for Fezziwig's Christmas party, I taught the children to dance the Sir Roger de Coverley. As far as the big girls were concerned, this was the most important part of the play. They had quite a discussion about their gentlemen partners. Henry was popular because he was the most graceful. It was not an uncommon sight during the month of December to see one of the girls take her partner into the hall to practice with him to be sure he would know the steps.

Albert and Warren had seen the movie version of the *Christmas Carol* and were able to give us much help. Warren did a good bit of the directing.

Everyone had a part in the dramatization all the way down in size to Clarence, who made a good Tiny Tim. The audience took part as usual in the singing of the carols and in their active appreciation of the dramatization.

WEDNESDAY, DECEMBER 28. And now I must think about planning for the rest of the year. I shall be expected to write a report for this course in curriculum which I am taking. Since it requires a great deal of time if it is to be worth anything to me, I think it would be better if I limited my writing to this for the next few months and not attempt to keep any other diary notes.

I have prepared a new program (see Appendix, pp. 256-257).

8

I Learn New Techniques

We began the textile study after Thanksgiving. During December the children had the experience of making linoleum block prints with which they printed Christmas cards, table-cloths, and scarves. They made batik wall hangings and tie-dyed bureau scarves, table covers, and window draperies. I spent some time, before the children began to design the gifts, teaching them about design. This I found to be a mistaken and backward procedure. The children were not really understanding. I was not considering how children learn best when I doled out subject matter in nicely organized form. I did not give the children an opportunity to experiment and to discover design for themselves. I was limiting them instead of allowing them to expand what design sense there was already within them. What saved the whole study was that the children enjoy working with their hands and once they actually began to do things, they began to learn and to enjoy learning. What are the next steps? How shall I begin after the Christmas holidays?

I plan to evaluate all along

Perhaps I should consider first what needs of these children might be met to some extent in a study of textiles. They need to have an understanding of the kinds of clothing to wear at the various seasons and for various occasions. The children need to acquire good taste in selecting new clothing. They need to make the best use of their clothing budget. They need to understand the problems of the consumer in purchasing clothing and to use this knowledge

I continually study the needs of the children, to meet them

wisely. They need to understand about labels and the stories they tell about the quality of the material and the workmanship, and the conditions under which the material or garment was made. They need to learn to read advertisements intelligently. They need to understand how changes are brought about in the world and living by inventions such as those used in the clothing and textile industry.

There is a need to fill among the adolescent girls who are at present much interested in themselves and in being attractive. The boys, and especially the big, slow boys, need to work with their hands, to do things that will open up a broader world for them within the range of their understanding.

Perhaps if I take a box of materials to school and we examine these and our clothing to try to find what they are made of, this might arouse interest.

TUESDAY, JANUARY 3, 1939. Today I started out by asking if the children knew of what materials their clothing was made. We found clothing made of cotton, wool, silk, and rayon, but not of linen. The children carefully examined the pieces of material from the box and kept asking, "Is this linen?" Then came the first question, after the children had made several mistakes, "How can you tell?" I turned the question back to the group. Helen said, "It wrinkles easily." Others pointed out that all the materials wrinkled. You couldn't tell that way. Albert said some cotton looked like linen and that made it hard to tell. Andrew said his brother could tell materials by feeling them. The children began to pick up pieces of material to feel them. While they were doing this Warren said that you could burn wool and tell by the smell. We tried this. The children easily recognized the animal odor of burning wool. There were some pieces that looked like wool but did not act or smell like wool during the burning test. Martha said that perhaps the material was mostly cotton with a little wool in it. She said she once got a sweater that was a mixture of wool and cotton. The children suggested burning other materials to see what happened. George burned silk while we watched. The children found that every piece of silk left a crust the way burned wool did and that there was a characteristic odor. Some pieces of material, which looked like silk but were not so soft, left stubby, charred ends. "That must be rayon," observed Ruth. George burned cotton and found that it acted like rayon. "That won't help us to tell them apart, will it?" muttered Albert. "It's easy to tell the difference between cotton and rayon, anyway. One's shiny and the other isn't," commented Pearl. "Oh, no, it isn't," Ruth contradicted. "The dress that I'm making in sewing club is made of broadcloth, and that's shiny." "But it's much heavier than rayon," retorted Pearl. "Miss Weber has a rayon dress that's just as heavy as my broadcloth and looks like it, too," Ruth said with finality. Since the time was almost up, I suggested that they look at materials they have at home and talk with their parents about ways of telling them apart.

WEDNESDAY, JANUARY 4. Today I asked the children what they had learned at home. Warren said that his mother told him that wool and silk are animal fibers and that is why they have that funny smell like feathers. Cotton and linen are vegetable fibers, made from plants. Ruth said rayon was a vegetable fiber, too. "Isn't it made from trees?" Warren said rayon is called a synthetic fiber.

The children liked the idea of making a collection for their notebooks of samples of the various kinds of materials, so we began to separate what we had into piles of cottons, woolens, silks, rayons, linens, and unknowns. "Can't we use the samples we got for our sewing club from the Lining Store?" suggested Mary. "That already tells on the back what it is and we can be sure." Mary brought them to the table and the children noted how the samples were cut and mounted.

While they were doing this, Sophia noticed how many different kinds of cottons there were and how different denim and nainsook are. I told the children that rayon had many names, too, but that since the rayon industry is new, we were not as familiar with these. Doris held up two pieces of wool and said, "There are different kinds of wool, too. This piece from the Lining Store is labeled wool crepe."

Warren, who had been quiet for some time, looked up from his busy sorting of materials and said, "We can't ever tell if we are right. What do factories that buy materials for clothing do? Do they have any way of being sure?" I told him that today it is practically impossible to tell materials apart without a microscope. As soon as the words were out of my mouth, I realized that we might possibly get one from Dr. Breed's school. What a fascinating experience this would be for the boys and girls!

MONDAY, JANUARY 9. On Saturday I was able to get a microscope from Dr. Breed, and I brought it to school today. The microscope disrupted the program of the whole day. The

Abundant interests impel into many fields of rich experiencing

little children too wanted to see what was going on. I mounted a cotton fiber under the microscope and each child took his turn examining the enlarged fiber. There were all sorts of awesome ejaculations. The children learned to distinguish the various fibers. They planned to make drawings of these for their notebooks.

At noon the children examined other things under the microscope. Warren used all his spare time reading in the Encyclopaedia Britannica Jr., studying the parts of a microscope and how it works.

TUESDAY, JANUARY 10. This morning we began to examine under the microscope fibers from the materials in the "unknown" pile in order to determine their nature. As the children suspected, many of the materials were made up of mixed fibers.

During all this time, I was the only one who handled the microscope. At noon Warren begged me to allow him to manipulate it. He said he knew all about how it worked and how to take care of it. I watched him work it for a while and then left him with a group of interested children. From where

I was working I could hear his voice. "Do you remember last year," he was saying, "how we used both our magnifying glasses together to enlarge what we were looking at? Well, that's the way a microscope works. Only it's stronger because often there are more than two lenses." He understood clearly what he was talking about and made the children understand it.

It was during this noon period that the children began putting pieces of material under the microscope to see the patterns of the weaves. They were interested only in how lovely the materials looked.

WEDNESDAY, JANUARY 11.   This morning I asked the children to look more closely at these weaves. They examined many pieces of material and found that three different kinds kept recurring. I gave May a book and asked her to see what she could find about weaves. May found that we were examining the three primary weaves. The children decided to put illustrations of these weaves into their notebooks.

When we were looking at a piece of satin cloth, Martha asked, "How is it done?" I asked the children if they would like to make looms and do some weaving themselves. They were enthusiastic.

MONDAY, JANUARY 16.   Together we planned a letter to send to Dr. Breed thanking him for allowing us to use the microscope. The letter had a warm, grateful spirit which showed clearly how much the microscope meant to the children. Doris, who is the present secretary, copied the letter in beautiful manuscript, and sent it.

TUESDAY, JANUARY 17.   I gave books to Ruth, Doris, May, and Sophia and asked them to find out about a Navajo Indian loom, a box loom, a lap loom, and a loom frame with a string heddle. I helped the girls to get reports organized to describe these looms to the group. The rest of the group, in the meantime, continued to work in their notebooks.

WEDNESDAY, JANUARY 18.   The girls reported today and the children listened so that each would be able to select the kind of loom he wanted to make. The primary children also listened. Several of them have expressed the desire to make looms and to do some weaving. Ruth said that, since a small Navajo Indian loom wouldn't be hard to make, the primary children could make this type. When the five- and six-year-olds felt put out, I promised them that they could make cardboard looms and weave pot holders of strips of material.

FRIDAY, JANUARY 20.   The boys made a memorandum of the lumber we would need for the various types of looms and after school we went to the lumber company to buy the materials. Doris wrote to the Industrial Arts Cooperative Service in New York for cotton and wool yarn. The children have decided to make pocketbooks and belts. The little folks will make table mats of heavy cotton cords on the Navajo-type loom.

FRIDAY, FEBRUARY 3.   For the past two weeks we have been making looms. I hadn't read the directions carefully, which was good because the children had to do a considerable amount of planning and following of directions on their own. This has resulted in increased independence. Every one of the

The children learn to think independently and to act on their thinking

older children, I am sure, could make another loom entirely without help. Edward, who is a poor reader, read the directions and made a box loom without help from me. He helped three others, who were also making box looms, to overcome their difficulties. George learned how to make a Navajo Indian loom and taught the primary children how to make them. He supervised the entire job.

This part of the study helped to fill a need and a desire on the part of the children, especially the older boys, to do things with their hands. They worked hard at reading directions because they had a strong purpose.

At last May is interested in something we are doing. She made a box loom with a little help from Edward, and is now weaving a pocketbook. All the other girls have been much interested since we began to examine materials.

FRIDAY, FEBRUARY 17. Another two-week period has gone by. The children have been busy with their weaving, which they always return to as soon as their other work is finished. All this time I've been wondering where we go from here. There haven't been any leads from the children, they are perfectly content to weave. In the meantime, I've been reading and reading about textiles until I'm saturated. This part of the study has taken about seven weeks. That seems like a long time. But how are we to judge this? As the study progresses, there may be outcomes other than those I have listed, outcomes which are not obvious as yet but which will help them to understand better what will come later. That, I think, will be one test of whether or not this period has been well spent.

I prepare in order to recognize what is significant in the experiences of the children

We have had no formal discussions during this whole time. We worked every period. When we needed to know something, we stopped, found out, and went on again. This technique seemed to be good, but I need to continue to evaluate it. The children have asked a few questions which helped to take the study forward for the most part. Next steps have been suggested by me when interest was high. This technique and these opportunities are new for the children as well as for me. It may be that increasingly they will raise the questions. This is part of what I must observe as the work proceeds.

What are the next steps? Through a study of the processes used in making cloth from the various fibers, for example, the nature of the wool, its care, the whole process of making it into cloth and clothes, what determines whether it is a good or poor conductor of heat, whether it can be washed or cleaned easily, whether it is expensive—through such a study I can see possibilities for meeting some of the health, the economic, and the social needs of the boys and girls.

Probably now I should try to guide this interest of the children in weaving into a deeper study of processes. So that I do not fall into the errors of the first part of this study by outlining subject matter to be learned, I think I shall start off by taking some raw wool to school and suggesting to the children that we wash it. The children have seen our neighbor's sheep shorn. They know where wool comes from. We will start with wool because it is the easiest fiber to spin and it can be worked more successfully than cotton.

Giving the children a stimulating experience seems to be a good way to begin and I shall continue to use it until I validate it or find some reason to reject it. These experiences should not be blindly chosen. An experience should open up possibilities for growth and for further experiences. It should arouse curiosity and set up strong purposes which will impel the children to learn.

I learn to select experiences which contribute to the children's growth

There are some questions I must ask myself as the study continues. Are they keenly interested? Are they able to understand? Are they using accurate varied facts as a basis for thinking? Are they learning to live with each other? Can they do something now about what they learn, no matter how small? Are they really increasing in understanding of the world in which they live?

TUESDAY, FEBRUARY 21. I took to school some unwashed raw wool from the Industrial Arts Cooperative Service and asked the children if they would like to make a piece of cloth from it. Immediately the question came, "How can we do it?" Since there wasn't enough wool to go around, I suggested that the girls wash the wool. They got together in a group and read to find out how. I showed the boys a wool card I had found in our attic. George and Edward offered to make two more like this one so that more than one person will be able to card at one time. They got their tools and began to work in the hall. I showed the rest of the boys three spindles with weights, which I had purchased from the Co-op. I showed them how to spin as my mother had taught me. This was much fun.

THURSDAY, FEBRUARY 23. To get us back into the spirit of what we were doing before the holiday, each group told the others what they did on Tuesday. Sophia showed us a clean piece of raw wool and explained the precautions they had taken to keep it from matting. George and Edward explained about the cards they had made and demonstrated carding wool. Albert demonstrated the method of spinning by hand with a spindle. We spent the rest of the time carding the wool and spinning. I suggested to the children that we keep a record of the time it takes us to spin and weave a small piece of cloth. I'm hoping that some valuable generalizations will come from this.

The children were so interested that they kept returning to the spindles all day long as they finished their other work. Each time, they recorded on the blackboard the number of minutes they had worked. Before the day was over they had used up all the raw wool.

FRIDAY, FEBRUARY 24.   Ruth has a small metal adjustable loom and the group suggested that we use this one to weave a piece of wool cloth. Since Ruth already knew how to work the loom, she set the warp threads and taught the others how to weave the woof threads. The children's records showed that it took four hours to spin twenty-seven yards of wool yarn and to weave two small pieces of cloth five inches by five inches. They were rough pieces of cloth, full of thick places. It takes a great deal of practice to spin an even thread.

The children made the remarks I had hoped they would be able to make. "It takes so long and it's so hard to weave by hand." "This is fun for us, but it wouldn't be if we had to make clothes for the whole family." "It takes a long time to make a suit or a dress this way. Did it take people in colonial times as long as this to spin and weave?" George found a picture of a small spinning wheel and decided to try to make one.

TUESDAY, FEBRUARY 28.   We received from Miss Moran an exhibit on the processes involved in the making of rayon. The children examined it with much interest. Martha asked, "Why can't we do this to show the processes wool goes through in being made into cloth?" Ruth suggested that we dye one of our pieces of "homespun" for this exhibit. We talked for a while about making an exhibit for our museum and the children suggested that we put into it the following articles: unwashed raw wool, washed wool, carded wool, homemade wool yarn, a sample of woven homespun, a dyed sample of woven homespun, and the legends to go with these. I suggested to the children that we might experiment with homemade dyes before we dyed the piece of homespun.

WEDNESDAY, MARCH 1. Together we read and discussed a bulletin from the Industrial Arts Cooperative Service on native dyes. The bulletin suggested making charts which show the results of dyeing cotton, wool, linen, and silk with a native dye, walnut hulls, for instance, using the following mordants: acetic acid, soda, alum, iron sulphate, and cream of tartar.

We made several such charts for our notebooks and left spaces for sample squares of materials. Tomorrow the children will bring bark of maple, white oak and red oak, sassafras, wild cherry and walnut, and some onionskins.

George, Edward, and Thomas completed the small hand spinning wheel and tried spinning some wool today. It didn't work very well and for us it was no faster than using the spindle, but it helped the boys understand the spinning process.

THURSDAY, MARCH 16. For the past week we have been experimenting with dyes. As the dyed squares of cloth dried, the children put them into their notebooks. They have been writing up the processes and results of their experimenting. May and Doris have been much interested but Pearl continues to be our chief dyer. She and Alice have been trying some experiments of their own at home.

We have spent most of the social studies periods discussing current events. The children are using their history and geography books as references whenever they need to get a background for the situations which the *Current Events* papers and the *Weekly Reader* bring to their attention. The current events section of their notebooks is by far the thickest section. They record all the places they study about on the large wall world map.

This morning Ruth said to me, "What a nice new sweater you have on, Miss Weber. Is it Angora?" "No, it's alpaca," I answered. "What's alpaca?" Ruth wanted to know. I explained, and Ruth stated, "I didn't know wool came from other animals besides sheep and goats."

During the social studies period I told the group of the morning's conversation. I showed the children the label in my sweater. They brought their coats and sweaters into the room to see if they could find other sources of wool. The children found labels that said "wool" and "worsted" and a Consumers Union label.

While all this was going on, Ruth found in a book that we get wool from yaks, llamas, camels, alpacas, sheep, and goats. "Of course, camels," she exclaimed. "I should have known. My sister has a camel's-hair coat." Andrew suggested that it would be nice to make a world map and to put on it pictures of wool-bearing animals. In the same breath he said, "I'll do it." He got his idea from a picture map showing the industries of New Jersey. This map is a great favorite with the children.

Before the close of the period I suggested to the children that we had raised several questions today which we do not want to forget. What is the difference between worsteds and woolens? What does the Consumers Union label mean? What are the animal sources of wool? We listed these questions on a chart for further study.

FRIDAY, MARCH 17.   The experimenting with dyes is finished now, as far as we are going to take it as a group. The onion dye with the alum mordant, a lovely yellow, turned out best for wool, so we used this to dye our piece of homespun. Pearl had the honor of doing this. After looking over the squares of grayed color, Warren remarked, "It's no wonder the clothes of the early settlers in our country were so drab."

MONDAY, MARCH 20.   Interest in reading labels is high. A man picked up William and Henry on the way to school this morning and the boys asked to look at the label in his coat. It was a coat made of llama wool. The man told the boys that it was an expensive coat. When the boys arrived at school they excitedly told us the story, and Henry asked, "Why are some woolen clothes so much more expensive than others?" We added this question to the chart we had started on Thursday.

Andrew wanted to work on the world map of sources of wool. In order to have the information for Andrew when he was ready for it, the children thought we had better begin the research on the question "What are the animal sources of wool?" While Andrew began to draw a map on a large piece of craft paper, the rest of the children turned to the geography books and other references. I suggested that if as they read, they should find answers to the other questions, it would be a good idea to note these references on bibliography cards and to place them in the card file as we have done in the past. As the children worked I moved around helping them to take notes. I helped the younger children in their use of the index and selection of references.

TUESDAY, MARCH 21. We began to discuss what the children had read. They made a list of wool-bearing animals and discussed how these animals live in their particular regions. They found good pictures of these animals for Andrew and showed him where on his map he should draw them.

Doris found that there were many kinds of sheep and added, "That's one reason there is a difference in price." Warren added, "Sheep require a great deal of care to keep the wool clean and free from foreign material. That makes a difference in price, too." It wasn't long before we could see an outline forming:

> The cost of a wool garment is dependent upon
> 1. the kind of sheep, goat, or other wool-bearing animal
> 2. the care of the animals
> 3. the process by which the cloth is made
> 4. labor.

Now our study and discussions can be more pointed. This is more technique of a new kind. We planned to consider the first item in the outline tomorrow.

WEDNESDAY, MARCH 22. We began to discuss the question, "How does the kind of animal from which the wool comes make a difference in the price?" While we were discussing this question, Sophia told us the difference between woolens and worsteds. The difference was apparent in the clothing of the children.

The discussion was not so smooth as it should have been. It is time again, I think, for the children to check on their discussion procedures.

THURSDAY, MARCH 23. We talked about the discussion of yesterday and the children listed the following points to keep in mind.

The children learn to act in consideration of each member of the group

1. Keep the conversation to the topic.
2. Listen carefully so that we do not ask questions which have already been answered.
3. Talk to the whole group.
4. Have the information in a form in which it can be readily given.
5. One speak at a time. Others await their turn patiently.
6. Speak courteously in making corrections or suggestions.

TUESDAY, MARCH 28. The children had found some interesting facts to answer the question, "How does the process by which wool cloth is made make a difference in the price?"

Thomas found that machines reduced the price of goods greatly. He stated that in 1700, when machinery was used for weaving, the price dropped from 50 cents to 9 cents a yard. "How did these machines come to be invented?" asked Sophia. We added this question to the others on the chart.

FRIDAY, MARCH 31. The notebook work lagged behind the discussions, so we have used the social studies periods as well as the English periods for the past three days to organize the material gathered and to get the stories written for the notebooks. We took time to check the vocabulary chart to be sure everyone understood all the words listed. The children learned to spell some of the words.

MONDAY, APRIL 3. The children read about the textile machines which greatly reduced the cost of woolen goods, and about how they came to be invented. They studied about the spinning jenny, about the spinning machine of Arkwright, and about the weaving machine of Cartwright. As I moved around helping the children, one by one they began to ask questions. Why were all the inventions made in England? Why did the people hate these inventions? Why was Arkwright called the "Father of the Industrial Age"? What were the factories like in those days? Why did women and children work in those early factories? Do these conditions exist today? We added all these to the question chart.

WEDNESDAY, APRIL 5. Yesterday we continued to read and study. We are finding a wealth of material but much of it is too difficult for the children to understand. I helped the children to use only what they could actually grasp, as evidenced by their ability to talk about it in their own words. Today we began to try to answer the questions we had raised. Henry, William, and Albert told the stories of the inventions of the spinning jenny and the machines of Arkwright and Cartwright.

May told the group that these inventions would naturally come about in England because the setup was already there. Groups of people were already brought together for spinning and weaving. England had division of labor. We talked at great length about the advantages and disadvantages of division of labor and I saw that the children really understood it. At Christmastime we had read about a clockmaker in the Black Forest. Doris said today, "Workers in a big clock factory today could never get the satisfaction from their work that this clockmaker did." "No," mused Warren, "but there is a kind of thrill in being a part of a big factory, I should think." "I'd like to visit a textile mill," said Thomas. "I'd like to see a big weaving machine. They must work fast."

During the English period Thomas wrote a letter to the Passaic Chamber of Commerce to ask about visiting a weaving mill.

THURSDAY, APRIL 6. Martha told the group that people broke up the machines because they were afraid the machines would take away their jobs. Manufacturers didn't like the inventions either, because they would have to make new machines and modernize their factories. "Invention of modern machines is one of the causes of unemployment today, too, isn't it?" asked Ruth. "Didn't a great many people leave our township for that reason, when reapers and binders and combines were invented and grain could be raised more profitably in the West?" "And didn't the coming of the railroad have a great deal to do with that, too?" added Warren. "We read not long ago in *Current Events* that people of the South are fighting the cotton picker because it would put millions of people out of work," Thomas reminded us. They are being helped to understand the world in which they live!

Mary told about the early factories. She stated that Arkwright had good factories where he enforced health rules and working conditions which were good for those days. Later children were introduced into factories because they found that they could run machines and be paid practically nothing. Women and children were paid less than men. There were long hours, low wages, unsanitary conditions. Goods were fairly cheap, much cheaper than they could be made at home. Machines in factories made it possible to produce goods in large quantities and this also reduced the price.

TUESDAY, APRIL 11. We have been reading to find the answer to the question, "Do these conditions exist today?" Pearl

The children begin to form conceptions of the responsibilities of society

brought in some newspaper pictures which showed children crippled because of work in factories and of children picking cotton in the South. The group is unusually interested in the labor problems raised by the coming of the factory system. We read and discussed laws that have been passed and efforts that are being made to better labor conditions for men and women and to eliminate child labor. We discussed what New Jersey is doing in regard to child labor. We discussed also consumer cooperatives, women's leagues, and the like which are trying to better conditions under which goods are produced. Warren brought in consumer magazines, and this noon Sophia introduced the group to a radio broadcast, "Consumers' Quiz," which she had discovered. Our school was wired for electricity this month and the first thing we did was to buy a small radio.

While we were discussing child labor, May read from an old book that a child labor law was to be made the Twentieth Amendment. She stated that it must be the Twentieth Amend-

The children learn to be critical and to check sources of information
ment by now. Ruth looked it up and found that the Twentieth Amendment had nothing to do with child labor. The amendment had not been approved.

Thomas told us today that prices of materials and clothing were raised somewhat due to better pay in factories and reduction of sweatshop labor. I pointed out to the children that when we pay attention to labels we are helping the cause of better conditions for labor and we will be rewarded by a better quality of goods.

WEDNESDAY, APRIL 12. The older girls in the 4-H Sewing Club have been studying the care of clothing. At our last meeting we began to consider how to store away winter clothing. I felt that this part of our work might well be extended to all the children in the school. We discussed this today and I suggested that it would be a good idea to have demonstrated the washing of a sweater, a woolen that could be made wet; and the cleaning of a wool jacket, a woolen that would be damaged by washing. "What do we know about wool that will help us to know how to handle the cleaning of woolen articles?" I asked. As the children stated the characteristics of wool, I listed them on the board. Under the microscope we found that the sections of the fiber telescope into one another and that the rod-shaped fiber is covered with scales. These make it possible for the fibers to shrink and mat if they are not handled properly. Wool fibers are less strong than cotton. Hot water and rubbing weakens and breaks them. Wool takes dye readily. Discolored woolens may be redyed. Wool is affected by heat and sudden changes in temperature. Wool, a poor conductor of heat, is a valuable winter fabric. It is not a good summer fabric as it holds odor and is affected by body secretions. Even in winter it is good to use shields in wool dresses. Wool absorbs a great deal of moisture and takes a long time to dry out. The children gave all these from their firsthand experience with wool. It was not merely a verbalization of something they had read. The children put these characteristics of wool into their notebooks. Doris thought we ought to put down the characteristics of the other fibers also.

THURSDAY, APRIL 13. Mary washed her sweater according to the directions she found in "Clothing Care," a bulletin of the Extension Service, New Jersey College of Agriculture, New Brunswick. She demonstrated while the group observed how to make a mild soap solution, how to wash the sweater and how to dry it. The children put the directions into their notebooks.

FRIDAY, APRIL 14. I made a detergent, the directions for which are also in "Clothing Care," and cleaned William's jacket. I also demonstrated how to press woolens. The children put these directions into their notebooks.

Doris and May asked to take home the detergent that was left over, so they could clean some of their woolens.

Word came today that children are not permitted to visit the factories in Passaic.

SATURDAY, APRIL 22. We left the study of textiles last week so that we could concentrate on preparing for the puppet show which we gave on Thursday night and last night and which we shall repeat tonight. All year, folks have been asking us whether or not we would have a puppet show this year. We advertised early and widely so that we would reach all the folks who wanted to come. On Thursday night, the little school was filled to overflowing so that some of the men, who had paid for their tickets, had to stand outdoors looking in at the windows. We gave them "rain checks" so that they could see the show on either one of the other two nights. Folks came from the next county fifteen miles away, from the county seat twenty-two miles away, from Pennsylvania and New York City. Tonight a group is coming from Newark.

The children are happy, but they are poised and restrained. They talked afterwards with the visitors with the assurance of those who know they do their work well. The scripts of *Nicodemus*, *Ferdinand*, *The Chinese Nightingale*, and a revival of *Winnie the Pooh* were original dramatizations of those stories, far from static. Each night the children changed and added to their performances.

The children develop self-confidence in their own ability and intelligence

I think these dramatizations have done more for these shy children in the way of wholesome personality development than any other one activity. The growth in judgment and intelligent management has been great. As I sit at the back of the room calmly enjoying the show and watching the reactions of the audience I am especially conscious of the scope of the growth. The children move in an orderly, quiet way behind scenes, each with his particular responsibility to perform, but so closely co-operating that any one of them can take over any task in an emergency. Here, social control rests with the whole group engaged in an enterprise to which all have an opportunity to contribute and to which all feel a responsibility.

This growth in organized co-operative action is the result not of accident but of careful planning. I have tried to create a situation in which the children do not follow a leader blindly but bring intelligent thinking to bear on the solution of their problems. The children have had many opportunities to plan, to carry out their plans and to evaluate them so that they were continually growing in the power to act more intelligently on the basis of each evaluation. This makes for democracy!

The children develop a sense of values to guide judgment and action

Between the scenes of the puppet show, the children sang the songs they have been learning since Christmas. They sing so beautifully that Dr. and Mrs. Breed asked us to sing at the Vesper Service last Sunday for the boys at the academy. We gave the following program:

Selections from the Masters:

    Bach—A Chorale
    Beethoven—Sing of Day
    Haydn—Echoes
    Mozart—Spring Is Coming
    Mozart—In Tyrolean Hills

Folk Songs

    Southern Appalachian—The Frog Went A'courtin'
    English—Frog in the Well
    English—Little Old Woman
    Irish—The Meadow
    Russian—Fireflies
    Russian—Canoeing
    Finnish—Dusk
    Italian—Street Fair
    Hungarian—Caraway and Cheese
    Dutch—In the Poplars
    Dutch—The Singing Bird
    Slovakian—Morning Comes Early

Mr. Allen, the hardware store man, from whom we bought the varnish stain for refinishing the desks last spring, came to me after the performance and said, "Do you know, Miss Weber, I've been examining every one of these desks and I haven't found a single mark on any of them! How do you do it? How do you do it!"

It is time again to evaluate what this part of the study of textiles has done for the children. It is meeting some of their health needs. The children have learned to brush the clothing they are wearing. Mrs. Sametis told me at the show last night that William brushes his jacket every day since I cleaned it, and hangs it up. They learned how to wash knitted woolens and how to clean spotted ones. The Andrews girls are cleaning all their winter clothes carefully before they put them away. The girls are using shields in their dresses to protect them and cotton dresses are laundered more frequently.

The study is meeting some of the economic needs. The children learned how to make their woolens last and wear well by learning the proper care of them. They learned to tell fabrics apart and so can give them appropriate care. They are learning to purchase fabrics wisely.

The study is meeting social needs. The children have a better understanding of the problems of the consumer in purchasing clothing. The girls, in their sewing club, **We begin to meet the needs of society by meeting the needs of the children** have been paying special attention to descriptions of materials, the weaves and number of threads, the twist of the thread, and the like. The children are paying attention to labels concerning the quality of the fabric and for the conditions under which it was produced. They have some appreciation of what goes into the making of clothing and of some of the changes brought about in the world due to inventions in the clothing and textile industry, and the problems that have come with them. Some of the children have an opportunity to use the knowledge they have gained in selection of clothing. The older children select their own clothing for the most part. William and Henry have interested their parents.

This study is meeting other needs. The adolescent girls found strong purpose in the study of clothing care. They used the 4-H Club bulletins and extended care of clothing to care of hair and nails. They are more conscious of good grooming.

The bigger boys had opportunities to work with their hands and to experiment. All the children learned and practiced a few good habits in carrying on a discussion. They learned to read to select important points and to share these with the group in discussion. The children are beginning to ask questions because they are interested, and because what they are doing is meaningful to them. They are learning to make more intelligent use of the newspaper and the radio.

What are the next steps? A study of cotton seems to have many possibilities for meeting the needs of the children and also for the formation of certain generaliza-

I make choices in selecting curriculum material

tions. Some of these generalizations which the children should be making are as follows: The way a garment is produced affects the price of the garment. Nations depend upon each other for raw materials. Because of the invention of machines and the coming of power, great changes have been made in ways of working and living. Nations trade when other nations have something they need. There is already some indication that the children are beginning to make these generalizations.

TUESDAY, APRIL 25. One of my friends gave me a book of photographs, *You Have Seen Their Faces*. It gives such a splendid picture of the problems of the South that I decided to show it to the group. Also, I was sure that questions would be asked, as it is a thought-provoking book.

It has taken us two days to study the pictures and read the captions which were actual statements made to the photographers by the farmers, the Negroes, and others, such as, "Somehow I've always done the best I could but it didn't get me anywhere" and "The auction boss talks so fast a nigger never knows what his tobacco crop sells for." As we studied the book, the children asked these questions: Why do the farmers in the South live so poorly? Do they have to live that way? Why don't they do something about it? Why can't the farmers make a living? These questions were too big to answer as they came up. I tried to keep the questions open by saying, "We ought to try to find out," and I suggested that we write the questions down so we won't forget. Helen acted as secretary. The children spent a great deal of their spare time looking through the book either singly or in groups and discussed it together.

THURSDAY, APRIL 27. Yesterday the group read to gather information about the South to answer the questions. Martha started the discussion today by saying, "I can tell how cotton is raised." Mary said that after Eli Whitney invented the cotton gin a great deal more cotton could be raised. Who was Eli Whitney? What did the cotton gin do? Why is so much cotton raised? These were questions which followed Mary's remark, and they were added to the question chart.

Andrew told us he was ready to put on his map the sources of cotton. Some of the children began to read for this purpose, while the others continued to read to answer the questions raised.

WEDNESDAY, MAY 3. Today we continued the discussion from where we left it on Thursday. Thomas told how the cotton gin came to be invented. The cotton gin could clean as much cotton in one day as several people could clean by hand. Since so much could be easily cleaned, the South began to raise much more cotton. Since so much more was raised, they needed a lot more people to pick cotton then. Cotton was cheap and there were many workers. Maybe that's why they couldn't pay them so much. I asked Thomas whom he meant by "they." He said, "The men who hire the tenants or lend them land and tools." A long discussion followed concerning cheap labor and Negro labor, and how they worked to the advantage of the plantation owners. The children could begin to see also how an invention like the cotton gin, freeing man from tedious labor, also brought problems with it. They had already discussed the cotton picker and the problems that lie in its wake. They returned to it again today, and realized what an unsolvable problem it seems.

The children learn to appreciate the complexity of human life and its problems

THURSDAY, MAY 4. Mary read the statement that the boll weevil is really a blessing. That statement was challenged by our new boy, Daniel. "How can any insect be a blessing?" "Because it made some farmers stop raising cotton," answered Mary. "Is that a good thing?" I asked. "Yes," came from many of the children. "If there is no cotton, the insects die because they have nothing to feed on. The ground has a chance to rest. The ground is poor because cotton has been raised there so long. It reduces the surplus." These were some of the reasons the children gave in answer to my question, "Why?" I asked, "I wonder if there are any other reasons?" We turned to our books to find them. We read that, although there were some changes for the better because of the boll weevil, they were small and not far-reaching.

MONDAY, MAY 15. The children have been reading and talking about the way the people in the South farm, how they market their cotton crop, and about the whole process from the gin to the manufactured article. They wrote up the stories for their notebooks.

While the children were writing stories today, Edward said, "There certainly are a lot of things that happen to cotton before we get it."

TUESDAY, MAY 16. I reminded the group of what Edward had said and asked if this had anything to do with some of the problems we had raised in the beginning. An excellent discussion followed. Cotton has to go through so many hands and all those who handle it want to make some money. The man who has the money to begin with is able to make more money, while the tenant farmer who begins with nothing and is kept ignorant doesn't have a chance. The manufacturer wants to make a large profit regardless, often, of how he does it. The lack of education keeps the people in ignorance. The children stated that the labor problem in the South was similar to the labor problem in the North. More perhaps has been done about labor problems in factories in the North, however. They drew on the knowledge they gathered during the study of wool. The children said that it usually is the first person in the line of production who has the hardest time. They compared this with the plight of the dairy farmer today in our own region and referred to our dairy study of last year. In the course of their discussion on the small amount of money the farmer gets for his cotton, Warren said, "Who tells what the price of cotton should be? How do they know?" We read to find out.

WEDNESDAY, MAY 17. It was difficult for the children to understand about exchanges. We took what we could understand of it. We found that the United States is an important factor in determining the price since it raises half the world's cotton. More than half the cotton England uses comes from the United States. Germany, Italy, and Japan also use United States cotton. There are exchanges in Liverpool and New York. These are places where cotton is bought and sold through contracts. The weather and insect plagues are closely watched by price setters. Climate, supply and demand, ease of transportation, all influence the price. England and Germany are trying to reduce the amount of cotton bought from the United States. England is experimenting with cotton to get better crops in Egypt and India. Germany is experimenting with substitutes.

THURSDAY, MAY 18. We read in recent issues of *Current Events* and the *Weekly Reader* that cotton was no longer "king." European demands for United States cotton are less. Rayon is a substitute fast taking the place of cotton. The children asked if this would increase the problem in the South and what was to be done about it. They discussed the problem of surplus crops, compared it with the problem of the surplus of milk and showed how conditions were similar—a surplus in the face of need for these products.

They felt that plowing cotton under was wrong but realized that it was a debatable question. They felt that teaching farmers the values of diversified farming was better.

SATURDAY, MAY 20. This part of the study has been interesting for several reasons. The only experiences involved were looking at pictures and reading. The children continually drew on past experiences and material gathered in other studies. All the questions and developments of the study came from the children. And, finally, for the first time, generalizations became apparent.

The children gather an expanding body of knowledge which helps them to understand better their own situation

This part of the study was difficult. Here is a problem that is an important national one, and one which touches the lives of all people. However, these children do not come into direct contact with it and, as far as I can see, there isn't anything they can do about it. For these reasons, I doubt if this study had as much value for these children as the wool study. The chief value was that it aided in forming generalizations to help understand their own situation. The generalizations I listed before the study began were stated, though not in the form in which I put them down. Other generalizations stated were:

> Climate is very important in the life and work of any people.
> One-crop farming has certain evils.
> Diversified farming is good for the soil, the crops, the people.
> Interests of manufacturers, producers, and laborers are different and often clash and cause problems.
> People who are kept in ignorance have no chance to better their lot.
> Even though there is "overproduction," because of problems in distribution this "overproduction" cannot be used where it is needed.

The children were thoroughly interested as was shown by the questions they asked, and their willingness to find material to help answer their questions. Their interest was to a great extent due to the dramatic quality of the material and I had to be careful to keep the discussions on a factual basis rather than on an emotional one. It was important to keep the study in the hands of the children, to keep their interest, or so much reading and discussion would have become monotonous and too difficult.

WEDNESDAY, MAY 24.   For the past three days we have been helping Andrew put on his map the sources of flax, silk, and rayon. It is a beautiful map, done in pastel water colors on illustration board. Andrew is very proud of it. The children listed on charts in their notebooks the characteristics of cotton, linen, silk, and rayon fibers.

This is where we left a profitable study. It was profitable to the children because it began to meet many of their needs, as has been pointed out. It was profitable, for **A summary** it taught me that old techniques will not do if education is to make a difference in the living of the children. We need to be continually evolving new techniques for new situations. I think I appreciate a little more fully the words I wrote last summer concerning the educative process and the making of curriculum.

WEDNESDAY, MAY 31.   During one of the science lessons this winter, I discovered that none of the children except the Hills had ever seen the ocean. I felt that a trip to the sea would be a worth-while experience for the children. Then one day, after I had related this fact to a friend who is interested in our little school, Mrs. Kollmar said, "Why don't you take them to our place?" Her home is right on the beach and is private.

And that is how I came to be visiting after school today the president of the Board of Education, explaining to him what such a trip would mean to the children, and asking him if we might use two school days since it would be safer to drive a number of cars to and from the seashore on weekdays than it would be on these warm spring weekends. He told us that we deserved a vacation, since we put in so much overtime at Stony Grove. And then, because he understood how much children can learn from such an experience, he granted permission.

THURSDAY, JUNE 1.   The first thing the children did was to write notes to their parents to get their written permission to go on the trip. On my way home last night I got enough

New Jersey road maps so that each child could have one, and now we began to study our route. We traced the direct route and then studied the picture map of historic spots on the back of the road map in order to plan to visit as many of these places as possible.

MONDAY, JUNE 5. We have been spending practically all our time this past week studying the significance of the historic spots we are going to visit. The children have been absorbed by the Revolutionary period and the part New Jersey played in that war.

Tomorrow is the big day. I don't believe any of the children will sleep tonight. We are taking only the children in the upper group, as it would be too difficult to look after the primary children on a trip of this sort. We promised to bring home for them as much seashore sand as we could.

THURSDAY, JUNE 8. It's over now, and today we were unusually quiet. None of us could find words to express how much the past two days meant to us. But whenever the children caught each other's eyes or mine, there was warm understanding.

We had left at 8:30 and made our first stop at Princeton where we saw the Princeton president's gardens, the Chapel, and Nassau Hall, which was a barracks during the Revolution, the dormitories, and the classroom buildings. From here we went to Tennent Church. They looked fondly at the 250-year-old oak in front of the church and tried to imagine what that spot was like when the tree was a sapling. Not far from Tennent Church we saw Molly Pitcher's well—both of them. We stopped along the road at a vine-covered eating place and bought milk to drink with the lunch we had carried from home.

At three o'clock we were driving down Barnegat reef with the ocean on our left, the bay on our right, and soft breezes between. The children could hardly contain themselves. As soon as they arrived they wanted to go in swimming. One of Mrs. Kollmar's sons, a veritable fish in the ocean, did lifeguard duty each time the children were in the water.

After a delicious supper some of the boys helped with the dishes while the rest gathered driftwood for the campfire. At dusk the campfire was lighted and the children wrestled on the sand and played hide-and-go-seek in the shadows of the dunes. Gradually they gathered around the fire and sang. Albert asked, "May we stay up as long as we want tonight?" "As long as you want," I answered. "Until twelve o'clock?" "Until twelve o'clock." "Oh, boy!" exclaimed all the children at once. But at 9:30 Ruth asked, "Do we have to stay up until twelve o'clock?" We had a good laugh and were ready for bed. The boys decided that they would get up early to watch the fishing boats come in.

At 5:30 the next morning I heard Tom's voice in a loud whisper on the other side of the partition, "Hey, War'n, you awake?" Warren answered, "Yes, do you hear that? The fishing boats must be coming in. Let's go." In less than a minute I heard their footsteps on the stairs. These were followed by another pair, and then another. By six o'clock we were all out on the beach and found the fishing boats just going out to sea to attend the nets. While the children waited for the boats to return, they enjoyed for the first time the pleasure of building sand castles and forts to keep out the aggressive water. They discovered sand crabs and dug them up just to watch the amazing speed with which they burrowed into the sand again.

The children watched the men as they sorted the many "funny kinds of fish," as the children called them. The fishermen were friendly and talked with the children. As Warren came in to breakfast he said, "You know, Miss Weber? They talk just like real fishermen." He was pleased that the fishermen he read about really existed.

Breakfasttime was fun. The children ate a tremendous amount. They poured prepared cereal over cooked cereal and flooded the mixture with milk. Then there were orange juice, an egg, bacon, toast, and all the milk they could drink. Lloyd, who came to our school for the first time on Monday, felt perfectly at home with us. When breakfast was over he stuck out his chest and patted his stomach and sighed pleasurably. "Mrs. Kollmar must be a taxidermist," he laughed, "because she has stuffed so many little animals."

This time it was the girls' turn to do the dishes. Since I had told the children they would have to wait for two hours before they could go into the water, they began to find ways of using up the time. Warren and Andrew took their sketch pads to the beach and each produced two good sketches. The rest of the boys, flat on their stomachs on the floor of the porch, surrounded a game of Chinese checkers. When the girls finished with the dishes they took a long walk on the beach. The tide was low yesterday morning and the children had a fine time in the water.

After another enormous meal, Mrs. Utter, Mrs. Kollmar's mother, told the boys and girls about her memories of the Civil War and also about her experiences in a California earthquake. Mrs. Utter is a fine storyteller and the children were spellbound.

When we were saying good-bye, Mrs. Kollmar told me she had never seen such a well-behaved group of children. That is a teacher's greatest reward.

On the way home we stopped at New Brunswick so that the children could see the Agricultural Experiment Station. While we were there we drove around the campuses of the New Jersey College for Women and Rutgers. At Bound Brook we stopped to see orchids.

We were at home by seven o'clock, and it was just beginning to rain. We didn't care, though—we had been favored with two warm sunshiny days.

Friday, June 9. We were back to normal again today and found ourselves swamped with work. There was the third number of our newspaper to get out. We held up the layout so that we could include articles on the trip to the seashore.

Also, we had to get on with plans for the Spring Festival.

During the winter, whenever it was not possible to play outdoors, I taught the children folk dances. The children enjoyed this so much that as the weather got warmer we continued to dance outdoors. One evening, soon after the electricity was installed, Martha visited the Young People's Club with her brother. When she saw the school grounds lighted up by the glow from the porch light, she had an idea. "Wouldn't it be fine," she exclaimed, "to have a festival to celebrate our electricity? We could do the folk dances outdoors and have floodlights and everything." So it was decided, and the young people offered to help. Our good friends, the Breeds, offered to lend us floodlights and extension cords.

Today we planned which dances we wanted to include. Henry was made chairman of the publicity committee to advertise the festival to the community. This is to be strictly a community affair and no admission fee is to be charged. Sophia is to appoint her committee to take care of refreshments. Ruth is to see that everything goes smoothly, and that the radio is turned on for social dancing at the end of the festival. Edward and George are responsible for seeing that there are receptacles around for the proper disposal of napkins and paper cups, and, as the group ordered, to see that they are used. Doris and May volunteered to see that any utensils we use are properly washed and that the kitchen is cleaned.

We spent much of the day reviewing the dances, first with the primary children and then with the rest of the group. We have the program satisfactorily arranged.

THURSDAY, JUNE 15. Sophia, Ruth, Doris, and May began to clean the kitchen as soon as they arrived this morning while the rest of us stood around and talked about the success of the festival last night. The dances looked pretty in the colored lights. This was our program:

1. European folk dances by the upper group:
   Children's Polka
   Rovenocka—Bohemian
   Csebogar—Hungarian

Come Let Us Be Joyful—German
Mountain March—Norwegian
Ritsch, Ratsch

2. Dances by the primary children:
   A'hunting We Will Go
   Shoemaker's Dance
   I See You
   O Where Has My Little Dog Gone

3. American folk dances by the upper group:
   Captain Jinks
   The Girl I Left Behind Me
   Pop Goes the Weasel
   Virginia Reel

4. Social Dancing

The young men had helped to move the piano outdoors, and then back into the room again before they left. All the young people danced and their parents were pleased. The parents were content to sit around and talk after the children had performed. The children moved among them with trays of lemonade and grape juice and stacks of homemade cookies.

As school is over tomorrow, we did little today except to get the schoolhouse ready for the summer.

9

We Learn to Live in a Democracy

SUNDAY, SEPTEMBER 3, 1939.   This summer has been a restful one. I spent much of my time outdoors hiking and swimming and now I feel luxuriously healthy.

I spent many peaceful hours on top of the hill overlooking the winding river, under my favorite apple tree. Often, when my eyes would get tired of reading, I'd roll over on my back in the grass and gaze up through the branches of the gnarled apple and watch the clouds drift by. I'd think about myself and all the wonderful things that are happening to me. All those things that I want for the boys and girls I teach, are coming to me too. I, too, am becoming increasingly aware of my capacities and of my place in the world. I study hard and listen to those who have had other and more experiences than I and I think I know the meaning of every word they say. I try, often painfully and discouragingly, to test these words and to turn them into action, again and again, and suddenly all the words take on new meaning. I realize that I did not really know before, but now I do. I am also aware that many of the things I now think I know, will take on new and fuller meaning as I continue to experience consciously. I have found that I can learn to do things I never did before. I, too, can meet life creatively and help to make it a better place for me and for my fellow men. It is the most wonderful, most encouraging and hopeful feeling one can have! I think I can understand a little better why Walt Whitman always wanted to sing about everything.

And I'd think often about the coming school year and all the new possibilities for growth it holds for all of us. I'd think about each of the children in turn. It will be good to be back with them another year, working together to improve our living. For no matter how impossible the way seems, if we do the little we see to do as we see it, the next step becomes clearer.

Little children, when they start out in life, are curious, exploratory human beings. They use all their senses to seek out the wonders of the world. They learn just by living fully. But not only that, they act upon what they learn. They make use of what they learn in similar or new situations. Then the children come to school and the school "ties" their senses. They must not talk. They must not move around. They must not feel. They must not see except what the teacher wishes them to see. For three years I have tried to bring back to these children this spontaneous desire for learning which they have in the first few years of their lives and which their parents and teachers, including myself, have been busy taking away from them. For, since I was brought up in the traditional school, I find myself, unless I am continually watchful, reverting to the kind of schooling I had. Gradually, I think, I have helped the children to desire to go on learning. This is the most important attitude which can be formed, for, without it, not only do they stop preparing but they also lose native capacities which would make it possible for them to cope adequately with the situations that come up in their living.

Now that the children do want to learn, the best way that I can prepare them for the future is to help them to get worthwhile meanings out of each present experience they have. Living in the present as fully as possible will prepare them for deeper and broader experiences later.

MONDAY, SEPTEMBER 4. Today eight mothers and six high school girls met at the schoolhouse with Miss Moran to learn how to can vegetables in the best way. Mrs. Prinlak left the new baby with Mr. Prinlak, who willingly took care of it so that his wife could get some new ideas on canning. Mr. Prinlak certainly must be revising his ideas about learning when they include even adult education!

Last spring the parents expressed a desire to learn more about making the most of their gardens. I called in Miss Moran and Mr. Lorenzo to help. They, in turn, secured the services of Miss Doerman, the food specialist, and Mr. Nissley, the garden specialist, from the State College of Agriculture. At a meeting on April 28, fourteen parents, young people, and children, representing more than half the families, met at the schoolhouse with the state specialists and the county agents to make plans for their spring gardens. We discussed our problems, received advice, and helpful printed material. Two future meetings were planned, one to learn better canning methods and the other to learn how to store bulky vegetables.

WEDNESDAY, SEPTEMBER 6. The children greeted each other and their teacher heartily, today. Mrs. Lenick told me that Sally could hardly eat her breakfast, she was so eager to get to school. The children seem to have lost all the shyness they usually have at the beginning of each year.

There are thirty children in school this year. (See Appendix, p. 253.) The Dunders moved to town soon after Christmas last year and Joseph was placed in an institution. Bertha Schmidt left also, as her mother moved back to the city. The Olseukis moved to the Williams place, far from the Prinlaks, which gave both families a pleasant, untroubled summer. Two new boys entered school last spring. Daniel Cole's parents bought the Olseuski farm in April. Mr. Cole was an automobile mechanic in the city but because of his health he was forced to give this up. Mrs. Cole is a friendly woman and added much to the fun of canning on Monday.

Lloyd Matthews came in June. When we heard there was a new boy in the neighborhood, we invited him to come to school for the last few days. His mother has been thanking me ever since, for she said that Lloyd is a nervous child who would have fretted all summer wondering about the new school and whether he would like us and be liked in turn. Lloyd went with us on the trip to the seashore and had the time of his life. This fall he is not a new boy, but one of us. Mr. Matthews is a landscape gardener who is looking for a place to farm. Mrs. Matthews had a happy time canning on Monday, too.

Mr. Ramsey is building some log cabins and is renting them to summer folk. The Moodys rented a cabin and spent the summer in Valley View. They decided to spend the winter here in order that Arthur, a six-year-old, might have the experience of coming to our school. Mrs. Ramsey thinks the school has done so much for Irene that Mrs. Moody hopes it will do the same for Arthur. Mr. Moody is an insurance agent and will have to commute to New York daily.

There are three beginners, another Prinlak, another Mann, and Robert Linden. The Lindens are caretakers of a boys' camp.

We started the first day properly enough by calling to order a club meeting for the purpose of reorganizing the club. Three committees were appointed, to evaluate last year's club meetings and to make recommendations for the coming year, to plan exactly what needs to be done in connection with each housekeeping duty, and to examine the constitution to propose additions or changes.

When we returned from play, I introduced the children to the books I had brought from the library, telling them interesting things about each book. The children made their selections and settled down to a quiet period of reading. While the others read, the five-and six-year-olds talked with me about their summer fun. They were especially intrigued with their new school clothes and the preparations they had made for the first day of school. They dictated a story about this and I put it on a chart. Each child began to make a picture of him-

self coming to school in his new clothes. Until 11:30, groups
II, III, and IV in turn had their reading periods. As the little
children finished their reading and their pictures, they went to
play outdoors with large balls.

During the story hour the whole school moved outdoors.
I told the primary children the story of "The Three Pigs"
and they dramatized it. Martha was with us because she will
be with the little folks tomorrow. The rest of the children
worked under the trees in their respective committee groups.
William helped the little children wash their hands before
lunch and he and Martha ate with them. The committee chairmen had a luncheon date with their teacher to discuss the
progress of the committee work.

The rest period was indeed restful. Pearl read silently as
she kept an eye on the little folks stretched out on the warm
grass in the sun. The older children sat relaxed listening to
Walt Whitman's poem "The Commonplace." We talked quietly
about what it means and we all felt lucky that many of the
wonderful things in life were free to us here in the mountains.

Following this, while the primary children worked with me
on spelling and number, the committees met to complete
the work they had begun in the forenoon.

At the end of the day, a meeting of the club was again called
to order. Martha acted as president pro tem and did a really
fine job. She called for the report of the Constitution Committee first. Warren reported that the committee was satisfied
with the constitution as it stands except for one thing. They
added that from now on the group should vote how the school
money is to be spent. He read the revised constitution to the
children and they voted to accept it.

Helen reported for the Committee on Housekeeping. They
had decided that it would be a good idea to make oak tag cards
listing on them what needs to be done in connection with
each job, as

Dusting (1)
1. Dust ledges around the room
2. Dust doors
3. Dust base moldings
4. Dust stove
5. Dust the two small cupboards
6. All this to be done in the morning before school

Dusting (2)
1. Dust desks and seats
2. Dust worktable
3. Dust piano
4. Dust library furniture
5. All this to be done in the morning before school

Librarian
1. Dust library in the morning
2. Keep cards from books in use in a box
3. Cross off the name from the card when a book is returned, put card into book and return book to shelf
4. Keep books in proper sections all day
5. Have office hours at end of the day to sign out books that are to be taken home
6. Make out cards for new books acquired

Then as the jobs change, the cards change hands also and everyone will know what to do. The group voted that the committee make the cards.

Albert's committee decided that club meetings are important and should be taken seriously. They felt that the president should be most carefully chosen and should be one who has given full co-operation to past presidents. The committee felt also that they would learn more about running their affairs if I took no part at all. They want to try to manage their club by themselves and to call on me for help when they need to. This was voted upon and passed.

Next came the election of new officers. Warren was elected

president; Helen, vice-president; Edward, secretary; and Andrew, treasurer. The group voted to spend some of its money for percale to make new cupboard curtains, for paint to clean up the little house and the furniture in it, for oilcloth to make a new world map to replace the one we filled with current events last year, and for lumber to build a new library table.

I sang all the way home tonight. This is going to be a wonderful year!

THURSDAY, SEPTEMBER 7. This day progressed even more smoothly than yesterday and the atmosphere was a happy one. Arthur Moody overflows with joy. As he sat at his desk drawing a picture of himself in his new high-top shoes, which he could not keep for winter, he kept mumbling emphatically, "I just love this school! I just love this school!"

This morning we began the usual sewing, painting, and repairing that puts our room and grounds into working order the first month of each school year.

We are still thinking about the school grounds. They were not filled in last year, for the WPA project was removed from Valley View.

FRIDAY, SEPTEMBER 8. We all felt today as if we had never been away from school at all. As soon as the children arrived at school they began to work at the activities they started yesterday. When it was just about time to clean up we had a visitor. While I was occupied in this way, Warren and Helen conducted the cleanup, planned the game with the group, supervised the play, called the group in on time to begin work. The children settled and worked for twenty minutes. Martha, with assurance, began the reading with the primary children. That, for the third day of school, shows a tremendous carry-over from last year.

Much credit goes to Mrs. Mann, who gathered up the boys who wished to go and took them for swimming lessons daily this summer. The Hill children found nice friends in some summer people who lived near them. Mr. Prinlak dammed up the stream so that his children would have a place to swim. There is one other element that is important. I have worked especially hard to build up self-respect in the four big boys. Gradually their work has been improving and last spring they felt so encouraged that they began to look forward to high school, as it no longer seemed an impossibility. They continually anticipated this year with questions such as these. "Will you give us writing lessons so that we can improve our writing?" "Will you give us extra time with our spelling?" "Will you teach us good ways to study?" It is little wonder that they were ready to get started.

WEDNESDAY, SEPTEMBER 13. I love to watch Andrew with the little boys who are painting. He wipes paint off their hands and speaks gentle words of warning about their clothes. He ties their aprons for them and teaches them how to fold their aprons to put them away.

Helen and Alice have been fine help, teaching the little girls to sew and to thread their own needles and to make their own knots. Verna has been like a little mother, teaching, giving advice, protecting.

The county librarian came while we were singing. As the older children selected their books, Helen and Martha gathered the little folks together and occupied them with singing games. One by one the older children each selected a book and found some shady nook and became lost to the world. The scene was so peaceful that I could not disturb it, so I postponed the art lesson until tomorrow.

FRIDAY, SEPTEMBER 15. Since the children are very much interested in current events these days, I thought I would use the social studies period to give them a beginning in learning how to evaluate what they read and hear. They are inclined to believe that everything which comes over the radio or is in the newspaper must be true. We talked for a long time today about the problem of the Polish corridor.

The high light today was the sandbox, which the boys

finished sinking into the ground in the playhouse yard yesterday. They filled it with the sand we had brought back from
the seashore for the little folks who could not go with us.
The little children could hardly wait until it was their turn
to play in the sand as the box is not large enough to accom-
modate all of the children at once.

MONDAY, SEPTEMBER 18. The paint on the little house was
entirely dry today. The primary children furnished it neatly
and played happily. By the time the morning physical education period arrived, they had a "roast" in the oven and, since
we could not leave that to burn, they continued to play in
the house through the physical education period. The little
children have grown much through their dramatic play. Their
vocabularies have increased, they are more self-reliant, they
are confident and poised, and their imaginations have developed. They do not have an opportunity to build up barriers
of inhibition. This playhouse has been worth many times
its cost.

The group is intensely interested in the situation in Europe.
We listen to the radio every morning before school and spend
a great part of our noon hour discussing what we hear.

TUESDAY, SEPTEMBER 19. Habits take a long time to form
and it seems we can never be sure they are fixed. We need
constantly to be checking. A little undercurrent of fooling
and waste of time is starting. Before it goes too far I think it
will be best to tighten up on privileges. In the fooling today
Pearl tore up an arithmetic paper of Verna's after Verna had
taken special pains to have a neat paper. Pearl thought it was a
great joke to see Verna doing it over. Every once in a while
Pearl exhibits this mean streak.

Helen fell back into an old habit today, too. She gloated
over everyone's misfortunes until she had the group quite
on edge. At noon, as we were playing two-o'-cat, Thomas
threw the ball to Helen and she missed it. Thomas could not
resist the temptation to rub it in. He said, "Why didn't you
catch it, you're so good!" Helen threw the ball at Thomas and

it would have hit him if he had not ducked. Thomas laughed good-naturedly, "You don't have to almost kill a guy." Helen left the game mumbling that she would bust his teeth in. The other children continued to play and the matter was ended and forgotten, I thought. In the afternoon, however, while I worked with the little folks and the older ones studied out-of-doors, Helen had a real battle with Thomas. She was on her way home before I knew anything about it. None of the children interfered, for they said, "She is better off at home if she feels like that." I called Thomas in and took away his privilege of studying outdoors for the rest of the week. The spirit of the rest of the children was fine. They gave an unbiased report of what had occurred and their accounts agreed. "They both have tempers and are show-offs," the children informed me. It was somewhat amusing, but it spoiled an almost perfect record since school began.

Each year we have given a dramatization of Christmas in other countries: Germany, France, and England. This year Mrs. Ramsey promised to help us with a Russian dramatization of a Christmas legend. She related the plot to me today and it is a good one. It makes provision for all the members of the group, especially the big boys. It has dramatic quality and opportunities for using lovely scenery and much Russian Christmas music.

WEDNESDAY, SEPTEMBER 20. Today was a decided contrast to yesterday. Warren took charge while I took a nature walk with the little ones. The children felt relieved that I would trust them after what happened yesterday. Helen and Thomas both promised to behave themselves.

On the walk, Richard found a katydid and we had a good time listening to it "talk" and being tickled by its feelers. Richard and Clarence are so much more alive than they used to be. Playing with Irene and Sally has been good for them. Florence and Richard kept calling to the attention of the group the beautiful things they saw, a tiny red maple, a cushion of bright green moss, and they would describe them in those terms. When we returned we made a terrarium and I sealed the battery jar. The children wanted to know how we would water it. I asked them to wait until tomorrow and perhaps they could tell me. We did not have to wait, however, for the dew began to form on the top of the jar this afternoon. Richard said, "I know. It's going to rain on it all by itself."

When I joined the little ones in their story hour, I announced, "I know a story." "Tell it to us," they all shouted. I told them about "The Mouse and the Sausage." When I finished I asked, "Now, who else knows a story?" Sally told the story of "The Three Pigs" delightfully and she held the attention of her young audience. Florence did well with "The Lion and the Mouse." Irene told a story of old Russia which she had read in her Russian folk-tale book. These children have learned to tell a story fluently and well.

THURSDAY, SEPTEMBER 21.   We stopped at three o'clock today to listen to President Roosevelt's address to Congress on the Embargo Act. I was afraid it would be difficult for them but all listened intently. Daniel played with things in his desk and Albert whispered to me and asked if he could do something else as he wasn't understanding the address. Warren and Helen remained after school to hear the whole of the speech.

The little folks put together their booklets of the stories they wrote about playing in the little house. The older primary children write good original stories. Eric still has difficulty. Irene, Elizabeth, and Florence write stories of nine and ten sentences.

FRIDAY, SEPTEMBER 29.   This has been a busy and fruitful month. I have managed to visit all the homes of the children and to use part of the drill period to have a conference with each of the older children. The co-operative spirit of both the parents and the children has been marked.

The children have organized their notebooks into sections marked by little tabs. Their notebooks include at present:

1. Things I need to do
2. My special needs
   a. My errors in written language
   b. My speech errors
   c. My errors in spelling in written work
   d. My arithmetic difficulties
   e. My reading problems
   f. Health habits I need to form
   g. Health defects I need corrected
   h. Daily cleanliness check sheet
   i. How I want to improve this year
3. My special accomplishments
   a. Books I have read
   b. Poems I like
   c. Poems and stories I have written
   d. Reports I have made
   e. Committees on which I have served
   f. Offices I have held
   g. Things I have made
   h. Things I have managed by myself
   i. Things I would like to do
4. Social studies
5. Science
6. Health
7. Current Events
8. 4-H Club Work

Each new year finds us on a higher plane of living. Visitors to our school this month have commented on the clean look of the schoolroom and the children. The children are beginning to have a greater respect for each other and their families. Thomas and his stepmother get along so much better. Helen's sisters are beginning to see that she does have some abilities. Helen may learn now that she does not need to assert herself. The children have shared willingly in the work that needed to be done whether it was cleaning or making adjustments in their self-government. They are building a sense of values as is clearly seen in their attitude toward those who are poor citizens of our group. Their standards of work are much higher than they have ever been.

The children have had folk stories, music, and dances, which are part of the heritage of every child. They have had much storytelling and dramatization, which frees them and makes them comfortable with language. Painting, clay modeling, sketching, and writing poems and stories have given them other mediums of expression. They are beginning to be genuine in their writing, expressing what they know and feel. They are increasingly interested in the writings of others. We love our library period when we informally share with each other the books we are reading. The children's tastes in reading are unusually good, as the librarian pointed out the last time she was here.

They have an increasing interest in the world and its relation to us.

There were problems, too, this month. I have learned to look at these from a new point of view. During all my years with the children new problems were continually arising and it seems that there will always be new problems as long as people live together. We must not regard these problems as irritating and inconvenient but must learn to face them and to do something about them. With this point of view, we cease to nag and blame children but seek to find the cause of the problem and together work out a solution. The children, too, have grown to recognize that whenever it is necessary for me to exercise direct control, it is not merely an imposition of my will, but that I am acting in the interests of the group as a whole, and they co-operate with me.

MONDAY, OCTOBER 2. This afternoon, Mr. Nissley, the garden specialist from the State Agricultural Experiment Station, met with the parents, some young people, and the school children, to teach them how to store vegetables. For an hour, on this damp day, we sat around the cozy fireplace in the Hill home and talked about ways of storing vegetables in the cellar and kitchen, in bins and barrels. Then we went outdoors and Mr. Nissley picked a good spot for an open pit and explained how to build one to keep vegetables fresh all winter. The Coles, the Matthews and the Manns, who came from the city and have only recently been farmers, asked many questions and were eager to learn. The children, too, asked questions and made contributions.

I could not help but feel a thrill as I watched the eager faces of children and adults learning together. I felt very privileged to be with a group that is making a small beginning in planning a better life for its members.

THURSDAY, OCTOBER 5. While I took the little ones on a nature walk this morning, the older children worked for forty minutes alone. When it came time for the physical education period, Andrew, who is president, helped the group make plans for play while they ate some fruit from their lunch. Then he excused them for play, supervised the play, and brought them in again for work. In the meantime, Miss Everett had come. Andrew gave her a copy of our school newspaper to read, and asked her to make herself comfortable until I returned. From behind the newspaper Miss Everett observed all that was going on. Whenever things go wrong in spite of our best efforts, Miss Everett and I use the phrase, "Democracy rattled." I found a little note on my desk when she left, saying, "Today, democracy did not rattle!"

This democratic control can come about only in a situation in which the children have freedom to work out the solutions to their own problems. Freedom of outward action has helped to do this, but I have worked hard not to allow such freedom to become an end, for then it is not freedom at all but enslavement to individual whims. The kind of self-control these children have really frees them to grow.

Democracy is far from rattling in other respects also. The children have been conducting their club meetings entirely by themselves this year. In other years I had continually to remind the secretary to write up the minutes. Now, the minutes are written regularly because of pressure from the group. There was much business to discuss today. After consulting the treasury, they decided to wait before buying new curtains.

They also discussed play at noon on the playground and made the decision that any person who spoils the fun of the others should be asked to leave the group. If he refuses to leave the group or continues to annoy in any way, a committee would come to me for advice. At the end of the meeting, someone remembered that new games and new teams had not yet been chosen. This was interesting. In other years choosing teams and games was the most important business and always came first. Then other business was dragged in, often just to have something to talk about. Gradually new business came to include matters the children really did want to do something about, until now they get at their significant business first and leave routine matters until the end.

On my way home, I thought about all this. We hear so much these days about preserving democracy. What does it mean and how are we to do it? It seems to me that in order to be fully aware of the advantages and responsibilities of democracy, to desire it, the children must practice truly democratic living in their schoolroom. But this is not enough. Since their school life is only a part of their whole living, they must also share in the democratic living of the community as far as they are able on the level of their maturity. To follow only these two practices would give us a very narrow sense of democracy. Since we live in an increasingly interdependent world, it is necessary for children to get an understanding of themselves in this world, in respect to place and time.

As I think back over the past three years in the light of this conclusion, there is one area lacking in the experience of the children. They do not have a connected picture of mankind's advance through the ages. They need to orient themselves in time as well as in space.

I am finding it good policy to use the social studies period for the first few weeks of school to have the children fix up the schoolroom. This gives us time to get settled and to iron out the difficulties we have in the beginning of the year. Also, I have an opportunity to study the children, to learn their interests and more about their needs. The social studies work, as well as all the other work of the school, should grow out of the problems which arise through the experiences the children have in their daily living. This year they are much interested in the war. We have gone back into history to understand certain phases of it, just as we have always used history to understand the current events. As I listen to their questions, I think it would be wise this year to capitalize on those that will take us back into the past so they can begin to orient themselves in time.

MONDAY, OCTOBER 16. The little children took a walk today to study the turning leaves. As we walked down the road the children remarked how beautifully the sun made the leaves shine and also that it was "raining" leaves. Richard asked, "What makes the leaves come off the trees?" We sat down at the side of the road and I helped the children to understand how a tree gets ready for winter. We examined branches for healed leaf scars. All the children learned to identify several trees they did not know before. These children like to smell things. They smelled birch and sassafras roots and liked these so well that they proceeded to smell everything in sight. They use all their senses when they take a walk. Seeds did not go unnoticed although the main emphasis was on trees. On Friday we had put our nature story books together considering them quite finished. When the children came back from their walk today they wanted to add another page with colored leaves. Arthur said, "I'd like my story to be, 'Here are some pretty leaves.'" He asked me to write it on the board so that he could practice it. It is no hardship for these children to learn to write. They have a purpose for writing.

TUESDAY, OCTOBER 17. In this week's issue of *Current Events* there was an article entitled "Our Free Press Celebrates a Birthday." We wandered away from the article in the discussion because several interesting questions came up:

1. How did the first free press come to be established in America and when?
2. Why didn't Reverend Glover's press escape censorship in America?
3. What made the press free?

We talked at length about the meaning of censorship and its place in the present war. Thomas pointed out that it was possible to give wrong impressions by leaving out things even though all the rest was true. In discussing the third question, we found that the press was made free through the statement of the First Amendment to the Constitution. Other questions came up. Why did we need a constitution? Why didn't they have one before 1791? How did the Revolutionary War make America free? How could a small country like America win a war against a large nation like England?

Andrew left us today. His father bought the farm he had worked so hard for. The group was sorry to lose its president and I felt all kinds of pangs at losing the curlyheaded boy. He belongs in this type of school where the kind of ability he has to offer is important.

This year I would like to acquaint the children with the County Library. After school today I took the first group to the county seat to get books for the rest. Florence, Elizabeth, Alice, and May had a fine time with the books, commenting "Albert would like this." "Here is a good picture book for the little ones." "The words in this are easy enough for Alex to read." "This book will help the big ones in studying about the Constitution."

On the way home, the sun was just beginning to set. The clouds were continually turning various colors and the mountains were red and purple in turn. We made up word pictures about them. It was such a happy time! The children were overflowing with conversation, whereas a year ago this group would have been silent.

Thomas was bursting with helpfulness today. He certainly has a tremendous ego. He thinks of everything in terms of himself these days. Now he pictures himself to be the "devil-may-care" type and won't comb his hair. It is when he is in helpful moods that I find these things out, for he hangs around and just talks, usually about himself. And yet, underneath each new pose you can see a sensitive, intelligent boy who has a nice face and a ready wit. One can't help but like him.

WEDNESDAY, OCTOBER 18. We continued the discussion of censorship from yesterday. In our *Current Events* there was a photograph of a French paper with a large black space over which was written "Censure." I asked the group if they had ever seen an American newspaper which had blank spaces such as this one. The children never had. "Does that mean that our newspapers print everything?" I asked. This brought us back to a discussion of propaganda and the difference between opinion and fact. Warren contributed much to the discussion. He told about the use of editorials and how we could find out how a paper stands on various subjects by reading the editorials and we could judge the articles accordingly.

I asked the children what newspapers they get at home and how they read them. This is what we found:

8 families get the New York *Daily News* once a week
1 family gets the New York *American* on Sunday
2 families get the New York *Times* on Sunday
2 families get the New York *Herald Tribune* on Sunday
1 family gets the Newark *Sunday Call*
All get the weekly town paper

Warren looks at the right-hand column and the headlines first. Edward also looks at the headlines. Albert looks at the "funnies" first and then at the news on the first page. Ten in the group look at the "funnies" first. Five read only the comics and nothing else unless they are looking for something for school.

Since the study seems to be taking an important direction, we chose two secretaries to take notes on our discussions. These will be kept in two separate notebooks for future use. Each day we shall select two new secretaries.

THURSDAY, OCTOBER 19. I brought seven different newspapers to school today all dated "Wednesday, October 18." We listed on the board what each paper considered the most important event and it became evident that the papers did not agree as to what was the most important, nor did they agree on the facts. Albert asked, "Why are the facts different in each paper?" The secretaries recorded the question because we could not answer it yet. The children also noted that the most important news was treated in the right-hand column.

FRIDAY, OCTOBER 20. After we had listed on the board the news each paper considered of second importance, the children made these observations. The papers differ on what they consider the most important news. What is the most important news in one paper occupies second place in another. Local news is important. War, which affects the whole world, is more important than local news. In all the papers the war news was most important but in two New York papers and in the Philadelphia papers local news occupied the place of second importance. Thomas commented, "I bet these would be the most important if there wasn't a war because people are mostly interested in the place where they live."

Richard brought three bricks from a brickyard he had visited to put into our museum. One was a wet-clay brick, the second a sun-dried one, and the third a baked one. Yesterday he brought in a small field mouse and he busied himself in all his spare time making an observation cage for it. At the end of the day he tucked cage and field mouse under his arm so that he could take it home and care for it properly over the weekend. The little children have been much interested in the museum since they have a section all their own. They spend much time studying it. The glass vial of steel filings and the magnets fascinate them. Florence and Clarence tried the magnets on everything in the room today, including their hair. Arthur spent ten minutes turning the big wheel on the spinning wheel which the big boys made last year, and watching the little wheel turn. Then he explained to me elaborately how it works, as if he had been the first to discover it.

Thomas came to me today and said, "Miss Weber, would you mind sitting in on our club meeting? We need some advice." The children were gathered around the president and secretary in an informal circle. Warren brought me a chair, asked me politely please to be seated, and then proceeded in a businesslike fashion to explain that they wanted a Halloween party and would like to have me help them with their plans. Program and refreshment committees were chosen. Helen and Martha, as chairmen of the committees, approached me when the meeting was over and asked if I would eat lunch with them on Monday to help them plan. The children love these luncheon "dates." It makes them feel so business-like and grown up.

MONDAY, OCTOBER 23. This morning on my way to school I was awed by the beauty of the earth. When I crossed the hill, I saw the little valley ablaze with light and color. The sky was heavy and dark and turbulent. The shadow of the sky fell upon the mountains in the distance and they appeared a deep blue. The light in the valley came in streams from behind me. I wanted to share this experience with the children. I described to them what I saw and suggested that we take a walk to enjoy it together. It would have been sacrilege to go on with the program I had planned when there was so much to be learned outdoors, so much that would remain perhaps only for today. As we walked, we talked of the things we saw, of the color of the mountains in the distance, of the shadows of the clouds on the mountains, of the patches of bright green where winter wheat and barley are growing, of the various blues, grays, and whites of the sky, of the color of the various kinds of trees, of the open quality of all the trees at this time of the year, of the deep color of the streams. Arthur walked beside me for a while looking intently ahead. "What are you looking at, Arthur?" I asked. "You're quite right, Miss Weber," he answered. "The mountains are blue."

When we returned, we sat for ten minutes and just talked. It was thoroughly enjoyable and refreshing. Warren wanted to paint some of the things we had seen. Since many of the children wanted to do this, we put aside the regular morning program. Helen and Martha did not paint. Instead, they put some finishing touches on sketches they had made on the walk. I have been encouraging the children to do this.

TUESDAY, OCTOBER 24. The children wrote some beautiful poetry about the things they saw yesterday. The best of these are going into our newspaper. The children do so much writing now that we can select and thus raise our standards. (See Appendix, pp. 261-264.)

The little children liked so much the hectographed copies of a song they composed that they want to create other songs and compile them into a booklet to give to their mothers for Christmas. Irene, Elizabeth, Florence, and Sally also want to make a collection of the poems they are learning and illustrate them for their mothers. During the story hour I told the little children the stories of "Discreet Hans" and "The Booby." When I finished they wanted to know what "discreet" meant. When I told them, Sally said laughingly, "The Booby was really smart and Discreet Hans wasn't discreet at all." Seven-year-old Sally had caught the implication of the words in these stories!

THURSDAY, NOVEMBER 2. The older children were glad to get back to the study of newspapers. We detoured for a few days to find out what Germany lost in the World War and why a man like Hitler would appeal to the German people. Today we looked through the papers and located the editorials. As the children dictated, I wrote on the board the topics covered by the various papers in their editorials. Then each child selected to read an editorial and also a news article on the same subject dealt with in the editorial, to compare them and to discover the difference between them.

MONDAY, NOVEMBER 6. The children had such a difficult time yesterday reading so much material in the newspaper that I decided to read to them instead. After all, my purpose is to help them to see the difference between an editorial and an article, and wading through much difficult reading material makes the children lose sight of their objective. I read an article in the New York *Times* on the proposed pact between Russia and Turkey, which had failed. I then read the editorial on this subject and the difference in the tone of the two was immediately seen.

TUESDAY, NOVEMBER 7. I read an article in the Easton *Express* about blood donors and then read the editorial on it and the children were quick to see the difference. Warren thought it would be interesting to read the Scapa Flow incident in all the papers. The contrast amused the children. The type in the New York *Times* was modest and the article was in the center of the page. It was careful to state sources as "The Admiralty said . . ." or "The German paper said . . ." The New York *News* considered this the most important incident on this date and used huge type on the front page. The third page carried the story, which used sources as "An eye-witness said . . ." or "It was believed . . ." The language was dramatic and it told about the attack in such a way that the children said you would think all of Scotland was fighting or hurrying to shelters. The *Times* used one sentence to mention air-raid alarms and dealt mostly with Chamberlain's report to Parliament.

WEDNESDAY, NOVEMBER 8. I read about the Scapa Flow incident in other papers today and again the contrast was strong. The children are beginning to distinguish between fact and opinion. The New York *Journal-American* did not have an article about the Scapa Flow incident but it did have an editorial. The editorial began with the incident, commented on the weaknesses of the British Navy, and blamed the whole thing on Roosevelt. Thomas could not see the connection and said, "He doesn't like Roosevelt, does he? It sounds as though he is using the Scapa Flow incident to get in an extra dig." Then we considered what a good paper tries to do in its articles. It tries to give facts which are accurate and which give true impressions. It quotes authentic sources and appeals to the intellect rather than to emotions.

FRIDAY, NOVEMBER 10. It is so satisfying to watch a group of children taking care of themselves. The children seem to teach themselves through the experiences they have every day. They are becoming more curious about the things they see and hear around them. Martha is probably the most curious and the most active. She finishes her daily work quickly, does considerable extra research or experimenting, creates poetry prolifically and then has time to spend for a story hour with the little folks. There are times when she gets silly and annoying. We usually ignore her until she gets over it. She is gradually finding that she gets more attention when she is cooperative and contributing.

Alice and Pearl have some artistic ability. Both girls are developing along these lines in a way I did not think possible. You never know what abilities are latent within a child until you have made possible all kinds of opportunities to uncover and develop them. There is something fine in all these Prinlaks that is worth cultivating. Stanley is a little shy when he arrives in the morning but he never fails to smile at me and say " 'lo." As the day goes on he loosens up more and more and takes an active and enjoyable part in everything. Elizabeth is a good friend of Florence's. Florence says, "I like Elizabeth, she is so good."

Walter Damrosch is on the air again and we listened to his program today. Martha was happy because she recognized at once the Beethoven selection as the one we sang last year. Many children have heard over the radio songs we sing in school.

MONDAY, NOVEMBER 13. We continued the newspaper study by reading the date lines to see how the news is gathered. They learned about the AP, UP, and INS news organizations set up so that even smaller papers, which could not afford to have correspondents in Europe, could get foreign news. The New York *Times* and *Herald Tribune* had many articles headed "by special telephone" or "by special cable." The children could see that it was only the larger papers that could do this.

We summarized today all we have learned about the difference between an article and an editorial. A good article is accurate, reliable as to source, gives all sides, and is not sensational. A good editorial expresses the views of the editor, uses facts accurately and is not petty. The children are ready to write some news articles and editorials for their own paper. Every day the children get more and more dissatisfied with the way they have set up their school paper in the past.

After the reading lesson, I told the group the Russian Christmas tale Mrs. Ramsey had arranged for us. The children like it and are eager to begin work developing the dramatization.

Lloyd asked to have his seat changed. He said that he and Warren are such good friends that the temptation to carry on social conversation is too great. He knew that if he could change his place it would strengthen his will power and improve his work. After the group had a good sympathetic laugh, we moved a few seats around and Lloyd settled down to business.

TUESDAY, NOVEMBER 14. The dramatization period proved to be interesting. All the children take part eagerly and confidently except the two new boys, Lloyd and Daniel. They are as silly as the other children were when we began dramatizing three years ago. Daniel did take a part finally and managed to contribute a few lines although he did it with a red face. The other children sympathetically did everything they could to make him feel at ease. They turned their questions to him to give him a cue and they directed him with their statements.

FRIDAY, NOVEMBER 17. We are continuing with our study of current events along with the study of newspapers. Martha gave a report on Wilson's Fourteen Points and was firmly convinced that if they had been carried out, we might not be having a war today. She backed her statements.

Walter Damrosch discussed canon and fugue today. The children had an enjoyable time picking out the fugue theme every time it occurred.

MONDAY, NOVEMBER 20. All the children in the upper group went together to see the movie *Mr. Smith Goes to Washington*. They enjoyed it thoroughly. We could hardly get Martha to come away.

TUESDAY, NOVEMBER 21. We discussed the film we saw last night and reviewed how a bill becomes a law, how bills are introduced, filibuster, parliamentary procedure, free speech, and control of newspapers by powerful men. Newspapers and censorship took on a new meaning for these children.

WEDNESDAY, NOVEMBER 22. For some time the little ones have been planning some sort of surprise for me. They have managed to keep it a secret. Today I was invited to sit in on their story period. Florence announced, "Miss Weber, our surprise is a play called *Rickety Rackety Rooster*. We are doing this because we love story hour so much." Then followed a unique dramatization that almost put me in tears, it made me so happy. I wish I could express in words the feeling they put into their little dramatization. Martha, who had directed it, sat next to me as we watched. She whispered, "You mustn't mind a few mistakes, Miss Weber. They are a little shy and nervous." All this was enough to give me a truly happy Thanksgiving.

MONDAY, NOVEMBER 27. The children have begun to think about reorganizing their own newspaper. Today we studied the commercial newspapers to list all the sections into which a paper is divided. We crossed off those we could not possibly have in our own newspaper, such as the financial page. We studied the commercial papers again and saw how fitting the names were. The children noticed that some papers had two names. Warren found a corner in the editorial page which said that the *Herald Tribune* was at one time two papers. The date of the merger was given. I asked the children why this was a good thing from the point of view of the two papers. The children gave reasons easily, that it would increase the circulation, that increased funds would pay for correspondents abroad and for better equipment.

When I entered the room after the club meeting today I was greeted on all sides by "This was the best club meeting we ever had." Warren told me afterwards that they learned a great deal from *Mr. Smith Goes to Washington*.

TUESDAY, NOVEMBER 28. What a busy day this was! We listed the departments we would need for our newspaper and elected an editor for each department. The children felt that to be truly democratic, the little folks should be represented on the staff and should elect their own editor for the children's department. Florence was elected editor of the Children's Page. Then the articles were given to reporters to write. As the writers finish their articles they are to give them to the proper editor, who accepts or rejects them and makes suggestions for improvement. When the morning physical education period came, the children wanted to be allowed to use the time to finish writing the articles as they were right in the middle of them and did not want to lose their train of thought. They had their play time at eleven, however, for they had been sitting still for a long period.

WEDNESDAY, NOVEMBER 29. The Christmas spirit is in the air and the children work feverishly to get many things done. The play is progressing. Christmas gift making turns part of the day into a workshop. The editors of the various departments squeeze in some time to correct news articles as well as to goad some slow reporters into writing them. The boys brought in some material for making Christmas wreaths and placed hemlock boughs around the room. The little children are finishing up poem and story booklets, music booklets of their original songs, and booklets about the study of the way nature gets ready for winter, as Christmas gifts to their parents. And with it all, there is always some time left to do the daily stint of reading, spelling, and arithmetic.

MONDAY, DECEMBER 4. We had some visitors from the Hawaiian Islands and the Philippines and again the children demonstrated how much factual material they have acquired just by following up the experiences they have in their daily living. The visitors were surprised that the children knew the name of the Philippine president and that they were aware of some of the islands' problems. The children asked the visitors if the Philippine people really wanted to be independent of the United States. The children also asked about the schools in the Philippines and the kind of country it is. The visitors sang native songs and talked in their native tongue. In turn, we sang American folk songs and did some American folk dances.

WEDNESDAY, DECEMBER 6. The newspaper staff met after school to put the paper together. We cut large sheets of brown paper, each representing a page in the paper. They began to think about the layout first. The staff decided on three columns, as less would not make it a newspaper and we have no room for more than three. They changed the name of the paper and chose to have a town crier as the symbol and "Hears All—Tells All" as the slogan. They decided that, since the newspaper study is the most important thing we are doing, the article concerning it should occupy the right-hand column and should have the largest headlines. They began to pin the articles on the brown paper where they thought they should go. At five o'clock we were still busy and the group did not want to go home.

THURSDAY, DECEMBER 7. This morning I decided that the rest of the children should have the experience this group had, since it was so enjoyable and valuable. While the rest of the group helped with the layout, those who met last night began to proofread and to rewrite articles. The children worked with a diligence that was satisfying to watch. Lloyd is a fine editor and insists on good quality in the articles. His pencil is busy putting question marks next to sentences that are not clear and in cutting out irrelevancies.

WEDNESDAY, DECEMBER 13. The first issue of the newspaper is out. (See Appendix, pp. 254-255.) We spent an hour reading it together and we know it is the finest piece of work we have produced. Albert said, "Boy, we're good." They want to give everyone they know a copy of the paper. They have a right to be proud! Thomas made an important comment today which gave me a lead as to the next steps. He said, "It has taken us a whole month of hard work to put out a twelve page paper. How can big newspapers get so much work done every day?" I suggested to the children that we might visit a newspaper plant after Christmas.

TUESDAY, DECEMBER 26. The last two weeks have been so busy that there was no time to write in a diary. I do want to record a few impressions of this period, however. The dramatization was quite successful, although for a while I was afraid it wouldn't be. Lloyd, who finally had an important part, got silly and did considerable talking and fooling behind the scenes. Before the entertainment he kept saying, "Oh, Miss Weber, I'm so nervous. Do you think I look all right? Do you think I'll do all right?" No one was important to the play but himself.

The group met the next day to clean up and to restore the room to its original working form. While we worked, the children discussed the play. They resented Lloyd's attitude and told him so. William was reprimanded for being so easily led by Lloyd. Henry and Daniel were commended for their fine work. The children were not at all satisfied with the dramatization and felt that it did not equal those of other years. Their main criticisms were that the group did not speak clearly enough nor did they put enough feeling into the conversation.

The audience enjoyed the dramatization and commended the children highly. From the conversation during the cleanup, I knew that the children were not flattered by these praises. Their standards are high and they diagnosed correctly what was wrong with their play.

The girls who have gone on to high school asked to continue their music at Stony Grove. We have been meeting every week since October. On the night of the Christmas entertainment the girls had an opportunity to sing. They sang "Lo, How a Rose," a sixteenth century melody harmonized by Michael Praetorius; "The Holly and the Ivy," an English carol; and "Silent Night," a German carol. All of them were sung in three parts. The girls had lovely tone and nice expression.

The children wrote much poetry this month and all of it was about things the children had experienced. The children loved the snow and delighted in getting covered with it from head to foot. Their observations were keen as their snow poems show. (See Appendix, pp. 264-265.)

SUMMER, 1940.   Complete diary notes were not kept for the rest of the year, but several things occurred which are worth recording. Most important of all was a study which grew out of interest in the newspaper.

During December I read *Jim of the Press* to the children. Although this book is written on the high school level, these children learned much from it because of the background of understanding about newspapers they brought to it. Armed with knowledge which they received through their study of the newspapers and with the insight which *Jim of the Press* gave them, they visited the Easton *Express* building on January 6. The children saw the composing room, the linotype battery and the whole process of making and printing a newspaper. They were so interested and asked so many questions that it brought forth a comment from our guide: "They haven't missed a thing, have they?"

On the way home the conversation was fluent. The children marveled at the speed at which everything was done. The linotype machine fascinated them most. How different this was from setting each tiny letter by hand. Mr. Matthews, who helped to transport us, told the children that when he was in China he had a small paper and had to set each article by hand, letter by letter. It was hard on the eyes, muscles, and nerves. Lloyd said that the man who invented the linotype must have been a very smart man. "Who invented the linotype and how did he get the idea?" he asked. Warren asked, "How long ago was printing invented? I saw pictures of old presses. They aren't anything like the ones we saw today." Albert was much interested in the way pictures were printed. He had examined carefully the tiny raised dots. "How did they make the dot?" he wanted to know. On the way home we stopped at the County Library and collected all the books we could find on printing and ordered others from the State Library Commission.

On the next school day we talked more about the visit we had made. We discussed for a while the tremendous influence of newspapers. Albert stated that we had the radio, telephone, telegraph, and other means of communication. Thomas pointed out that there were certain values in a paper not afforded by these others. You can pick up a newspaper whenever you want and read it over any number of times to get the facts in mind. It was at this point that the group thought it would be a good idea to have a paper come to school each morning for the rest of the school year. I was authorized to use some of the money from the treasury to order one. The children were much interested in the paper all year and spent much of their spare time singly and in groups reading it. A few would always gather around to skim through it as soon as the paper arrived in the morning. Its contents became the topic of conversation for many noon hours. Pearl, especially, got much joy from it.

When the children began to read about printing in the books we had brought back from the library, they became so interested in what they were finding that they began to read aloud to each other. "Whew, listen to this," one would say, and the others would stop to listen as he read. One book said that John Gutenberg invented printing. Another said that it was not John Gutenberg at all but the Chinese who did. They did manage to take some notes for future discussions. Lloyd had never taken notes on this kind of reading before, so I took a little time to teach him how to go about it.

In the discussion that followed, the children agreed that we needed to find out more about the following topics:

> Gutenberg
> Invention of movable type
> Printing before Gutenberg
> Invention of the printing press
> Improvements made in the printing press
> Spread of printing through Europe and to America
> The linotype
> Coster, Fust, and Caxton
> Printing of pictures

Each child selected the topic in which he was most interested and began to do the research for it. Warren went to the town newspaper office to find out more about the linotype. Since this paper comes out only once a week, the newspapermen were not busy and had time to give to him. Warren had read in Compton's Encyclopedia how the linotype operates, and was able to explain it to the men. They were so impressed by what he knew that they allowed Warren to work the linotype and to make a slug of his name and address. Warren exhibited it proudly to the group and said he would put it into our museum for a few days.

After two days of reading, we discussed how printing was invented. Through the discussion we found that it really was the Chinese who first invented movable type but that, since they did not have an alphabet, it was impracticable. It was difficult to keep 40,000 characters in some sort of order. Edward asked, "Why don't they adopt an alphabet? How did they come to have the system which they use?" Daniel wanted to know how we got our alphabet. The children read that John Gutenberg got his idea for printing by movable type from playing cards that came from China. "How did the Europeans get the cards from China?" they wanted to know. Martha read that it was the invention of papermaking which made printing practicable. Henry wanted to know what they used before they had paper. How is paper made? Henry is also much interested in Marco Polo, so much so that he continually has part of the group reading over his shoulder as he points things out to them. He found that it was Marco Polo who created interest in the East and made it possible for Gutenberg to be playing with Chinese cards. We listed these topics we wanted to know more about:

> Invention of the alphabet
> Invention of paper making
> Writing materials before paper
> Marco Polo
> The Crusades
> China in the time of Marco Polo
> Europe at the time of Gutenberg

There were now enough topics to go around and each child selected one. Then began a series of research periods, reports, discussions, and more research. They made contributions and asked questions which sent the reporters back to their books again. As the reports were made, the topics were broken down into more detail. For instance, "Europe at the time of Gutenberg" got to be too big a topic and was divided into:

> Monks and monasteries
> Castle life and warfare
> Towns and guilds

"Invention of the Alphabet" gave rise to:

> The Incas and their writing
> The writing of the American Indians
> Legends and the *Song of Roland*
> Egyptians
> Phoenicians
> Greeks
> Romans

As we read and reported, our notes became more and more voluminous. The children had notes on their own research and some had notes on the reports of others. What to do with all this material became a problem. It was too valuable to discard and yet in its disorganized form it was not worth much. Thomas said in jest, "We ought to make a book, we have enough material for one." I surprised him by saying, "Why not?" The more we thought about it, the more it seemed a sensible thing to do. It was then that we really went to work, being careful to keep our notes accurate and full. As the children read and came across material suitable to a topic someone else was working on, a bibliography card was made for the reference and given to the person working on that topic. As the children were ready to report, they signed up for certain days. The group would listen, giving suggestions and criticisms.

Thomas reported one day on the Crusades. He had a difficult time of it, for he was trying to use the words of the book as he read from his notes. "Say it in your own words, Thomas," I suggested. "Forget your notes." Then followed an exciting tale of the Crusades with all the gory details. He barely mentioned the Children's Crusade, and Helen suggested that he get his material for this from *Boy of the Lost Crusade*.

When Albert gave his report on the monks, Martha said to him, "Have you read *Gabriel and the Hour Book*? That is a beautiful book. Miss Weber, you ought to read it to us."

Some of the reports were unusually well prepared. Lloyd gave a report on the evolution of the book. He had on the desk before him small reproductions which he had made of the steps in arriving at our present book form. As he talked, he demonstrated. He showed that the oldest book form was a parchment scroll which stretched often sixteen or seventeen feet in length. Lines were written across the scroll and the scroll unrolled from top downward. In the Buddhist scrolls, the writing ran the entire length of the scroll which was unrolled sidewise. This was no inconvenience though, as it was not actually read. The Hebrew scrolls of law had the lines written in columns so that the page form could be easily seen. The page form of this scroll gave someone the idea of folding it like an accordion and putting it between blocks of wood. This made it much easier to store the books. Lloyd picked up each of his scrolls in turn and demonstrated exactly what he meant. He folded the Hebrew scroll before the group. Then he picked up a pair of scissors and cut the pages of the folded scroll to show how the next step came. Now it was possible to write on both sides of the leaf and our modern book form came into existence. He put his illustrations into the museum.

The research was hard for Edward and George and they were not much interested until we began to experiment with making paper. These boys made a deckle and mold for us following the directions in Bonser and Mossman, *Industrial Arts in the Elementary School*. We made some rag paper, following directions given in this book also. This paper was successful. Our experiment in making parchment was not so successful, however, as we did not stretch the lambskin properly. We also wanted to make paper from papyrus and ordered some from the Industrial Arts Cooperative Service. They get papyrus from Florida and as this year was an unusually cold year in Florida, all three crops were frozen.

The children continually added to the museum. They added wood pulp, a piece of commercial parchment, homemade parchment, homemade rag paper, cardboard type molds which we got from the Easton *Express*, engraved copper plates, colonial wax tablets, replicas of Babylonian clay tablets, a plaster replica of the Hebrew Code of Laws, and a newspaper photograph of the group, taken while we were at the Easton *Express* and published in the paper the following Monday. We added to the library also and the shelves became so crowded that they were inconvenient. The boys met one weekend and added shelves the whole length of one side of the room under the windows. The books and museum pieces were spread out. It added much to the attractiveness of the room as well as to the efficiency. Warren exclaimed, "Our room doesn't look like a school any more." (See Appendix, p. 260.)

The children visited the County Library in groups for books. They have learned to love books and care for them affectionately. Although we used several hundred books this year, the children did not lose or deface a single one.

When all the material was gathered, the group became an Editorial Board. We listed on the board all the topics about which we had found information. We studied the list to discover the organization best suited to it and grouped the topics in this way:

About Newspapers:
    Printing a newspaper
    The linotype
    Printing pictures
    Printing presses

About the Invention of Printing:
    Invention of movable type
    Life of Gutenberg
    Printing before Gutenberg
    The Crusades
    Marco Polo
    Life in the Middle Ages
    Castle life
    Towns
    Monks and monasteries

About the Alphabet:
    Invention of the alphabet
    Incas
    Writing of the American Indians
    The *Song of Roland*
    Cave writing
    Egyptian hieroglyphics
    Phoenicians spread the alphabet
    Romans spread the alphabet

About Writing Materials:
    Egyptian inscriptions
    Skins used by the shepherds

Clay tablets of Babylonians
Chinese rag paper
Evolution of the book form
Papyrus scrolls

About Early Civilizations:
Egyptians
Greeks
Romans
Babylonians
Rosetta stone
Sumerians
Assyrians
Chaldeans
Phoenicians

About Modern Writing Materials:
Pens
Pencils
Paper
Bookmaking

There were fifteen children in the upper group. (The Cartwrights had moved away after Christmas.) I selected five of the most capable children to serve on the first editorial committee: Warren, Helen, Martha, Lloyd, and Thomas. The rest of the children were divided up among the other five committees. On the first day, I met with the first committee and helped them to learn how to edit material. We followed this procedure:

1. Read all the material to be familiar with the contents.
2. Organize the material and divide into chapters.
3. Compose topic paragraphs to tie the chapters together so that it will make a running story rather than isolated topics.
4. Make any changes necessary in the body of the chapters to bring out the point of view indicated in the topic paragraphs.
5. Go through the whole, correcting English and spelling errors.

I left the group to do the work by themselves. When they were ready, Martha reported to the group. She outlined how they went about their work and then read the topic paragraphs for criticisms.

This committee had divided the material into four chapters in this order:

> Printing a Newspaper
> The Linotype
> Printing Presses
> Printing Pictures

They began the first chapter with:

> The newspaper is one of the quickest ways of informing us of recent happenings. How a newspaper does this is a fascinating story.

To tie the first chapter with the second, they wrote:

> If it were not for the linotype, the printing of newspapers would be a much slower process. Due to the brilliant and ingenious mind of Ottmar Mergenthaler, who invented the complicated linotype machine, we are able to keep informed of events almost as soon as they occur.

At first Martha said "genius mind." Lloyd said they had argued about this in committee. He thought it should be "ingenious." I asked the group what they thought; as no one knew, I suggested that they look in the dictionary. They could not tell even then, until I suggested that they look at the letter in italics. Henry found "n" after "genius" and "adj." after "ingenious." "I know," he said, "it should be ingenious, because it is an adjective we want."

They began their third chapter with:

> Printing presses were not always the efficient machines they are today. The earliest presses were very simple and crude.

The fourth chapter began:

> Pictures make up an important part of newspapers. They are prepared for printing in a very interesting way.

Each member of this committee then became the chairman of one of the other committees to guide them in their editing. As each committee was ready, the members reported to the group for suggestions and criticisms. They considered the suggestions and made further corrections. No one ran out of work, for even after the organizing was done, there was much correcting of English and spelling to be done and some rewriting. The children worked over the stories again and again. Each story went through the hands of practically every member of the group. Many of our chief difficulties were brought up and discussed during English periods. The result was a piece of work of remarkable accuracy and beauty of expression. It took several months of hard work to achieve this but it has been extremely worth while.

Group II put their material into six chapters.

The Invention of Movable Type
Printing Before Gutenberg
The Crusades and Printing
Marco Polo
The Spread of Printing
Books in the Middle Ages

These were the topic paragraphs they composed:

Chapter 5. Reproducing by means of engraved blocks was a slow and difficult process. It wasn't until the invention of movable type that printed material became available to more than a few people. We credit the discovery of printing with movable type to John Gutenberg.

This topic ties up this section with the preceding section and then goes on to tell of the life of Gutenberg and how he invented movable type.

Chapter 6. As we have said, the Chinese before the time of Gutenberg had already invented a kind of printing.

Chapter 7. The invention of movable type and printing might have come at a much later date if it had not been for the Crusades. The Crusades opened up a new world to Europe.

They ended the chapter by saying:

Some of the Crusaders brought back playing cards such as the ones from which Gutenberg got his idea to invent movable type. It was due to the invention of printing that enough books could be made about the travels of Marco Polo and others to start men on the idea of sailing dangerous and unknown seas to find a new route to the East.

And they began the next chapter like this:

Marco Polo should be mentioned as well as the Crusades for the interest he aroused in the East and because this interest led to the discovery of many things.

The last paragraph in this chapter explains the first:

When Constantinople was captured by the Turks and there was much trouble in the East, people could no longer go safely by the old routes to get these luxuries. It was then that Columbus tried to find a route to the East by sailing West. The Crusades and Marco Polo not only opened up the way for printing in Europe but for a new civilization as well.

Chapter 9. Printing spread rapidly over the countries of Europe after the invention of movable type.

This chapter goes on to tell how books came to be printed all over Europe and ends with this paragraph:

When books came to be printed in the languages of the various countries, people became interested in reading and in getting an education. This was responsible for many changes in the world. The fact that some people could read had a great deal to do with the spread of the Protestant religion.

Chapter 10. Before books were printed there was little interest in learning. During this time there was one group of people who kept learning alive by copying by hand the scrolls of the ancient world. They were the monks.

This chapter describes the living of the monks and contrasts this with the living in the outside world, in the castles, and in the towns, and ends by saying:

It was into this kind of world that John Gutenberg was born and it was this kind of a world which produced printing.

The other committees treated their material in the same way. Five other chapters were added to the book:

Inventing the Alphabet
Writing Materials
Early Civilizations
Modern Writing Materials
Bookmaking

As we gathered information, we delved into ancient backgrounds whenever we needed to and then came up to the present again. In order to help develop a sense of time, we used the device of the time line. At the end of the study we decided to include this chronology in the book. We also listed a bibliography.

The children made the following illustrations for the book:

> Old Wooden Press
> Punch and Matrix
> A Crusader
> An Illuminated Manuscript Page
> Various Ways of Keeping Records in Former Times
> > Peruvian Quipu
> > Notched Stick
> > Birch Bark
> > Wampum
> Egyptian Hieroglyphics
> Chinese Characters
> How We Got Our ABCs
> Writing Materials
> > Egyptian Papyrus Roll
> > Babylonian Cuneiform
> > Greek Wax Tablet
> How Our Book Form Came to Be
> How a Modern Book Is Made

Since we worked right up to the last day editing the book, it was necessary for the children to return to school for a few days in the early summer. At this time the children folded and marked paper for the pages and traced the illustrations. I typed the entire book. The children sewed the signatures and we all had a hand in binding the book in bookbinding board and vellum. Helen cut a linoleum block, showing a scroll, for the end papers. It became a beautiful book, and very valuable to us. A friend of mine offered to reproduce copies of the book exactly as we made it. The book was photographed page by page. There were enough books reproduced so that each child could have one for his own. We presented the County Library and some of our friends with others.

We had one other interesting experience in this study. On

May 25, we visited the Metropolitan Museum of Art in New York City. Warren had carried on a correspondence with the museum and had acquired a guide for us. Mr. Grier took the children on a tour to see some of the authentic works of the writing of the early civilizations. He taught the children to read some of the symbols in the Egyptian hieroglyphics. He showed them examples of Egyptian, Cretan, Greek, and Roman writing and writing materials. The children saw Babylonian clay tablets, Greek wax tablets, and Egyptian papyrus scrolls. The illuminated manuscripts fascinated them most. Mr. Grier brought the parchment manuscript from the museum library and turned the pages while the group gazed in wonder and admiration.

The children also saw mummies, mummy cases, ancient Egyptian jewelry, and implements of work and war. They saw pyramids, Roman houses, and a monastery. They saw feudal armor. There was even time for a half-hour movie which showed how the museum explorers find and strip Egyptian tombs and how a mummy is unwrapped. Many things were cleared up for the children which they did not quite understand through their study.

As I look back over this study I feel that I have accomplished my purpose. The children have done thinking that is important in developing understandings and ideals. This thinking has been continually tied up with immediate experiences or the ideas would have been barren and meaningless to the children. The children have a better understanding of their place in the world.

The rest of the school year was as rich as this part. This study could not have been so fruitful or meaningful if it had not taken place in an environment in which children are constantly having rich experiences and are continually being helped to understand and solve the problems which arise in their daily living.

Two other incidents should be recorded, both of which are testimonies to the fact that, whenever there is equality of opportunity in education, the gifted children not only do not suffer and become mediocre but are able to develop their capacities to the maximum.

One day this spring I gave a standard achievement test to the older children. Since it took all day to give it, I had the problem of finding something for the little children to do in the meantime. Martha offered to take care of them. The night before the testing, Martha took books home and made out some lesson plans which she showed me the next morning. They were as carefully thought out as my own plans, even to the extent of stating the purpose of each lesson. Martha helped the little children with the gardening around their little house. They took a walk and Martha helped them to write a story about the things they saw. They continued with their reading and with spontaneous dramatization during the story hour. Martha helped them wash up for lunch and then supervised the noon period. The children played games, sang, painted, and modeled in clay. Before they went home, Martha helped them with spelling and numbers. When a child of twelve can be with a group of little children for a whole day and keep the group happy and busy with worth-while tasks, she is being educated in the fullest sense of the word.

The second story also concerns Martha. We had a puppet show as usual this spring. There were three performances at the schoolhouse, and we were invited to take the show to the town high school and to Blair Academy. The primary children gave the story of *Little Black Sambo*. It was entirely produced by Martha. She helped the little children make the puppets and creatively to work out the dramatization. Martha helped the little children to select the ones who would finally take the parts. Eric was Little Black Sambo. Martha was able to bring out of that shy little boy latent abilities which I had not been able to reach. Martha also taught each child what his responsibilities were so that on the evenings of the entertainment she was able to sit on the audience side of the curtain to watch the results of her efforts. When it was over, Martha caught my eye and we two teachers knew we had done our work well.

POSTLUDE

At the end of this fourth year, I left Stony Grove. If I have been successful in making these children real to you, you are asking, "What has happened to them? What are they doing now?" The answers to these questions are so important that the purpose of this book would not be fulfilled without them.

Anna Olseuski and Olga Prinlak were the first to leave our school. Anna went to the town high school, graduated with honors, and left our community to do secretarial work in a large city.

Olga was not allowed to go to high school as Mr. Prinlak, at that time, did not believe in an education, especially for girls. Olga went to New York to do housework. With her first savings she had her teeth attended to. Since then she has sent money home regularly to help clothe the younger children. She has done much to persuade her parents that the younger girls should go on to high school.

Frank Prinlak, Ralph Jones, and Catherine Sametis left Stony Grove in June, 1938.

For some time Frank was employed on a large fruit farm. One day, on my rounds about the county, I stopped to have lunch at a diner. The waitress was saying to a man at the counter, "I'll bet you're sorry to lose Frank." "Sorry!" exclaimed the man. "Why, he's the best worker I ever had. You can bet if it were anybody else than Uncle Sam, he wouldn't get him!" They were talking about Frank Prinlak. Frank is now in the navy.

Ralph is in the ground force of the air arm of the navy. For a while after he left high school he was employed in a garage and later in war work. Ralph did not do well in high school. His only interest was in mechanics. He is now doing the kind of work he likes, as his last cheerful letter shows.

One evening this spring I was invited by Catherine and Sophia to have dinner with them. The house was clean and in order, quite a contrast to the way it looked eight years ago when I first stepped into it. The girls had prepared the dinner. There was roast chicken; mashed potatoes; snap beans; an apple, turnip, celery and lettuce salad; vanilla pudding; coffee for Mrs. Sametis and myself and milk for the others. The salad recipe was one Catherine had learned from one of Miss Moran's demonstrations. As I watched Catherine cut the apples, leaving the red skin on, and deftly toss the salad with a spoon and fork, I realized that this was not merely a company procedure, but that Catherine had had plenty of practice.

Both girls were wearing dresses they had made. Sophia showed me her new spring clothes, which she had carefully planned and purchased. Catherine showed me the lovely cretonne the girls had bought to make a cover for the living-room davenport.

The main talk of the evening centered around the problem of whether it would be advisable for the girls to go into war work or to go to New York to start on the secretarial career for which they were prepared. Since Catherine graduated from high school she has been secretary and assistant to a doctor in a near-by city. Sophia graduated from high school last spring. After considering all sides of the question, the girls made the decision to go to New York this fall. They will live with their aunt and uncle until they find what they want to do.

Later that evening Mrs. Sametis said to me, "Do you know, I never thought I'd be proud of my children, but I am."

In the fall of 1939, Sophia Sametis, Doris Andrews, Mary Olseuski, and Ruth Thompson went to high school. At the end of that school year, the high school awarded certificates of merit for scholarship and good citizenship to three students from each of the undergraduate classes. Anna was one of the three juniors. The three freshmen who received the certificates were Ruth, Sophia, and Mary. Stony Grove pupils make up about 4 per cent of the total high school enrollment, and yet almost 50 per cent of the students receiving the awards were former pupils of Stony Grove.

Doris and May left the community that year and I have lost track of them.

Mary has a secretarial position in the city.

Ruth graduated from high school last spring and is now married to a fine young aviator. She is eagerly looking forward to making the home she has dreamed about. Ruth will undoubtedly make a good wife and mother. She has an unusual amount of good, practical common sense.

Thomas Lenick, Edward Veniski, George Prinlak, and Warren Hill left Stony Grove in the spring of 1940. We allowed Helen Olseuski to go on to high school also, for she was maturing rapidly and needed the challenge of association with her peers.

In two months' time, Warren had made enough of an impression upon the more sophisticated town children to be elected president of the freshman class. The following year, Helen was elected president of the sophomore class. When Helen and Warren were juniors, they revived their interest in puppets and, with their art teacher, taught their classmates how to put on a show. Helen was valedictorian when she graduated this spring.

George did not go to high school. He spent some time in the Civilian Conservation Corps and left it with a fine record. He is now in the navy.

Edward went to high school until he was sixteen, and since the high school had nothing for him, he left it to work on the farm. To be sure, he took the right course for him, vocational agriculture, and while he was in the agriculture laboratory he was happy, but a vocational course is not the whole answer, by any means, for these slow-moving children.

If the high school had been willing to start where Edward was, it could have taught him much more. On each level of increasing maturity, Edward could have learned more about getting the full meaning from printed matter, from the newspapers, magazines, books, farm publications, etc. He could have learned to express himself more adequately. He could have been helped to make his maximum contribution to his new, enlarged society. In other words, Edward could have continued to grow along all the lines described in this story.

Education should be thought of as growth, and this growth an ever-present process for as long as life lasts. It stopped being that in high school for Edward, and for how many other children in the country! Instead, these children sit, patiently waiting for the day when the law allows them to "quit." What a waste for our democracy of human resources!

Thomas went to high school with high hopes. He was going to make something of himself. He was going to show his stepmother that he did have good "stuff" in him. Thomas lasted six months. He came to me one day and said, "I've quit, Miss Weber. I get into trouble with all my teachers because I can't learn what's in the books. I'm just wasting my time there." I talked with Thomas for a long time to renew his faith in himself, to try to prove to him that he wasn't entirely at fault because he found no meaning in high school. Thomas got a job in a photographer's laboratory in a small factory. He soon earned enough money to buy a secondhand car in good condition. From then on he visited me frequently. His well-groomed appearance and confident manner assured me that all was well with Thomas. One day he told me how much he had saved, and when I asked him what he was saving for, he said, "Well, someday I want to get married, and you know that takes a great deal of money."

Thomas read the papers regularly and we used to have lengthy discussions on the government and the state of affairs in the world. His opinions were based on facts and were without blind emotion. Thomas is now in the navy. He is one member of the armed forces who really knows what we are fighting for!

Andrew Dulio and the Cartwrights left Stony Grove during the winter of 1939-1940, and Lloyd Matthews left at the end of the same year. The Cartwrights left the neighborhood and I lost contact with them.

After Andrew moved, he finished out the year at his new school and then went to work on his father's farm. One day, some time ago, when Andrew was still at Stony Grove and I was visiting at his home, he took me out to show me his father's animals. It was then that he said he would rather be a farmer than anything else in the world. He had his arms around the neck of a cow and was rubbing his cheek against hers. His face lighted up as he remarked, "She's such a nice cow, Miss Weber."

Lloyd left because his parents bought a farm in another state. Mrs. Matthews told me that spending a year in our neighborhood was one of the best things that ever happened to Lloyd. From a self-centered boy who almost spoiled our Christmas play, he matured considerably and became an efficient president and one of the most capable editors our school paper ever had.

In September, 1942, Pearl Prinlak, Albert Hill, and Daniel Cole entered high school. Pearl is taking the Commercial Course, while Albert and Daniel are taking Vocational Agriculture. Daniel is doing unusually well and shows promise of becoming a fine farmer.

Martha, also, was a freshman in high school that year. Four years ago, after all the Joneses but Ralph and Martha were married, their grandmother decided that she would retire and take her much-deserved and long-overdue rest. Mr. Jones and Ralph moved to town, and Martha went to live with one of her married sisters.

Martha entered the seventh grade of the town school and the next two years were unhappy ones for her. She found herself in an undisciplined class with a weak teacher. She resented the whole situation and became one of the leaders in continually devising new pranks. When I talked with her and suggested that she join the local 4-H Club and the Girl Scouts, she said, "They don't do anything. They're so silly." When I reminded her that she wasn't doing anything to help change the situation, she echoed Ralph's attitude of a few years before, "What's the use!" Martha was beginning to go through the adjustments of adolescence and there was no one to help her. I could not be close enough to the situation to make a real difference.

Now that Martha is in high school, things are no better. She is not doing the work of which she is capable and is wasting her many fine talents. What an opportunity the high school is missing!

What about Stony Grove in the four years since I left it?

In spite of the fact that the salary was meager, that the boarding place was unattractive to a girl raised with modern conveniences, and that the neighborhood lacked urban recreational facilities, a young girl with fine recommendations took the position. It was to be her first year of teaching. What she lacked in the way of maturity we thought would be made up by her other qualifications. She knew music, art, and literature. She had been an excellent student and had been elected to Kappa Delta Pi in her junior year.

Since we were aware of the difficulties of the situation, we gave the young teacher a great deal of help. When I told the children I had taken a position as a helping teacher, I also explained to them that it would be fine for them to have a new teacher, that a new teacher would bring new ideas into the community just as our new pupils and new families always did. In fact, I did such a good job and the children began to look forward to the new teacher with such eagerness that, I must confess, I felt somewhat lonesome those last few days. There were none of the usual fond farewells, which of course, was the way it should have been. It wasn't until a week after I had left that the children remembered to give me a parting gift and a party.

For three days the new teacher watched me work with the children, and she helped where she was able. During this time I acquainted her with the school and the records of the children, and we made the plans for the first week.

For that first week, while the teacher allowed the children to share in the directing of their activities the program of the school continued normally and the teacher learned much from the children. On the following Saturday, however, in spite of all the advice she had received, the teacher worked at the schoolhouse rearranging furniture and changing the charts on the bulletin boards.

When the children arrived on Monday morning, they rebelled. In the first place, as an outsider, before she had been completely accepted by the group, the teacher had taken the liberty of making changes in matters that concerned the group, without regard for the children who, in the past, had always shared in making decisions which concerned them. The children resented this. But their resentment might have passed if the changes had been good ones. The children had learned how to make the best use of light as they worked at the various kinds of activities, in order to prevent eyestrain. Now they found all the desks facing the windows. They had learned that the bulletin board has a more valuable use than that of a display space for pictures. They had used the bulletin board for notices, for charts regarding housekeeping duties, and for other charts of this kind to which they had to refer frequently. Now the children found their charts high above the teacher's desk out of their reach, and on the bulletin board were pictures of animal pets which could have been easily seen if they had been placed in any other part of the small room. No doubt, the teacher had been taught, as I had, that a good way to start a unit of study was to put some attractive picture on the bulletin board, but what had she learned about children sharing in the learning process? What had she learned about sizing up the situation and acting intelligently upon what she found? Like most of us in this highly civilized world, she has spent so much time learning what someone else thought or did that she has had no time to learn to do original, critical thinking.

These are some of the incidents which made the children lose faith in the ability of the teacher to guide them.

The parents, too, were wondering. Didn't she care about

them and the children? She never took the trouble to visit them. They knew it wasn't schoolwork that kept her too busy to visit them, for she was out frequently with companions they thought she had chosen unwisely. The teacher knew nothing about rural customs and codes and did not care to learn.

The teacher began to be more and more careless about her appearance and the appearance of the room and after a time the children stopped caring also. They began to refuse to do housekeeping duties and to "work for the teacher."

The situation gradually became worse. At first the children tried to talk it out with the teacher, but this resulted, as time went on, in bickering and complaining. Finally, "She knows it all, let her do it," came to be the way out of all responsibility for them.

This is not the first time a group of children have reached a high degree of self-control one year and then have thrown over all discipline the next year with another teacher. If, under circumstances such as I have described, the children had not been critical, if they had docilely accepted what they had decided, through their own thinking, was wrong, then indeed the work of the previous four years would have failed to accomplish its purpose.

But children, being immature, need a guide. This fact has been recognized since man began to live with man. If it were not so, there would be no need for teachers at all. It is because these children lose faith in the one who is supposed to guide that they become confused. Then they have no one to help them to resolve the conflicts, which they, in their immaturity, are not capable of resolving for themselves.

The following year, a mature, experienced teacher helped the children to regain some of their good habits. Unfortunately, because of ill-health, she stayed only one year.

Then, because the war-created shortage made it impossible to get a teacher, a member of the community who had done some teaching in the past offered to help out. She was aware of her limitations and was honest with the children. The children respected this attitude and, instead of taking advantage of the situation and shirking their responsibilities, they assumed greater responsibility.

That summer, Alice had said to me, "Do you know who our new teacher will be, Miss Weber? We'll have to teach ourselves, won't we?" And that is exactly what the older children did. If they disagreed on certain points in the lesson, they discussed it thoroughly until they came to some agreement. They had a list of items to discuss with the helping teacher each time she visited them. They continued to read books of all types. They persisted in carrying out all the activities suggested by their textbooks. At the end of the year, when the children were given an achievement test, they scored far above the average for their grade.

What the children could do by themselves, they did. But immature children with limited experiences cannot be expected to do the whole job that needs to be done. These older children were in the second, third, and fifth grades during the fourth year described in this book. After what they had been through in the three years following, to have retained so much self-reliance shows how effective education, properly conceived, can be. If a few short years can make such a difference, think of the kind of citizens we could develop if every child could have training in creative, democratic living for the twelve years that he attends the public schools!

Gradually, the schoolhouse became more and more run down. Doors and walls were black and sticky with finger marks. Dust hung heavy over moldings, picture frames, books. The door of the little house swung on its hinges in the wind. The wild-flower rock garden grew up with weeds and gradually disappeared. Now and then a persistent little wild flower would defiantly raise its head. It was fighting, like the children, against forces over which it could have no control.

Our school was becoming the counterpart of most of the one hundred thousand other one-teacher schools in the country, and it was headed for the same fate.

Last spring the Board of Education felt that it would be better to close the school and to transport the children to the town school. They put the matter up to the community. The community turned out in a body and voted the proposal down. Only two families, both of which have moved into the community recently, voted for it.

The parents told me, "The war won't last forever. Perhaps someday we'll have a good teacher again. The school is the only thing that holds us together." These people know that a small school can be effective in the community, and they are not willing to give it up.

Last week I visited the schoolhouse. This summer it has been completely repaired and repainted inside and out. As I drove away, I took one last glance at it. There it was, a small, white, boxlike structure shining in the sun, just as it had been eight years ago when I first confessed my faith in it. My heart pounded furiously. "Someday they will have a good teacher," I thought. Someday all children will have good teachers. This is the chief hope of Democracy!

August, 1944

Appendix

The Children
Second Year, 1937-1938

	Age
Grade 8	
Ralph Jones	14-7
Catherine Sametis	16-2
Grade 7	
Ruth Thompson	12-3
Sophia Sametis	11-8
Doris Andrews	12-3
Mary Olseuski	11-10
Frank Prinlak	15-8
Grade 6	
May Andrews	10-3
Warren Hill	10-7
George Prinlak	13-4
Edward Veniski	11-10
Thomas Lenick	12-7
Grade 5	
Helen Olseuski	9-0
Andrew Dulio	13-2
Grade 4	
Albert Hill	9-3
Pearl Prinlak	11-1
Martha Jones	9-9
Joseph Dunder	14-5
Verna Cartwright	12-2
Alex Cartwright	13-1
Gus Cartwright	14-2
Grade 3	
Alice Prinlak	9-8
William Sametis	8-8
Walter Williams	8-1
Henry Mann	7-9
Grade 1	
Richard Cartwright	9-6
John Dunder	9-4
Joyce Williams	6-4
Irene Ramsey	6-1
Beginners	
Elizabeth Prinlak	7-8
Florence Hill	5-9
Charles Willis	5-1
Eric Thompson	5-1

The Children
Third Year, 1938-1939

	Age
Grade 8	
Ruth Thompson	12-3
Sophia Sametis	12-8
Doris Andrews	13-3
Mary Olseuski	12-10
Grade 7	
May Andrews	11-3
Warren Hill	11-7
George Prinlak	14-4
Edward Veniski	12-10
Thomas Lenick	13-7
Grade 6	
Helen Olseuski	10-0
Andrew Dulio	14-2
Grade 5	
Daniel Cole	9-5
Albert Hill	10-3
Pearl Prinlak	12-1
Martha Jones	10-9
Joseph Dunder	15-5
Verna Cartwright	13-2
Alex Cartwright	14-1
Gus Cartwright	15-2
Grade 4	
Alice Prinlak	10-8
William Sametis	9-8
Henry Mann	8-9
Grade 2	
Richard Cartwright	10-6
John Dunder	10-4
Irene Ramsey	7-1
Bertha Schmidt	7-6
Elizabeth Prinlak	8-8
Grade 1	
Florence Hill	6-9
Eric Thompson	6-1
Sally Lenick	5-11
Beginners	
Charles Willis	6-1
Clarence Cartwright	6-5

THE CHILDREN
Fourth Year, 1939-1940

	Age
Grade 8	
Warren Hill	12-7
George Prinlak	15-4
Edward Veniski	13-10
Thomas Lenick	14-7
May Andrews	12-3
Grade 7	
Helen Olseuski	11-0
Andrew Dulio	15-2
Lloyd Matthews	11-11
Grade 6	
Daniel Cole	10-5
Albert Hill	11-3
Pearl Prinlak	13-1
Martha Jones	11-9
Verna Cartwright	14-2
Alex Cartwright	15-1
Gus Cartwright	16-2
Grade 5	
Alice Prinlak	11-8
William Sametis	10-8
Henry Mann	9-9
Grade 3	
Richard Cartwright	11-6
Irene Ramsey	8-1
Elizabeth Prinlak	9-8
Grade 2	
Florence Hill	7-9
Eric Thompson	7-1
Sally Lenick	6-11
Grade 1	
Clarence Cartwright	7-5
Charles Willis	7-1
Arthur Moody	6-5
Beginners	
Stanley Prinlak	7-5
Paul Mann	5-2
Robert Linden	6-1

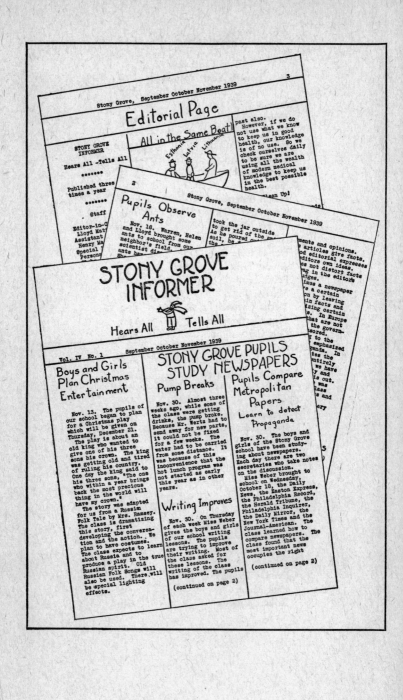

Editorial Page

All in the Same Boat!

Esthonia   Latvia   Lithuania

STONY GROVE
INFORMER

Hears All —Tells All

• • • • • •

Published three
times a year

• • • • • •

Staff

Editor-in-C...
Lloyd Mat...
Assistant...
Henry...
Special...
Person...

past also.
However, if we do not use what we know to keep us in good health, our knowledge is of no use. So we check ourselves daily to be sure we are using all the wealth of modern medical knowledge to keep us in the best possible health.

Pupils Observe Ants

Nov. 18. Warren, Helen and Lloyd brought some ants to school from our neighbor's field. ... scientist did. ants hav...

took the jar outside to get rid of the ... As he poured ... soil, he ... the ...

...ments and opinions. ... articles give facts. ...od editorial expresses ...ditors own ideas. ...s not distort facts ...g in the editor's ...dges. ...ison a newspaper ...s a certain ...on by leaving ...n facts and ...zing certain ...s. In Europe ...hat are not ...the govern- ...sored. ...ng to the ...emphasized ...nda. In ...es the ...ntirely ...we have ...y and ...s out. ...was ...ass ...and ...ry

STONY GROVE INFORMER

Hears All   Tells All

Vol. IV No. 1   September October November 1939

STONY GROVE PUPILS STUDY NEWSPAPERS

Boys and Girls Plan Christmas Entertainment

Nov. 13. The pupils of our school began to plan for a Christmas play which will be given on Thursday, December 21.

The play is about an old king who wanted to give one of his three sons his crown. The king was getting old and tired of ruling his country. One day the king said to his three sons, "The one who within a year brings back the most precious thing in the world will have my crown."

The story was adapted for us from a Russian Folk Tale by Mrs. Ramsey. The class is dramatizing this story, first developing the conversation and the action. We plan to have costumes. The class expects to learn about Russia and to produce a play in the true Russian spirit. Old Russian Folk Songs will also be used. There will be special lighting effects.

Pump Breaks

Nov. 30. Almost three weeks ago, while some of the class were getting drinks, the pump broke. Because Mr. Wertz had to send away for new parts, it could not be fixed for a few weeks. The water had to be carried from some distance. It was because of this inconvenience that the hot lunch program was not started as early this year as in other years.

Writing Improves

Nov. 30. On Thursday of each week Miss Weber gives the boys and girls of our school writing lessons. The pupils are trying to improve their writing. Most of the class asked for these lessons. The writing of the class has improved. The pupils

(continued on page 2)

Pupils Compare Metropolitan Papers

Learn to detect Propaganda

Nov. 30. The boys and girls of the Stony Grove school have been studying about newspapers. Each day there are two secretaries who take notes on the discussion.

Miss Weber brought to school on Wednesday, October 18, the Daily News, the Easton Express, the Philadelphia Record, the Herald Tribune, Philadelphia Inquirer, the Daily Mirror, the New York Times and the Journal-American. The class learned how to compare newspapers. The class found that the most important news occupies the right

(continued on page 2)

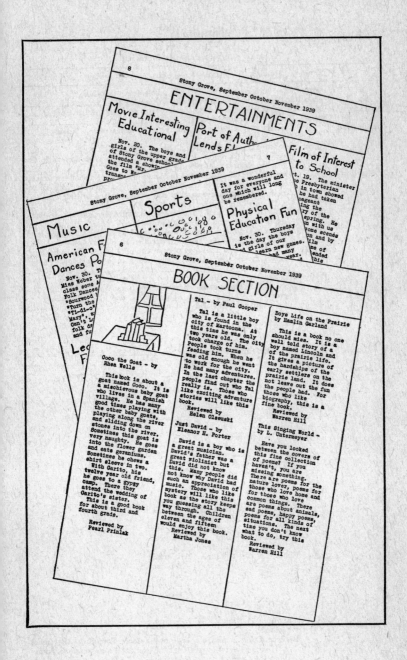

ENTERTAINMENTS

Movie Interesting Educational

Nov. 20. The boys and girls of the upper grade of Stony Grove school attended a showing of the film "Mr. ... Goes to Wa... trans...

Port of Auth... Lends Fl...

Film of Interest to School

...t. 19. The minister ... Presbyterian ... in town showed ... he had taken ... pageant ... ing the ... ry of the ... spring. He ... with us ... ome scenes ... on and by ... film ... me of ... ended ... his

It was a wonderful day for everyone and one which will long be remembered.

Music

Sports

Physical Education Fun

Nov. 30. Thursday is the day our boys and girls of ... learn new games. ... had many ... year. A

American F... Dances Po...

Nov. 30. T... Miss Weber t... class some s... Folk Dances ... "Sourwood M... "Turn the ... "Ti-di-a ... Mary", a ... Gan", L... folk d... and fu...

Lea... F...

BOOK SECTION

Coco the Goat - by Rhea Wells

This book is about a goat named Coco. It is a mischievous baby goat who lives in a Spanish village. He has many good times playing with the other baby goats, playing along the river and sliding down on stones into the river. Sometimes this goat is very naughty. He goes into the flower garden and eats geraniums. Sometimes he chews a shirt sleeve in two.

With Garito, his twelve year old friend, he goes to a gypsy camp. There they attend the wedding of Garito's sister.

This is a good book for about third and fourth grade.

Reviewed by
Pearl Prinlak

Tal - by Paul Cooper

Tal is a little boy who is found in the city of Martoona. At this time he was only two years old. The city took charge of him. People took turns feeding him. When he was old enough he went to work for the city. He had many adventures. In the last chapter the people find out who Tal really is. Those who like exciting adventure stories will like this book.

Reviewed by
Helen Olesuski

Just David - by Eleanor H. Porter

David is a boy who is a great musician. David's father was a great violinist but David did not know this. Many people did not know why David had such an appreciation of music. Those who like mystery will like this book as the story keeps you guessing all the way through. Children between the ages of eleven and fifteen would enjoy this book.

Reviewed by
Martha Jones

Boys Life on the Prairie by Hamlin Garland

This is a book no one should miss. It is a well told story of a boy named Lincoln and of the prairie life. It gives a picture of the hardships of the early settlers on the prairie land. It does not leave out the fun the people had. For those who like biography, this is a fine book.

Reviewed by
Warren Hill

This Singing World - by L. Untermeyer

Have you looked between the covers of this fine collection of poems? If you haven't, you are missing something. There are poems for the nature lover, poems for those who love home and for those who love common things. There are poems about animals, sad poems, happy poems, poems for all kinds of situations. The next time you don't know what to do, try this book.

Reviewed by
Warren Hill

Program for the Primary Children

	Time	Monday	Tuesday	Wednesday	Thursday	Friday
Social Studies Physical Education	8:45	Plan work for the day with the whole group together				
	9:00	Social Studies and Science with the teacher				
	9:20	Social Studies and Science activity with an older child or alone				
	10:00	Physical Education with the teacher				
		Active games	Rhythms	Active games	Rhythms	Singing games
	10:20	Get Irene started on reading. Others get ready to work				
	10:25	Charles and Clarence—Reading Readiness conversation with the teacher. Others read silently				
Reading and Creative Work	10:35	Richard, Eric, and Sally read to each other, with the teacher. Charles and Clarence play in the play corner until 11:00. Florence, Elizabeth, and Bertha use easel or clay or do creative writing				
	10:50	Elizabeth, Bertha, and Florence read to each other, with the teacher. Richard, Eric, and Sally work in workbooks				
	11:00	Elizabeth, Bertha, Florence work in workbooks. Richard, Eric, and Sally play in the play corner. Beginners use easels or clay				
	11:15	Elizabeth, Bertha, Florence play in the play corner. Richard, Eric, and Sally use easels or clay. Beginners play in play corner or alone at seats				
Story Time	11:30	Health— whole group together with teacher	Dramatization Older child tells story and little children retell and dramatize.	Same as on Tuesday but with teacher	Creative stories and poetry	Story telling to each other, with an older child
Lunch	12:00	Hot Lunch and Outdoor Play				
Rest	1:00	Rest				
Music	1:15	Music				
		with teacher	with an older child	with teacher	with an older child	with whole group
	1:30	Spelling for Eliz., Flo., and Bertha, with the teacher. Irene studies arith.	Arithmetic for Eliz., Flo., and Bertha, with the teacher. Others study spelling.	Check all spelling	Same as on Tuesday	Same as on Wednesday
Drill on Skills	1:40	Spelling for Eric, Richard, and Sally with teacher.	1:45 Arithmetic for Rich., Eric, and Sally with the teacher.			
	1:50	Check Irene's arith.		Arithmetic for Irene. All others study arith.		
	1:55	Spelling for Irene. Others study spelling	2:00 Check Irene's arith.			
		Beginners play in play corner or out of doors. Sometimes they meet with one of the primary groups for incidental number work. Sometimes they meet with an older child.				
	2:05	Primary group goes home.				

PROGRAM FOR THE UPPER GROUP

	Time	Monday	Tuesday	Wednesday	Thursday	Friday
Planning	8:45	Plan work for the day with the whole group together............				
Social	9:00	Study Social Studies and Science alone............				
Studies	9:20	Social Studies and Science conference, discussion, activity, study, with the teacher............				
Physical Education	10:00	Physical Education with a pupil leader in charge............				
	10:20	Study Reading, groups V and VI. Groups III and IV work on Weekly Readers.	Study Reading, groups III and IV. Groups V and VI work on Current Events.	Same as on Monday	Same as on Tuesday	Study history and geography backgrounds for Current Events, map study, etc.
Reading	11:00	Reading, group III with the teacher, group IV with the teacher	Reading, group V with the teacher, group VI with the teacher	Same as on Monday	Same as on Tuesday	Conference and discussion of Current Events with the teacher
		All others not reading with the teacher, check on health record daily, write for newspaper, correct English errors, write for Social Studies, Science, and Health, keep notebook up to date, etc.				
Creative Expression	11:30	Health, with the teacher	English, with the teacher	Puppets, poetry, newspaper, alone	Creative stories and poetry, with the teacher	English, with the teacher
Lunch	12:00	Hot Lunch and Outdoor Play............				
Rest	1:00	Rest............				
Music	1:15	Creative writing, alone	Music, with the teacher	Creative writing, alone	Music, with the teacher	Music, with the teacher
	1:30	Study spelling errors, put score on graph, alone.	Check pre-test in spelling, dictionary study, alone.	Study spelling, alone.	Study arithmetic, alone.	Study spelling, alone.
Creative Expression		Spend remaining time at easels or with clay or with hobbies. These activities will occupy most of this time.				
Physical Education	2:05	Physical Education with the teacher............			Teach a new game.	
	2:20	Spelling, pre-test				Spelling, final test.
Drill on Skills		Arithmetic Give help where needed. Groups III and IV	Check groups regularly. Groups V and VI	Groups VII and VIII	Club meeting	
	3:10	Housekeeping Duties............				
	3:30	Dismissal............				

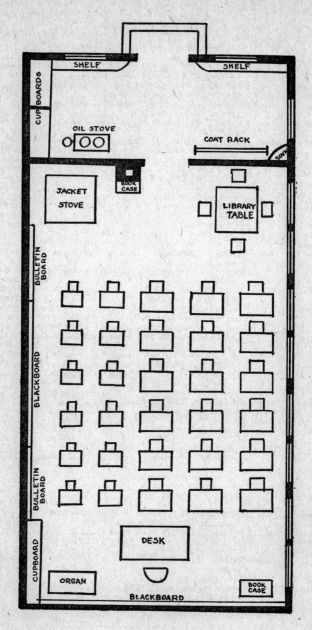

Figure 1

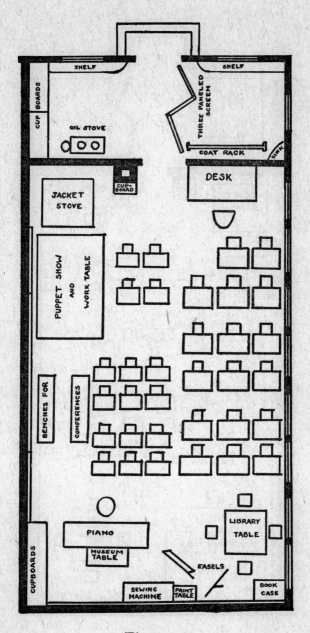

Figure 2

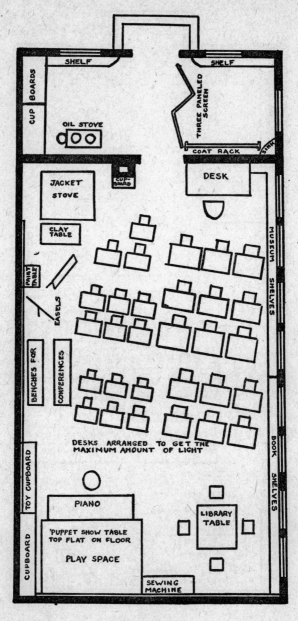

Figure 3

THE CHILDREN'S POETRY

Pitter Pat,
Pitter Pat,
Says the rain.
The river has currents,
The lakes are high,
When the rain goes
Pitter Pat.
When the rain goes
Pitter Pat,
The thunder booms,
The lightning flashes,
When the rain goes
Pitter Pat.
—William Sametis

Pitter pat, pitter pat
The rain falls into the trees.
When the clouds stop shedding their silver drops
You can smell the fresh air that comes from the soft, damp ground.
The sun peeps out from behind a gray cloud
And shines like a washed off diamond.
—Henry Mann

Perhaps it will rain.
The sky is getting blacker.
The rumbling of thunder
Bangs and clatters with all its might.
The lightning lights up the sky for a second.
Crash! Boom!
Then all is still.
Perhaps it will rain.
—Albert Hill

Put the spindle in your hand,
Then twirl!
         twirl!
         twirl!
Pull a little wool out,
Then twirl!
         twirl!
         twirl!

Out comes an uneven thread,
Because I am not used to it.
Then twirl!
    twirl!
    twirl!
—ALBERT HILL

The sea is splashing on the shore.
The surf is pounding more and more.
The gulls are screaming,
The sun is beaming
Down on the seemingly endless water
On the ocean floor.

Near the shore the beach is sandy.
Crabs and shells are always handy.
Near the beach a store sells candy.
Now isn't that just dandy?
—MARTHA JONES

On the horizon the day is breaking.
Over the country side a faint cry of a cock is heard.
Slowly the sun peeps around a gray cloud.
People are stirring, making ready for work.
Little by little the birds and bees begin to work.
The sun mounts higher into the sky.
—HELEN OLSEUSKI

The sun rises red on the dewy meadow.
Its crimson red throws dull shadows.
The reflections of the sun light up a sailing cloud.
Soon the air is filled with melodies
And the sweet fragrance of the dawn.
—PEARL PRINLAK

The dawn comes creeping o'er the woods and fields,
Peering over hills into valleys,
Making flowers brighten and trees turn their leaves.
Sunlight rushes into the valley and everything is
    cheerful and gay.
—WARREN HILL

In a small meadow covered with flowers
Of crimson, gold, blue and yellow,

A small trickling brook finds its way.
The sun shining above sends its rays of sunshine down.
A small mound of earth feels a soft push.
Suddenly a little green plant lifts its face
To the glorious feeling of being alive.

—MARTHA JONES

There is a glowing fireside
Warm and snappy
With the fresh smelling logs upon the hearth.
A sleek, shiny-eyed cat
Yawns and stretches out before the fire.
An old lady sits by the fire
Sound asleep,
Her knitting in her lap.
A sly little mouse
Looks out of his hole
At this contented scene.

—MARTHA JONES

A little mouse scuttles
Between the furrows of smooth dirt
Hunting for lost kernels of corn.
He hears the thud of a human's foot
And hurries to his hole, hungry.

—WARREN HILL

There is a square of golden, creamy butter
On a light pale pink plate
On a snow-white table cloth.
It is lifted
On a piece of warm, brown toast.
It melts all over
And trickles slowly down the sides
On to the plate.
Eager hands wait for it to cool off.

—MARTHA JONES

Up, up, up I go,
Up above the sea of clouds I see below.
Now I am higher
Than the rain
And the snow
And the trees.

I look down and see a sea of rolling clouds.
I see the high breakers
And the rolling tide
In the clouds.
Now I am coming down,
Down to the hard earth.

—ALBERT HILL

There are fiery red maples
Singed with yellow, bronze and orange.
The green pine and hemlock
Pierce the splotches of ochre-colored birch and hickory.
The mighty oaks with their brown cloaks
Blot the mountain side.

—WARREN HILL

A little green field
Lay on the valley floor,
Nestled against the mountain side,
Flashing brightly in the sun
In the warm afternoon.

Leaves swishing and swirling
Sailed high over the treetops.
The little green field was peaceful,
Contented at heart
With such cheerful friends around.

—MARTHA JONES

SNOW POEMS

The snow is crusty, deep and thick,
Higher than our boots and galoshes.
The snow cones and drifts and swirls.
The tops of dunes are set in curls.

—ALBERT HILL

The long drifted snow banks pile up
Like waves on the ocean.
The waves are ready to spill
But they stay, held back by something.

—PEARL PRINLAK

Huge trees that have stood the storms of years
Fall to the earth under the weight of the ice
That is caked on their branches.
The tremendous strain tests the trees strength.
Now and then through the stillness
A tree gives way to the icy weight with a crash.
Then all is still again.

                —WARREN HILL

The tall branching trees
With thin white ice
All hang to the ground.
They look like the water flowing out of a fountain.
The water running between the trunk and its icy coat
Looks like tiny black bugs pushing to the ground.

                —ALICE PRINLAK

INDEX

Adolescents, adjustments of, 55-56, 155-156, 158-160, 185. *See also* Young People.

Apple industry, study of the, 154, 155, 156, 162-163

Appreciation of music, 112, 163-164, 219, 221

Arithmetic, 5, 13, 40, 208

Art, *see* Batik, Block printing, Book making, Carpentry, Christmas cards, Christmas gifts, Clay, Design, Dye experimenting, Lettering, Painting, Paper making, Puppet making, Room planning, Scenery for dramatizations, Screen, Sketching, Tie-dyeing, Wall hangings, Weaving, Wool processes.

Batik, 166

Beginners, *see* Five- and six-year-olds.

Block printing, 166, 236

Board of Education, xv, 117, 191, 247

Book making, 236. *See also* Records, study of.

Bulletin boards, 31, 35, 138, 245

Carpentry, 57, 79, 82, 85, 91, 92, 94, 95, 101, 105, 136, 138, 145-146, 149, 170-171, 230

Character development, *see* Democratic living, experiences in; Needs, discovering; Needs, meeting.

Christmas, *see* Christmas cards, Christmas Carol, Christmas gifts, Christmas Story, Russian legend, Sabot of Little Wolff.

Christmas cards, 44, 166

Christmas Carol, 165

Christmas gifts, 45, 109, 166, 217

Christmas Story, the, 45, 47

Civics, 116-117, 180-182, 184-185, 212-213, 214-215, 217-219, 220, 221,

225-226. *See also* Helpers' Club; Newspaper, school.

Clay, 82, 101

Club Agent, xv, 65, 199

Clubs, *see* Forestry club, Helpers' Club, Sewing club.

Columbus, dramatization of the life of, 19, 22, 25, 31, 36

Community, history of, 57-58, 60-65, 68-71, 75, 78, 80; present day, 120-124. *See also* Apple industry, Dairying, Government.

Community problems, 37, 55, 82-84, 103-105, 114-115. *See also* Mother's group.

Conducting, 54, 68, 71, 112

Conferences, personal, 7, 25, 26, 41, 44, 49, 55-56, 63-64, 68, 73, 158-159

County Library, xv, 56, 204, 209, 213, 226, 231

County Superintendent, xiv, 112, 117

Creative writing, *see* Original poetry, Original stories

Current Events, 55, 100, 108, 109-110, 118, 175, 189, 204, 205, 207, 212, 221, 223

Dairying, study of, 124-134, 140-142

Dancing, *see* Folk dancing, Rhythms.

Democratic living, experiences in, assuming responsibility, 12, 26, 43, 73, 140, 203; appreciating the complexity of human life, 134, 141-142, 187; appreciating national problems, 180-181, 185-190, 207, 221; appreciating other peoples, 13, 184, 195-196, 206, 223; appreciating world problems, 100, 142, 155, 204, 217; checking sources of information, 181; co-operating for the group welfare, 151, 178, 183, 209-210; developing curiosity, 57, 198, 219; developing leadership, 35, 203, 224, 238; developing self-confidence, 46,

266

106, 144, 183, 204; developing
self-discipline, 97, 203, 210-211;
developing a sense of values,
155, 160, 183, 208; evaluating results of plans and activities, 42,
45, 138, 183; participating in
community living, 209-210, 211;
planning and carrying out activities, 18, 25, 44-45, 96-97, 200-
203; recognizing the worth of
others, 36, 46-47, 208, 224; re-
specting the rights of others, 16,
69, 178, 222; sharing in the solution of problems, 12, 93, 155, 160;
sharing tasks, 12, 21, 79-80, 100,
149, 208; using an expanding body
of knowledge, 185-190, 225-237;
using intelligently means of communication, 186, 204; writing a
constitution, 20, 200, 201; *See
also* Helpers' Club, Housekeeping,
Playing together, Social Studies.
Design, 92, 166
Discipline, *see* Adolescents, adjustments of; Democratic living, experiences in; Individuals, adjustments of; Needs, discovering;
Needs, meeting.
Doctor, 91-92
Dramatic play, 70, 76, 78, 129, 151-
152, 205
Dramatization, *see* Christmas Carol,
Christmas Story, Columbus, Dramatic play, History of Valley
View, Indian life, Mozart, Puppet
shows, Rip Van Winkle, Russian
legend, Sabot of Little Wolff,
Spontaneous dramatization.
Dye experimenting, 175, 176

English, *see* Language.
Evaluation, the teacher's, 48, 57,
72-73, 80, 90, 104-105, 120, 141-
142, 146-147, 157-167, 171-173,
184-186, 191, 207-212, 237-238
Excursions, *see* Trips.

Five- and six-year-olds, 17, 18, 38,
70, 73, 81, 84, 89, 95, 101, 106, 118-
119, 135-136, 139, 140, 151-152,
153, 200-201, 205, 206-207
Folk dancing, 165, 195-196, 223
Forestry club, 10, 20, 24, 28, 33, 39,
41, 43, 93, 95, 97. *See also* Club
Agent, Plot study.

Funds, how acquired, 27, 48, 65,
144; how spent, 49, 65, 82, 85, 92,
149, 181, 203, 226

Games, 7, 21, 28, 34, 36, 130-131,
135
Geography, 55, 60, 90-91, 100-101,
109-110, 117, 125, 127, 130, 131,
142, 176, 177, 186-189, 204, 223
Government, study of, 115-117
Grouping, 4-5, 6, 8, 9, 25, 34-35, 58,
59, 81, 118, 256-257
Guidance, *see* Adolescents, adjust-
ments of; Conferences, personal;
Democratic living, experiences in;
Individuals, adjustments of;
Needs, discovering; Needs, meet-
ing.
Guidance, vocational, 117, 120-124,
219. *See also* Apple industry,
Dairying, Newspaper, Records,
Textiles, Work experiences.

Handwriting, 40, 65, 152, 212
Harmonica practice, 7, 23, 24, 54,
59, 112
Health, 9, 10, 15, 24, 34, 86, 88, 92-
93, 94, 99, 153, 184-185, 201,
208. *See also* Doctor, Hot Lunch,
Mental and emotional health,
Nurse, Physical education, Sex
education.
Helpers' Club, 12, 15-16, 19, 35, 50,
69, 101, 126, 155, 160, 200-203,
210-211, 216
Helping teacher, xiv, 52, 57-58, 70,
72, 75, 120, 157, 210
History, 11, 19, 54, 57-58, 60-65, 71,
75, 78, 80, 115-117, 121-125, 134,
141-142, 157, 173-174, 178-181,
186-189, 192, 194, 211, 213, 217,
220-221, 226-237
History of Valley View, dramatization of the, 80
Home Demonstration Agent, xv, 38,
54, 57, 198-199
Home visits, 7-8, 10-11, 13, 14, 16,
17, 18, 20, 24, 28, 77, 81-84, 160,
162, 207
Homes, study of, 34, 35, 51, 64-65.
See also Playhouse.
Hot lunch, 27, 42, 44, 46, 52-53, 54,
56-57, 70-71, 79, 119
Housekeeping, 12, 18, 21, 39, 42, 52-
53, 55-56, 119, 201-202

Indian life, dramatization of, 25, 36

Indian life, study of, 19, 23, 25, 31, 32-33, 36

Individuals, adjustments of, 7, 23, 26, 44, 63-64, 68, 71-75, 77-78, 87-90, 102-105, 205-206, 209

Language, articles for newspaper, 138, 139, 223-224; bibliography cards, 155, 229; book reviews, 138, 255; capitalization and punctuation, 14-15, 22, 39, 208, 224, 231-234; composition and story writing, 35, 65, 69-70, 76, 78, 207, 228, 231-234; conversation, 4, 70, 75-77, 99, 126, 205, 206-207; discussion, 23, 76, 109-110, 178, 228; editing, 224, 231-234; grammar, 119, 233; interviews, 68, 69, 75-76, 117, 127, 129, 140; in daily program, 9, 14, 22, 118, 256-257; letter writing, 71, 74, 129, 131, 135, 152, 170, 179, 191; note taking, 62, 64, 69, 123, 129, 214, 227, 229; proofreading, 224, 232-234; reports, 25, 47, 124, 170, 201-202, 208, 228-230, 232-233; script writing, 25, 51; speech training, 114; usage, 14, 22, 39, 76, 208, 231-234; vocabulary, 39, 40, 51, 70, 108, 205, 208, 217; *See also* Creative writing; Dramatization; Handwriting; Library period; Motion pictures; Newspaper, school; Notebooks; Reading; Spelling; Story period.

Lettering, 18-19, 24

Library period, 9, 15, 36, 59, 89-90, 96, 200, 209. *See also* County Library.

Management, *see* Grouping, Helpers' Club, Hot lunch, Housekeeping, Notebooks, Older children help, One-teacher school, Outside help, Playing together, Program, Routine matters, Whole school activities.

Mental and emotional health, *see* Adolescents, adjustments of; Conferences, personal; Democratic living, experiences in; Individuals, adjustments of; Needs, discovering; needs, meeting; Sex education.

Mother's group, 27, 38-39, 42, 47, 56, 64, 79, 100, 198-199, 209-210

Motion pictures, 128, 149, 165, 221

Mozart, dramatization of the life of, 153, 163

Museum, 9, 18, 30-31, 60, 67, 92, 149, 215, 230, 259, 260

Music, *see* Appreciation of music, Conducting, Folk dancing, Harmonica practice, Original songs, Reading music, Rhythms, Singing, Singing games.

Needs, discovering, through home visits, 8, 10-11, 13, 14, 20. 24, 28-30, 53, 81-84; through observation, 6-7, 10, 11, 15, 21, 23, 32, 38, 40, 46, 63, 102-104, 155, 167; through personal conferences, 25, 68

Needs, meeting, through conferences, 7, 25, 26, 49, 55-56, 63-64, 68, 71, 158-159; through daily program, 8, 19, 20-21, 22, 45, 119, 153-154; through democratic living, 12, 35, 46-47, 48, 93-94, 146-147, 149, 151, 155, 160, 183, 201-203, 208-212; through enriched experiences, 7, 9, 10, 19, 26, 30-33, 57-58, 70, 85, 140, 165, 171, 173, 191-194, 198, 209, 211-212, 216-217, 237; through group play, 11, 15-17, 36, 93-94, 130-131; through housekeeping activities, 12, 21, 39-40; through increasing skill in using the tools of learning, 14-15, 40, 70, 151, 204; through individualized instruction, 13, 14-15, 23, 128, 227; through informal situations, 26, 46, 71-73, 126, 144, 204, 205, 223, 224-225; through opportunities for creative expression, 15, 26, 106-107, 143-144, 165, 182-183, 206, 209, 220, 238; through opportunities to evaluate experiences, 42, 45, 113, 151, 178, 224; through opportunities to initiate and plan activities, 25, 36, 44-45, 96-97, 216; through parent-teacher cooperation, 14, 27, 56, 77-78, 79, 160-162, 207-208, 209-210; through trips and outside experiences, 32-33, 57-58, 67, 70, 97, 131, 191-194, 237; through using children's interests, 26, 57-58, 90, 93, 195, 204, 205; through using the resources of the community, 10, 32-33, 43, 57-58, 115-117, 120-121, 216-217, 221

Newspaper, school, 35, 42, 43-44, 67, 79, 105, 106, 138, 220, 221-224

Newspaper, study of the, 204, 212-226

Notebooks, 17, 35, 39, 70, 152, 207-208. *See also* Progress books.

Nurse, xv, 92

Objectives, the teacher's, *see* Evaluation, Purposes.

Older children help, 36, 43, 76, 94, 109, 119, 135, 138, 139, 140, 152, 203, 204, 238

One-teacher school, 1, 11, 57, 104, 119, 143, 244-248

Original poetry, 35, 36, 43, 152, 209, 217, 225

Original songs, 217

Original stories, 89, 96, 101, 209

Outside help, 57, 59, 61, 65-66, 68-69, 95, 112, 115, 117, 140, 169, 191-194

Painting, 98, 101, 119, 152, 217

Paper making, 230

Personality development, *see* Democratic living, experiences in; Needs, discovering; Needs, meeting.

Pets, study of, 4, 11, 13, 17, 18, 31

Philosophy, the teacher's, 1, 10, 12, 32, 40, 44-45, 46, 48, 72-73, 104, 106-107, 120, 173, 190-191, 197-198, 209-212, 237

Physical education, *see* Folk dancing, Games, Playing together, Rhythms, Singing games.

Playhouse, 85, 91, 92, 94, 95-96, 98, 101, 106, 129, 135, 151-152, 205

Playing together, 7, 11, 14, 16-17, 19-20, 27, 28, 34, 35, 36, 50, 71, 76, 93, 130-131, 135, 141, 145, 150

Plot study, 137-138, 138-139, 142-143, 145

Post Office, study of the, 124, 125, 126, 131

Program, the daily, 3-5, 8-9, 18, 22, 44-45, 58, 81, 109-110, 118-119, 153-154, 165

Progress books, 49, 56, 139

Puppet making, 57, 59, 61, 79

Puppet shows, hand, 67, 75, 79, 129; string, 26, 47, 51, 53, 57, 59, 61, 63, 66, 79, 96, 136, 143-144, 150, 182-183, 238

Purposes and plans, the teacher's, 3-12, 20-21, 25, 26, 32, 40, 44-45, 46, 49, 57-58, 61, 85, 86, 90, 104, 106-107, 120-121, 148, 157, 165-167, 172-173, 186, 211-212

Radio, broadcasting, 164; use of, in school, 181, 195, 205, 207, 219, 221

Reading, 4, 6, 9, 11, 16, 22, 38, 40, 58, 62, 64, 70, 73, 77, 118, 125, 130, 136, 153, 171, 177, 208, 226-230, 255, 256, 257. *See also* Library period.

Reading music, 53, 68

Records, the study of, 211, 225-237

Resources, neighborhood, Apple orchards, 154, 156; Brook clay, 82; Community history, 57-58, 120; Dairy farm, 129; Indian lore, 32; Local government, 117, 120; Natural environment, 10, 43, 120, 137, 216; Schoolgrounds, 8, 62, 65-66, 150-151, 195; Schoolhouse, 12, 39, 105, 198-199

Resources outside of the neighborhood, Agricultural Experiment Station, 194; Books, 231; Broadcasting station, 164; County seat, 117; Department store, 97; Doylestown Museum, 60; Industrial Arts Cooperative Service, 175; Library, 213; Metropolitan Museum of Art, 237; Movies, 128, 221; Newspaper establishment, 225; Newspapers, 204, 215, 226; Post Office, 126; Princeton University, 192; Quarry, 60; Radio, 181; Seashore, 191-194; Tennent Church, 192; Trains, 75; Walker Gordon Dairy, 131

Resources, people as, Agricultural Agent, 140-141; Board of Education 117; Breeds, the, 47-48, 57, 169, 184, 195; Cellist, 112; Chairman of Township Committee, 117; Club Agent, 65, 199; County Superintendent of Schools, 117; Dairy farmer, 129; Home Demonstration Agent, 38, 57, 198-199; Lumber Company proprietor, 92; Old residents of the community, 62, 68; Parents, the children's, 56-57, 79, 100, 115, 206, 226; Publisher, 236; Puppeteer, 59, 66; State Food Specialist, 199; State Garden Specialist, 199; State Landscape Specialist, 65-66; Teacher's brother, 68; Teacher's father, 95; Visitors to school, 46, 223

Rhythms, 59, 118, 136

Rip Van Winkle, the pageant of, 144, 146

Room planning, 3, 18, 30-31, 85, 98, 146, 149, 230

Routine matters, 1-28, 40, 49, 52-53, 70, 85, 96-97, 114, 146, 149, 153-154, 200-202, 203, 210. *See also* Older children help.

Russian legend, dramatization of a, 206, 220, 224-225

Sabot of Little Wolff, dramatization of the, 106-114

Scenery for dramatizations, 36, 79, 108, 111, 113

Schedule, the daily, *see* Program.

Schoolground beautification, 8, 9, 17, 19, 23-24, 59, 62, 65-66, 68, 70, 76, 81, 128, 129, 135, 138, 150, 152, 153, 203

Science and nature study, 8, 9, 18, 34, 43, 58-59, 92, 93, 99, 117, 142, 167-170, 181-182, 206-207, 212. *See also* Dye experimenting, Forestry club, Museum, Pets, Plot study, Schoolground beautification.

Screen, three paneled, 85, 96, 97, 98

Sewing club, 38, 57, 97, 99-100, 101-102, 126, 181, 185

Sex education, 88-89, 126, 160, 165

Singing, 5, 9, 37, 48, 49, 68, 74, 112, 128, 164, 184, 225

Singing games, 196, 204

Sketching, 96, 105, 111, 194, 217

Social Studies, 9, 11, 14, 19, 25, 33, 54, 55, 57-58, 85, 90-91, 94, 100-101, 105, 106-107, 118, 256, 257. *See also* Apple industry, Columbus, Community, Current Events, Dairying, Government, Homes, Indian life, Newspaper, Pets,

Playhouse, Post Office, Puppet shows, Records, Sabot of Little Wolff, Textiles, Trains.

Spelling, 5, 9, 22, 23, 35, 40, 45, 76, 118, 151, 208, 232, 233, 256, 257

Spontaneous dramatization of stories, 139, 201

Story period, 18, 36, 139, 201, 207, 221

Summer activities, *see* Vacation activities

Textiles, study of, 157, 166-191

Tie-dyeing, 166

Training, the teacher's, xiv, 86, 148, 156

Trains, study of, 70-78

Trips, on a train, 75; over an Indian trail, 32; to the County Court House, 117; to the County Library, 213, 226, 231; to the Doylestown Museum, 58, 60; to the Metropolitan Museum of Art, 237; to a newspaper establishment, 224, 225; to places in the community, 68-69, 75, 120, 129, 156; to places outside of the community, 79, 164, 184, 238; to the Post Office, 126; to purchase dress patterns and materials, 97, 100; to the seashore, 191-194; to the teacher's home, 67; to the Walker Gordon Dairy, 131

Vacation activities, 82, 86, 93, 139, 143, 148-149

Visitors, 46, 160, 223

Wall hangings, 68, 71, 78, 166

Weaving, 85, 91, 109, 170-172

Whole school activities, 34-35, 36, 39, 41, 42-43, 75, 79-80, 85, 106-107, 109, 128, 130-131, 145-146, 163, 170-171, 195-196, 216-217, 222

Wool processes, 172-182

Work experiences, 12, 39, 42-43, 65-66, 79, 85, 94, 149, 222-224, 231-236, 238

Young people, 10, 37, 104-105, 114, 196, 198-199, 209, 225